Dog Zen

Everything You Need To Know To Transform Your Dog

Mark Vette

AS SEEN ON TV

RANDOM HOUSE
NEW ZEALAND

I dedicate this book to my recently passed and much loved father Captain Gordon Vette, who revealed to the world the real cause of the Erebus airline disaster, a special man, father and mentor of mine, and my late dear mother Heather Vette, who gave me my love of nature and dogs. Her last words were 'Nature is a beautiful thing!' She continues to inspire and support me. Both go on in me and this work.

———————

Contents

Prelude

The first time I saw a wolf in the wild I was awestruck. Like a grey ghost slipping through the underbrush, head in the classic lowered carriage, it was focused on the invisible prey ahead. Gliding with each step, dropping its nose to the ground, scenting at intervals, agate eyes glistening. We were 50 metres away, watching through binoculars, yet it seemed only a few metres.

A second wolf was following, an invisible thread of scent joining them together; a third was up on the ridge working the flank. The snow was light, and the day cold. A snap of a branch from one of our team and the wolves froze instantly, fixing their stare over to where we were. They were gone in a blink, evaporated into the forest. The scientist I was with said, 'That's it: you've seen your first wolf, and now you won't see them again for dust.'

He was right. We didn't see them again until we were airborne over Isle Royale (an island in the Great Lakes in the United States), radio-tracking the wolves as part of the late Durward Allen's inspired wolf ecology study. This work gave us some of the early wild-wolf research findings, and for me it brought back the childhood feelings of awe and excitement when I read Farley Mowat's *Never Cry Wolf*. I was hooked.

My love affair with dogs started at a very young age — well, maybe not a love affair, as my experience was more one of overwhelming anxiety and frustration. Given Scott, an unruly 45-kilogram German Shepherd, as a young boy of six, I learnt very quickly what it was like to be faced with a dog that caused havoc in your life. Chasing chickens and biting people, running away and much more — all of the frustrations experienced by the many dog owners I was later to meet in my clinic over 40 years. I swore I would find out what made Scott tick. He was also my best mate, sleeping in my under-the-stars bed made of covers at night (Mum never knew, or so I thought), and with me during the day exploring the 'wild forests' of Chamberlain Road, West Auckland. Together we travelled our imaginary wild, me and my wolf mate. The night dreams were great, the day time realities more challenging. Thankfully, with the help of my grandfather, a dog trainer in World War Two, I slowly and painfully learnt my first lessons about working with these awesome creatures.

There started a life-long obsession to learn everything I could about dogs, to solve these problems humanely and intelligently, and to continue to enjoy the awe and wonder dogs bring into my life. Fast-forward 55 years and I have had the great fortune to spend my life with dogs and wolves — learning what makes them tick, and growing an enormous respect for their intelligence and love, and for our unique bond with these remarkable beings.

I went to live with and study the wolf (the North American clade — group sharing the same ancestor as the dog) 40 years ago, and was awestruck by this magnificent species. I was amazed by just how many of its behaviours were exaggerated dog behaviours, or, more correctly, how dogs showed toned-down wolf behaviours. I discovered that a wolf isn't a dog, and that although they share 99.96 per cent of their genes, they are also very different. A wolf could never live with us in our homes safely and cooperatively, but a dog can . . . Why is this? What can we learn from the wolf, and how did a dog become a dog? These questions took me on an amazing, life-long journey to discover the evolution of the dog and its co-evolution with us; how dogs joined our families, contributing to our lives in so many ways.

So here is where I have landed: *Dog Zen*, the art and science of dog behaviour — my dog behaviour and training philosophy; all that I have learnt in my 55-plus years of working with these magnificent creatures. My journey started with a frustrated six-year-old boy with a German Shepherd too big for him, and wound its way through the plains and forests of northeast America and into my behaviour clinic and the multitude of dogs I have had the good fortune to meet, train and transform through the years. How grateful I am to share this with you.

Me and My Dogs

Mark is a world-renowned animal behaviourist, zoologist and trainer, with a unique combination of academic studies and 40 years of applied clinical consulting and treatment. He has worked as a lecturer and consultant to academic institutions, welfare organisations and industry. Mark draws on his deep understanding of wolf behaviour, developed in the US under the renowned behaviourist Professor Erick Klinghammer, to provide deep insights into the progenitor of the dog and dog behaviour.

Mark has also trained a variety of species for film and television, including movies such as *Narnia, Lord of the Rings* and *The Last Samurai*. Mark has led three television series to date: *Purina Pound Pups to Dog Stars, Dogs Might Fly* and *The Funny Farm*. As part of his advocacy of animals Mark has achieved five world-first animal performances, including driving dogs and flying dogs.

If you were to ask Mark where his most profound insights come from it would be from his 40 years of Zen practice under the guidance of his Great Zen Master Thich Nhat Hanh. Dogs too are his 'Dog Zen Masters'. He continues to learn much from these amazing beings that have been at his side all his life and he never ceases to be amazed by their presence and joy.

Here, Mark introduces you to his dogs.

Blue is a tri-coloured Beardie Huntaway rescued by me out of the back of a small urban garden where he had worn a deep track circling through boredom. He was 3 years old then and went on to become super smart with a film and commercial CV as long as Lassie's tail. The highlight was being cast as Yogi Bear's dog! At 12 years of age he

is now gracefully retired on my property at home. The most loved and affectionate of dogs.

Tommy is a champion pure-bred Parson's Jack Russell I met while casting for a TV commercial body double. His first 3 years were very limited, contained in a breeding environment. He has gone on to undertake some TV commercials but his restricted early environment has limited his abilities. His main role is as the beautiful, loved companion that enticed my partner into my crazy life.

Monty is an SPCA-rescued Giant Schnauzer cross selected specifically for the SPCA, FCB and Mini driving dogs project. Little did we know that underlying his mischievous face was a complex bundle of issues masking his real talents. With love and therapy, he has become an intelligent, fun-loving dog. Joy and love ooze from every pore and his karate-like tail is in constant wag motion! With 100 million tweets to his name, his highlight was featuring on David Letterman as the world's first driving dog — not bad for a dog so close to being put down.

Reggie is a Labrador-German Shepherd cross, one of the 12 dogs we rescued for our UK-based TV series *Dogs Might Fly* on dog cognition with Ádám Miklósi and Victoria Stilwell. It was love at first sight for us both. He came with dog–dog aggression generally motivated by his obsession with his toys. Once we had established our special bond he became the most intimate and affectionate dog, super intelligent and rock solid in temperament. He has learnt one of the most complex sequences of behaviours ever taught to a dog and became the world's first flying dog on 18 October 2015. A bond that special couldn't be broken so I brought him back home to New Zealand — and oh how glad I am that I did.

Porter is really Jazzy's dog, but spends time with me too. Jazzy trained him for Driving Dogs and he is also a star on TV and film. He is mischievous, but the most playful, loving dog — especially with Nalu, his human sister.

Opposite from top left clockwise: Blue, Monty, Reggie, Tommy, Porter.

Introduction— Love is Understanding

To truly love our dogs, we need to understand them — what they need, how they communicate and how they learn. If we know this, then we can act in ways that will support and love them. A beautiful saying from my teacher, Zen Master Thich Nhat Hanh, says it all: Love is understanding. To truly love someone, some being, we must first truly understand them.

What I want people to come away with after reading this book is a deep appreciation of the dog, and a wonder of the human-dog relationship that has evolved and co-evolved over millennia. First and foremost, we must understand that dogs are dogs: they have their own culture, language and way of understanding the world. And importantly, we need to acknowledge that, just like us, dogs are not and cannot be perfect. We are asking them to live in our human world, which is fundamentally foreign to them. It is therefore our responsibility to support and mentor them to live safely and happily in our complex world. Why do we do this? Because we love them, and want them to be happy. We want to have a harmonious and loving relationship with them. Unifying our two disparate cultures — the dog and the human — is the role of Dog Zen, my dog behaviour and training philosophy . . . a new paradigm.

Dog Zen invites us to see dogs in a larger perspective. They are our Dog Zen Masters, our teachers — certainly they are mine. One of the meanings of Zen is to look, to see, to understand, so one of the purposes of Dog Zen is to cultivate an ability to observe, to read and to have insight into our dogs. By helping build our understanding we can truly see the wonder of dogs; that they are not something to own and bend to our will, but are separate, extraordinary beings to be cared for and nurtured. By understanding our dogs, we can build a harmonious relationship and work with them more effectively to help them live in our world.

Our relationships with dogs are not just about 'sit', 'down', 'stay', 'wait', 'good boy', 'bad boy'. They are more akin to the relationship we have with a family member — driven by love, trust, appreciation, respect and joy. Do we know why we are in a relationship with our dogs? Do we even know that we are in a relationship with our dogs? That it's not merely a one-way street but a dance of two partners, from different worlds, cultures and perspectives. And, like any partnership, the key to success lies in understanding what it is like to walk in their shoes (or would that be paws?), to understand their perception of the world.

This book explores why we love our dogs so much, and how they love us, how they came to be in our lives and what truly makes up this wondrous being, the dog. To do this we will go back to where dogs came from, how and why they became our best friends, and why they are able to understand us and read our gestures, emotions and behaviours.

From our deepened understanding of the dog we look at the key principles of Dog Zen training. Dog Zen is primarily a system of rearing and training that relies on 'doing things at the right time', during the critical socialisation and learning periods. That old adage 'prevention is better than the cure' is certainly true here. If you do the right things at the right time you will reap the most beautiful relationships. However, all is not lost for older or rescue dogs. Dog Zen also looks at what can be done to fix things when they invariably go astray. Yes, we can teach old dogs new tricks!

When human relationships can feel fraught and challenging, the unconditional love of a dog can ease our hearts. Though let's not romanticise this too much. Our relationships with dogs can also be difficult and distressing when dogs show inappropriate behaviours, like biting a child or another dog. Then we can be faced with the challenges and complexities of a relationship gone awry, and sometimes even more difficult because of the risks and consequences. However, if we are willing to shift our perspective from merely training our dogs to building a relationship with them — the bond — then our training and lives together will transform.

The wolf is the dog's ancestor

I am often asked why it is useful to look back to the wolf and other early dog ancestors to understand our dogs of today.

Over the past 10 years, the genetic research around wolves and dogs has exploded. We now know that genetically dogs are 99.96 per cent wolves. The wolf provides the 'chassis' (both physical and behavioural, so to speak) of the dog, supplying the foundational aspects of dog behaviour and social order. By looking back at the evolution of the dog from the wolf, we can explore the origins of dog behaviours. What they meant in the wolf, the proto-dog (the wolf that first began to associate with humans — the beginnings of the dog) and later the dog itself; what the evolutionary drivers were that moulded these changes. It is helpful, therefore, to look at these original behaviours in the wild, and investigate the meaning of them to help illuminate many dog behaviours. This gives us an understanding of what these behaviours are and why they evolved. From there, we can meaningfully understand how we can best bond with and train our own dogs.

However, don't be fooled: the 0.04 per cent that differentiates the dog and the wolf makes a huge difference. The change that drove the evolution of the dog from the wolf via the proto-dog to the dogs we know today transformed the dog's focus from the pack to the human in unprecedented ways. This changed both the nature of the bond and dog intelligence. No wolf would be safe left alone with our children, whereas a properly bonded dog would save them from even a wolf, love them like their own, or maybe even more. We took the reins through domestication and shaped one of the most amazing, unique and genetically diverse species on Earth. In so doing, we created one of the greatest symbiotic collaborations — truly man and woman's best friend!

The 'Zen' in Dog Zen

There are two aspects to the 'Zen' in Dog Zen: the practical aspects of being in a calm, learning state; and dogs as a door or teacher for us to live more in the present moment. For us being in the present moment, concentrated and aware, is critical to being able to grow and live a happy life. In training and rearing your dog, having the dog in

Mark at Wolf Park, Indiana, living with and studying these beautiful animals.

The wolf pups investigating the world. This grows the brain connections.

a state of calm awareness and concentration (a learning state) is also critical for learning, and therefore training.

From learning psychology, we can identify these states and know that if an animal or human isn't in a learning state (also called 'para-sympathetic arousal' or 'rest and digest'), then no learning is possible. Dog Zen uses this understanding to induce the learning state as a central principle in its training. I especially emphasise this state when I teach a Dog Zen 'down'. It is a unique part of Dog Zen, and it goes hand-in-hand with re-creating in adult dogs the optimum learning state that puppies experience during the formative period (1-4 months of age).

The other aspect of the 'Zen' in Dog Zen is that in many ways dogs are our teachers, often the last semblance of Nature in our complex, left-brain-dominant world. One of the highest states in Zen, sometimes called 'enlightenment', can most simply be described as being fully in the present moment. Dogs do this all the time. This may seem silly to some, but it is a profound state of presence that gives them some of the qualities that we admire — loyalty, trust, love, play, joy and much more.

What greater doorway to experiencing this presence than with our dogs? Maybe we all have experienced that moment of pure joy and peace as we watch our dogs, whether they are rolling on the grass, napping in the sun or jumping blissfully into the pond. They don't have regrets about yesterday or fears for tomorrow: they are truly in the moment, every inch of their being experiencing and enjoying the very thing they are doing. What would life be if we could all just be like our dogs in that moment?

Dog Zen has been built from 40-plus years of my academic and clinical experience. But equally importantly, it is built on a lifetime of loving dogs. It is critical that our approach has a sound scientific understanding, but please let's not leave it there. The relationship with a dog is one of our most cherished relationships, so it is also built on love. Bringing both the science and the love of dogs together is the aim of this book: hence we have *Dog Zen*, the art and science of dog behaviour.

Alongside this book is its online companion, dogzen.com — a compilation of over 30 videos that take you through the practical 'how to's of the Dog Zen techniques covered in this book. It provides additional step-by-step video instructions to deepen your understanding.

I hope it, and this book, go some way to building your understanding of these glorious beings that share our homes and our hearts. And, through that, I hope it helps you build a harmonious relationship that will carry you and your dog through your lives. So let's begin.

MY GIFT TO YOU

WANT TO SEE MORE?

I hope you'll enjoy reading this book, and that it will give you immense value in your relationship with your dog!

I know dog training can be challenging, and sometimes there's nothing like seeing how it's done in the flesh.

My Dog Zen online training programme gives you access to 30 comprehensive training videos, with me *showing* you exactly how to do all of the training techniques covered in this book with your dog. It's the closest thing to having me there to train your dog personally!

To thank you for purchasing this book, to enjoy a month of access to Dog Zen for only $1, head to www.dogzen.com/checkout and enter the coupon code DOGZEN1

All the best in your training endeavours,
Mark

The Dog

1

Why do we love our dogs so much?

Our long-evolved collaboration with dogs has led us to become two of the most successful mammalian species on Earth, and the collaboration continues! What is unique is our amazing bond, a relationship based on trust, cooperation, honesty and love. It is this that separates dogs from all other species, and what ultimately brought them into our homes and families. Once you have experienced such a special bond, you know how remarkable it is.

BLUE: OUR MUTUAL SEARCH FOR AFFECTION

My dog Blue is a very affectionate Beardie who regularly comes up and nudges my arm. 'Come on, mate,' I suspect he's saying. 'Enough work, it's time for a pat, don't you think?' I don't know about you, but

I've experienced a few cups of tea all over my lap upon such a loving nose nudge. Dogs always seem to have a paw on your foot or be lying on your feet. My ergonomically correct footrest seems to have turned into a fluffy Beardie that applies a warm lick to my foot at intervals.

It's not surprising they want to be so close. The ancient wolf ancestor slept in huddles, and I imagine 30,000 years ago hunter-gatherers in the midst of an ice age enjoyed the warmth of their dogs' fur-blanket bodies on bitterly cold nights.

What an extraordinary history we share with our beloved dogs. They have been with us for millennia, warming our hearths and hearts, sneaking into the innermost reaches of our lives more than any other species. As I look down, it's not a chicken or a pig lying at my feet, but a rather cute Jack Russell — so what is it about dogs that makes us love them so much?

'Biophilia' is the word used to describe human beings' long-held fascination with fauna and life processes. We have kept pets for tens of thousands of years, running the whole spectrum from monkeys to snakes, parrots to cats, but the first domesticated by far was the dog. How surprising that it was a predator!

There are an incredible number of benefits found in this relationship, for both humans and dogs. It is often physical contact that draws us to animals. We are a highly social animal, so we have a deep penchant toward love, connectedness and relationships. Dogs and humans share this innate drive for contact and touch. Research shows that wolves touch six times an hour, and as pups they are thermotactile (heat-seeking): the pup's head is like a probe for finding warmth and contact. We particularly love animals that are neotonised; that is, show baby-like attributes. What we will see later is that part of the evolution of the dog has been the juvenilisation of the wolf, resulting in dogs taking on more wolf-pup-like characteristics, involving both behaviour and underlying physiological features.

Many studies have shown that most urban dog-owners got their dogs for companionship, and that dogs fulfil our need for social connectedness and friendship. It was recognised very early on that dogs play an important role in family life, and are organic members of these groups. In one study, 65-80 per cent of respondents regarded

Blue and his signature
film move.

their dogs as family members. In a US study, over 71 per cent of people said they carried a photograph of their dog in their wallet, 62 per cent of dogs had their own chair, 55 per cent got birthday presents, and 13 per cent had their own bedroom.

Studies have also revealed that the emotional bond between dogs and their owners is proven to bring many benefits to us, like decreasing stress (as measured by lowered blood-cortisol levels), improving the longevity of our lives, and fulfilling our emotional needs in distressed situations. A 2012 study measured various degrees of attachment between owners and their dogs. Owners who had higher oxytocin levels (sometimes known as the 'love hormone') and lower cortisol levels (the stress hormone) when interacting with and petting their dogs tended to have closer bonds with their dogs. A number of recent studies have shown that petting a dog lowers blood-cortisol levels and decreases stress. Research shows — and it's my experience, too — that dogs are good role models for a better, healthier lifestyle; they encourage us to walk, be in Nature and meet people.

Dogs' attachment relationship or bond to their mentors (that is, their owner and immediate family) is almost identical to the attachment relationship between the human mother and her infant. Humans even have specialised brain cells in their amygdala (one of the emotion centres of the brain) that respond preferentially to animal images. One study revealed that when a person was showed images of 'cute' animals, they performed difficult tasks more diligently than people who viewed 'normal' animals or food. This suggests that the maternal-like hormones (probably oxytocin and vasopressin) stimulated more-caring responses. Studies of women shown images of their own children and dogs also showed that they evoke very similar responses in the brain compared with unknown dogs and children, suggesting that maternal feelings might extend to animals.

This thankfully is a two-way street, as dogs also live for social fulfilment and connectedness. In fact, recent research has shown that a dog's central focus, even over and above their own species, is us. Dogs also have similar hormones to humans; they also produce oxytocin, which has been shown to be the main neuro-chemical influencing the bond between humans and dogs. We both enjoy our interactions, derive support and cooperate at an unusually high level.

Many studies are now looking at dogs' ability to experience empathy and caring, their responsiveness to human gestures and their bonding hormones — even the fact that dogs most likely have 'mirror neurons' like humans do. Mirror neurons allow us to sense what another being is experiencing. I can feel it in myself as I watch Tommy's joy as he rolls on the carpet having a good scratch. I can't help but smile at his happy noises.

The possibility that dogs do have mirror neurons is considered rudimentary proof that dogs may have a 'theory of mind'. That is, where an animal understands that the 'other' has a separate mind and a different view or perception of the world. I can see it in Tommy, my very food-driven terrier, when he looks around furtively as he eats the neighbour's cat food. Clearly aware it's a habit I'm likely to be unhappy about, he gobbles more rapidly than normal, sneaking looks to see if I'm about to interrupt his happy delight. Traditionally, theory of mind was only attributed to humans, but it is now also formally attributed to chimps, bonobos and orangutans. While this is still controversial in dogs, more and more evidence is showing that dogs also have it.

Dogs truly are members of our families, and, through their acute ability to follow our gestures and learn by observation, they can learn the family rules of engagement and synchronise their behaviours with ours. I know myself that being with my dogs, throwing the ball, going for walks and swimming in the ocean is fulfilling, joyful and calming. My dogs seem to express unconditional love and joy, bringing me back to Nature and my own inner peace.

I have experienced, in a number of cases with my clinic dogs, what appear to be symptoms of depression after the death of an owner or a companion dog. Evidence shows that dogs mourn, and mourning occurs in animals that have strong bonds. The attachment relationship is strong in dogs, and indicates that they, too, may have a sense of empathy and love. Their hormones and physiological responses appear to be similar to those of dolphins and elephants.

CRYSTAL AND EBONY: DOGS MOURN, TOO

When Crystal, a Labrador, lost her dog mate of nine years, she stopped eating. Her owner, Jenny, said it took Crystal months to come right.

Julie lost her husband, Chris, from a heart attack, and their Doberman, Ebony, mourned for weeks with the rest of the family.

She lost weight and was lethargic, and they were so worried about her deteriorating health that trips to me and to the vet were needed. For Ebony it was important to make sure she was given lots of socialisation with other dogs to distract her and provide her with a purpose and stimulation. Julie walked her with friends' dogs, got her out and about and did lots of ball play. In many ways this is what we might also suggest for people, and so it was helpful for Julie as well. For a short period of time Ebony was also put on anti-anxiety drugs to help her get out of sympathetic arousal and into the learning state.

The many roles dogs play

Dogs are loved by us in the West today mainly for companionship, yet many certainly still have jobs, too. Dogs' cooperative skills and strong focus on us have made them great collaborators and assistants. Long ago they served purposes that improved our ability to survive and thrive, and they probably wouldn't be around today if they weren't originally useful to us. Some scientists have speculated that they even saved us from extinction in prehistoric times when we were under heavy competition from other large predators (particularly during the mini ice ages).

Early functions included guarding, hunting, tidying up our waste, and later herding and pulling loads, to name a few. One of the less savoury behaviours (in human terms) goes further, as eating our waste, including faeces, is common in village and pariah dogs even today.

We see evidence in today's herding dogs of just how much of an advantage dogs would have been to early humans. Their social competence skills are clearly demonstrated as they work in a coordinated fashion with the shepherd. They have an ability to 'take turns', moving one way, then responding to a command to move the other way, coordinating and harmonising with the needs and aims of the shepherd. This is also evident in guide dogs, where one study showed how they take turns in decision-making and have the ability to understand our aims or goals. They have been shown to be able to both lead and be led, taking over when appropriate.

Our bonds can and should start young, like Nalu with these pups.

Our bonds are driven by the same oxytocin in dogs and children. My daughter and granddaughter loving this pup.

In conclusion

What is most critical about our relationship with our dogs is that we can have the same emotional physiological response to our dogs as we do to our human loved ones. The mistake, so easily made, is when we therefore treat them like humans. You can see where the confusion can come from, when our body is responding in the same way as it would to our beloved human friends.

However, this is the critical part: we must treat and guide our dogs in a way that is helpful to them, from their perspective. Guiding them to live in a human world as though they were human will not help them. It can cause them confusion, fear and stress. So this is our challenge — love them with all our hearts *and* treat them the way these animal beings need us to treat them. We are the ones who have asked them to live in our modern human world, so it is up to us to understand them and help them to do that. It is up to us to be the loving mentors for our dogs.

To help us understand the dog's world, the next part of this book will look at how and why the dog came to be in our lives, and then at what the defining features are that make a dog a dog.

Becoming the dog

We know how much we love our dogs and what an amazing collaboration it is, but how did they come to be in our lives? How is it possible for a descendant of a wolf to end up in our living rooms and our hearts?

I know from having lived with wolves that they cannot be trusted to be left with young children, fowl, livestock or food — and they certainly don't take 'no' for an answer. A recent study from the Wolf Science Centre in Austria showed that while dogs can be taught not to take food in the presence of caregivers, wolves could not. I know from training wolves on the set of a Narnia film and at Battle Ground Wolf Park that when we used chicken drumsticks while clicker training, we were sure to wear gloves — fingers taste as good as chicken legs to a wolf, even a so-called tame one!

In this chapter we will venture through the pivotal events shaping the evolution of the dog, from the wolf through the proto-dog to the village/pariah dog. While the dog is a dog and not a wolf, as we have seen, the wolf is a significant ancestor to the dog (99.96 per cent) and has contributed important features to the dog's make-up. So we look back not only because it is a riveting tale, but also because it provides a helpful guide to the defining features and behaviours of the dog.

I have had a long love affair with wolves, and 40 years ago was fortunate enough to have access to some of the greatest scientists and trainers in dog behaviour. Professor Erich Klinghammer (student of Nobel Laureate Konrad Lorenz) was my first mentor, and he taught me much. At the time, his research centre at Battle Ground Wolf Park in Indiana housed two packs of wolves and a mixture of dogs and other canids (members of the dog family). The study group was tight-knit, and we lived and studied close to the hand-reared wolves.

I was exploring my thesis hypothesis that the herding behaviour in dogs was modified wolf-hunting behaviour. At that time, we strongly suspected that the gray wolf was the primary ancestor of the dog, although in 2015 the ancestor was in fact identified as a now-extinct sister species. What struck me most about wolves was how similar to dogs their core behaviours were, but also how different they were in significant ways. This period proved to be the most enlightening of my life in terms of understanding dogs, through studying wolves.

The old Lupomorph model

It's worth touching on some old research that people often get confused about. Forty-plus years ago the world's imagination was captured by research on the wolf and how it related to dogs. The now-discredited social order model that was developed, the Lupomorph model, describes wolves as if they were aggressive despots, tough leaders of the pack with strict linear hierarchies maintained by aggressive dominance.

This old theory was based on observations of unnatural zoo-formed wolf packs made up of older, unrelated wolves who were unable to leave. In the wild, wolf packs are made up of kin-related family members. Within these egalitarian family packs, dynamics are mediated by threat signals with very little actual aggression, whereas interactions

Professor Erich Klinghammer and me, during studies at Wolf Park in Indiana.

Me at Wolf Park in Indiana.

PARK

between separate packs are often severe. Unrelated wolves will often attack or kill wolves they don't know. Without the ability to leave, as would occur in the wild, the social dynamics of unrelated zoo packs become disruptive and aggressive. In addition, thinking that the wolf is the direct ancestor of the dog, and not considering the proto-dog and pariah/village dog's place in dog evolution, also contributed to this misunderstanding of dog behaviour.

Describing dog behaviour based on this unnaturally occurring activity proved misleading and created the ill-informed 'dog as an aggressive dominant leader' theory. This theory does not play out in wild wolf or feral dog packs. What we do see is that the leaders of these packs have the most connections and are the most liked.

What is understood today is that dogs did evolve from ancestral wolves and that although dogs are significantly different to wolves in many important ways, the wolf alongside its successor the proto-dog provided dogs with significant attributes that underpin them today.

The evolutionary path to today's dog

2.1 FROM WOLF TO DOG — THE MOST UNLIKELY OF TALES

Our understanding of the dog has evolved incredibly in the past 10 or 15 years, but there is still some debate around the ancestral pathway dogs took to become dogs and join up with humans. A recent study has confirmed that the ancestors of dogs joined humans at least before agriculturalisation, some 12,000–14,000 years ago. It is even possible that it started with our very early ancestors as they began to imagine and create the first simple tools 3.6 million years ago, or a little later when we first used fire, 1 million years ago. At the very least, it was early in the reign of *Homo sapiens*, and certainly once we came out of Africa 43,000–45,000 years ago, that our relationship with wolves or at least proto-dogs may have begun.

The beginnings of the canids started with the ancestor of the wolf. Ten million years ago, early canids radiated out into three divergent arms. The most successful arm arose seven million years ago during the start of an ice age — as the climate cooled, the first real canid ancestor started to appear. It was called *Canis ferox*, and it resembled a hairy type of coyote with a small body and a bull-terrier-like head. This ancient ancestor to the wolf evolved through a number of iterations until some two million years ago, when one of the dog's most significant early ancestors — the Etruscan wolf — emerged.

About 1.7-1.9 million years ago, the Etruscan wolf ventured from North America to Asia across the Beringian land bridge, and on through to Eurasia and Africa. This activated the historically significant 'Wolf Event', so known because of the wolves' domination of Europe, where they successfully competed with many much bigger predators, such as giant hyenas, sabre-tooth tigers and many more. They went on to adapt into almost every possible niche and environment — from ice and desert to tropics and mountains — and became the most successful predator of their time.

Through this period, wolves began to form into kin-related family packs, enabling them to hunt larger prey and protect group members. The social coordination needed to hunt prey improved their sociability and their social brains. The need for more complex communication with larger numbers of group members grew the connections in their brains (a process called 'gyrification'), making them more intelligent, with a greater behavioural plasticity (flexibility) and adaptability. Through this they developed a social order, with a key role of helpers evolving to assist in raising the young. This attribute would contribute significantly to the evolution of the dog.

At the same time, one of our early ancestors, *Homo erectus*, started travelling from Africa through the Levant (a historical geographical area around the eastern Mediterranean). *Homo erectus* had evolved from our early ancestors, who had moved down from the trees in Africa as the temperature warmed and the savannah grasslands took over from the forests. *Homo erectus* evolved from these ancestors who had hunted on the plains, and became the early hunter-gatherers. Following a similar trajectory to wolves, they too developed complex social orders motivated by hunting. Tools, fire, art and culture followed.

The first evidence of a meeting between *Homo erectus* and the Etruscan wolf occurred about 1.7 million years ago, soon after the wolf crossed from North America. Little is known about how or if any relationship formed. However, it was cold, and competition would have been strong among the many large competing predators, such as the saber-tooth tigers, giant hyenas and huge bears. By 30,000-40,000 years ago, the two most successful predators were *Homo sapiens*, in their large bands of hunter-gatherers, and the Etruscan wolf. Many of the other predators, except the wolf and the giant bears, were made extinct within 10,000–15,000 years of *Homo sapiens* arriving around 43,000 years ago.

This is when we think the amazing co-evolution story began properly. It is hard to imagine that man and wolf separately could have out-competed the other, more powerful predators. Certainly the wolf had dominated the land for nearly two million years, but when humans arrived they changed the landscape and out-competed most except the wolf. Is it possible that a collaboration with the wolf is what saved both man and the wolf from extinction? Together, did they out-compete the other top predators of the time? Did this need bring together humans and wolves, later to become dogs, into a unique and symbiotic relationship?

What we do know is that the social brains of *Homo sapiens* and the canids grew in a parallel evolutionary trajectory. And somewhere over those next tens of thousands of years, the descendent of the Etruscan wolf started to hang around human hunter-gatherers, and is believed to have self-domesticated.

With the dog's direct ancestral wolf species now extinct, we are left with just the modern gray wolf to reflect on what the wolf has brought to the dog.

The gray wolf is adapted to hunt for large prey, like elk and moose. This is a specific niche very different from other canids, like the coyote and jackal, which can be social but are more inclined to be solitary and kill small prey. The drive to capture large prey helped the wolf evolve a social order so that it could communicate across multiple pack members. This grew its sociability, social communication and ability to co-operate.

The wolf pack normally centres on a mating pair in a monogamous bond that breeds first in a 'whelping' (birthing) and then a 'rendezvous' den over a four-month period. The pack settles temporarily for that four-month period, to raise the pups to the stage where they move out into the world. This is the very important 'formative period', a short, intense time of optimum learning, where the pups spend most of their time in a learning state. This time is critical to the pups' development into stable, mature pack members. Also known as the critical period for socialisation (CPS), it is a key attribute of dogs today.

The pack is kin-related, having a mum, dad and the kids, as well as uncles and aunts. The older siblings disperse to form their own packs from around one to four years of age, but before that they become the very important 'helpers'. Their role is to help Mum and Dad raise their younger siblings to adulthood. While there is a social order with a hierarchy, where younger adults are subordinate to the elders, this is more like a parental or uncle/aunt relationship: ordered yet subtle, with mainly postural language and signals mediating the interactions. The older wolves 'mentor' the young, a bond that is very important in aiding learning and social integration. It is this critical helper role that receives the pup as it moves away from Mum, mimicking our bond with our dogs, which we will explore later in the book.

The most important factors that I believe contributed to making the wolf the progenitor of the dog are its intelligence, neuro-plasticity (flexible brain, resulting in adaptability), its peer-to-peer social communication system, and its ability to form amicable social bonds similar to humans.

But of course the story doesn't end there. We all know that a wolf is a wolf, and the dog became a dog. There are significant differences which make the dog distinctly a dog, and this is what we will explore next.

2.2 PROTO-DOG AND SELF-DOMESTICATION

So what created the titanic shift of the wolf's attention to humans and put in place the beginnings of the dog?

There is a huge dossier of scientific research trying to find the answers to where and when the wolf began to join up with man. Some of the oldest findings go back to nearly 40,000 years ago. There are five different sets of findings of animals with wolf- and dog-like features, in Southern Siberia, the Czech Republic, Belgium, Russia and France, ranging from 31,000 to 36,000 years ago. This may indicate different possible origins, or at least false starts to the process of self-domestication. Self-domestication is the process of wild animals living around and adapting to humans, without direct human selection or breeding.

One very interesting finding in France, at the entry to a famous cave with ancient human paintings, is a set of footprints preserved in mud that show a young boy with a large dog-like animal (between wolf and dog size) walking beside him for 30 metres. The ash from the torch

The wolfpack is a kin-related group.

he carried is dated to around 26,000 years ago. What an evocative and amazing find — surely no wolf would be walking beside a child holding a fire torch? This companion must have been the earliest form of the dog, the proto-dog.

In places such as Israel and Germany there is clear evidence going back 14,000 years of dogs living with humans, but there is also paleontological evidence that long before these dogs there were proto-dogs living with us. New research shows how the proto-dog evolved with the hunter-gathers, before the advent of agriculture. Revised mitochondrial DNA analysis puts this at around 25,000–30,000 years ago, but possibly much more. Some early analysis even puts it at 145,000 years ago! The most likely best current estimate, however, is about 18,800–32,100 years ago, not long after we arrived from Africa where there were no wolves.

It is difficult for paleontologists to discriminate between wolves and proto-dogs as they evolved into dogs, because the differences are subtle. There is plenty of evidence of what is described as wolves found in our habitations and our burial sites. We know that some of these will likely turn out to be proto-dogs as our techniques get better and the story becomes clearer.

For the purposes of this book, it is not important to pinpoint exactly where and when during the hunter-gatherer days self-domestication happened, but rather that it *did* happen. So instead, let's explore what the evolutionary pressures and opportunities were that created the change, and what this tells us about the dog today.

The latest, most convincing research suggests that the wolf self-domesticated to take advantage of man's waste and rubbish, which increased in volume as we became more successful hunters and gatherers. Just like seagulls, pigeons and rats, early wolves are likely to have congregated around our settlements to pilfer and clean up our food and faecal waste. While this started with the hunter-gatherers around 40,000 years ago, it really took off when early humans started to settle into fishing and hunting settlements and later into agricultural villages. This created more concentration and continuity of resources for the wolf to take advantage of. It is this shifting focus from hunting to scavenging that established proto-dogs as a separate subspecies.

Researchers that have watched wolves around dumps have found that wolves are largely active only at night. It is speculated that the more courageous and confident wolves got bolder and started to scavenge during the daytime when humans were around. It is thought that these wolves that could eat near humans and not get too stressed (which would stop them eating) developed a selective advantage. It is these more friendly, confident wolves that would have led to our first proto-dogs. Nature had started the selection for confidence, and its resultant companions friendliness and docility, that would lay the foundations for the dog. As these more docile wolves became successful in their adaptation to the human niche, the genetic traits of friendliness and docility were further strengthened. The docile wolves were successful, so they got to breed. What's more, it was more likely that they were breeding with each other, therefore strengthening the selection of the docile gene or gene complex.

We have learnt a lot from studying the domestication of pigs, horses and chickens, where there are plenty of records and research. However, information is far more limited in terms of the domestication of canids. The only good model of a documented domestication process in a canid is the Silver Fox breeding programme established at the Institute of

Cytology and Genetics in Novosibirsk, Russia, which began in 1959. The study, spanning over 50 years, followed the deliberate domestication of foxes for ease of management in fur production, the primary selection criteria for which was docility. This study demonstrated that docility evolved (through artificial selection) within the controlled Silver Fox population over between 8 and 40 generations. When you consider that over the course of the proto-dog's history we may be talking about 200,000–400,000 generations, we can see that there has been plenty of opportunity for extensive evolutionary change.

The Silver Fox research also suggested that increased docility was paired with smaller adrenal glands, which would have produced fewer 'fight–flight' hormones, so it is likely that the docile wolf would have been less fearful of humans. Together with a delayed and extended formative period that saw changes to the hypothalamus (the centre in the brain for the fight–flight hormones) in the docile foxes — changes similar to those we see when comparing dogs with wolves. The extended formative period allows time for more brain connections that increase social intelligence to become wired, and allows for longer periods of social development. It is believed that the natural selection for juvenilisation of the wolf caused the delay and extension of the formative period.

Alongside the increasing docility came all the hallmarks of increased juvenilisation: that is, the 'puppy-isation' of the proto-dog. As we saw, the hallmark of a formative period is that the pup is in a period of an extended learning state. As the brain capacity increased, its intelligence and ability to learn increased. This provided more opportunity for dogs to build complex relationships and learn to read our gestures, as well as more readily cross-foster with other species (bond with and include them in the family). These were all significant attributes of the proto-dog, and the concentration of these saw the beginning of its separation from the wolf. With the proto-dog's growing awareness that the critical food resource came from humans (as they were now scavengers), more and more their focus concentrated on us, until as research has indicated, ultimately humans became more important to them than even their own kind.

As mentioned earlier, it is unlikely that today's gray wolf species would have made that confident leap toward humans, because they are very shy and wary of us. Rather, it has been speculated that the actual ancestral species may have had an adaptive mutation that predisposed it to be more confident, be less frightened and have the ability to cross-foster onto multiple species.

Once proto-dogs started to hang around humans, it is likely that a number of other benefits to both species started to consolidate the relationship. We were both relatively small and less powerful than many of the other predators of the time. It is probable that the proto-dog's presence and barking (due to its territorial protectiveness inherited from the wolf) alerted us to threats. Other benefits could have included hunting with us (which would have directly improved our chances of survival), cleaning up waste so that other predators and scavengers were not attracted, and acting as body warmers, to name a few.

We know that some of the current hunter-gatherers, such as the Tanzanians and the Congo tribes, use their dogs like modern-day pig hunters do in the West. These dogs are highly valued amongst these tribes, and in some cases they are valued even above children, reflecting how critical they are to the group's survival.

Purely scavenging around hunter-gatherers by itself may have been difficult, and it has been hypothesised that humans may have deliberately fed and kept proto-dogs as pets, like Aboriginal people do with Dingos. It's likely that pups of these proto-dogs could have been taken in and reared through the formative period, socialising onto humans and the other species in the villages. Those kept in the villages could have continued to mate with wild wolves, but if socialised to humans may have whelped in the village.

This self-domestication of the wolf into the proto-dog became the 'raw material' from which dogs emerged. Human-led domestication then refined this process more and more over time.

2.3 VILLAGE AND PARIAH DOGS

To really understand what made the dog a dog, we are best to move ahead a little in time to when we truly settled down and created permanent villages. This would have created even more concentrated and reliable waste sources, providing resources for the proto-dogs. Around 12,000–15,000 years ago, at the beginning of agriculture, we start to see an increase in the numbers of dogs, and populations forming. These dogs slowly evolved into the dog we see today in village, pariah and dump dogs (free-ranging dogs not owned by anyone) — they are the direct ancestors of our dogs.

It has been estimated that there are 850 million village and pariah dogs in the world today, compared with the 150 million dogs owned by people, demonstrating just how successful a niche human waste has been for dogs! These village and pariah dogs are living examples of proto-dogs, advanced and evolved yet not pet dogs (although they could become pets if taken in at the right age).

These dogs exist due to the pressures of natural selection; they are not bred like our domesticated pets, which are now directly influenced by humans. As the last remnant link back to the proto-dog, they provide an excellent opportunity to see dogs in their natural situation before we began breeding them, and so understand the evolution of the dog.

Interestingly, a defining feature of pariah and village dogs is that they are all very similar in type, colour and size. If pet dogs enter these wild populations, their gene line gets integrated back into the typical 10-15 kilogram tan-coloured pariah dog over a short number of generations.

Probably the best studies of modern pariah dogs are those of a population that lives around villages in West Bengal and of dump dogs in Mexico. Through these dogs we can see the emergence of dog attributes, the foundation of all dogs today. Mating with the gray wolf has also added some genetic variability, too.

The pariah and village dogs are not migratory hunters anymore; instead, they are scavengers and small-animal hunters. Their food is generally found in the village surrounds, concentrated in areas like dumps and latrines, and its availability is regular. They can, and do, still hunt small prey, but critically not as a pack. The wolf social structure of a family pack with a monogamous pair of wolves is no longer necessary in this niche, nor are the accompanying hierarchies. Instead, the dogs form loose packs that don't protect territories like the wolf, and are promiscuous or forming short-term pairings. They are much more tolerant of having a large number of dogs around, although they can compete over short-term resources.

So what replaced the old hierarchy? Feral dog studies have shown that the leaders of these packs, far from being the dominant despots that were once proposed, are instead the most liked and connected with the most 'friends'. The pups are often left to their own devices early in the formative period, as resources are readily available. They are often very aware that humans are the source of the resources they need, and so humans can become a focus for their behaviour.

They have the capability to bond with humans, and often actively 'adopt' humans if possible.

Since resources are more evenly distributed and competition is lessened, the hierarchical structure becomes more context-specific; i.e. their response varies, depending on the reliability of the resource and whether it is worth defending. Interestingly, because food resources are smaller and more discrete than a large kill, dogs don't share food — 'possession is nine-tenths of the law'. As the value of the resource goes up, so does the protectiveness. This is called resource holding potential (RHP), a new hypothesis to help explain how dogs might resolve conflict when they don't have a linear hierarchy.

Dogs still have conflict at times over controlling a resource or access to a mate or an area. In this case, according to RHP, each dog judges who wants it more and they assess the risk of a fight. This can be influenced by how bold that dog is and who won before. Fighting is uncommon, but threat displays are used to displace other dogs. This is largely signalling and posturing, and the more strongly motivated

One of 850 million village/pariah dogs — the true ancestor to the dog.

dog normally wins the interaction.

These dogs mature earlier than wolves, and reach sexual maturity earlier. By eight months most are in puberty, and by a year old females can reproduce. Dogs are smaller and more efficient at converting food than the much larger wolves, so can survive on smaller energy inputs. They aren't constrained by the demands of the wolf's niche of searching, finding, hunting and protecting territories. This gave the proto-dogs, and now dogs, a significant adaptive advantage, and allowed them to out-compete wolves and most other canids in adopting and holding the human village niche.

Further research suggests that as dogs began eating human scraps, those that could digest cellulose succeeded better. Studies suggest that this rice-digesting gene is also linked to increased friendliness to humans, and so it has been called the 'rice-nice gene combination'. This increasing friendliness enhanced their human focus and attachment — yet another driver for that all-important evolutionary trait: docility.

Due to their human orientation, dogs' attachment relationship is especially focused on the caregiver (mentor) as compared with the wolf, which is more generalised onto the whole pack. As wolves move to a new pack after puberty, wolves and therefore dogs have an ability to redirect their attention and affiliation onto new individuals outside the group. This keeps their ability to change and adapt open much longer, and enhances their ability to learn and re-bond as their environmental and social context changes — a great attribute in our highly variable modern world. We use this attribute of dogs to build our own bond with them as their mentor.

Finally, dogs' unique capability to cross-foster onto other species, while retaining their sexual preference for their own species (and so continue to breed and evolve into their own specialised species, *Canis familiaris*), was also a defining attribute that allowed dogs to so successfully live with us. Their ability to live with other important domestic species like chickens, pigs and sheep; if they had continued to predate like their wolf forefathers this would have quickly ensured a one-way ticket out of the village.

So what about the 150 million pet dogs, the ones more familiar to us in our homes and hearts? How did they take that next step or two on this evolutionary tale of wolf to dog?

2.4 HUMAN-LED DOMESTICATION AND BREEDING (DESIGNER DOGS)

From the original village and pariah dogs up until 5000 years ago there wasn't a lot of variety — we had, roughly, only 30 or so proto-breeds. However, now there are well over 400 breeds! What an incredible influence modern humans have had on the dog.

'Domestic' means relating to home and of the family, and refers to dogs when we take over their care and management, and influence their breeding. This is different from self-domestication, which is a natural process; domestication is a variant of evolution that is driven by human need and desire. We are effectively designing the dogs we want or need.

When dogs started to congregate around our villages, they were generally not owned by anyone, but hung in and around, providing various functions. Slowly various opportunities might have come up to take them into our homes, the most obvious being the raising of orphan pups. The more they shared our homes, the more we would have discovered how useful they were, and the more we would have been driven to take control of their domestication. No other pet serves more varied purposes and functions than a dog. They wouldn't have been kept if they weren't useful.

As the roles and functions of dogs grew, they became more and more important to humans, migrating globally with us by 9000–10,000 years ago. While we now know from modern genetics that all dogs relate back to the now extinct sister taxa of the gray wolf, which came from the Etruscan wolf from Eurasia, they also mated with their local wolves, of both taxa, which further diversified them in different ways. For example, a 35,000-year-old fossil from Siberia showed that wolves contributed DNA to Northern Huskies through ancient inter-breeding.

As humans became more centred on agriculture and stayed in one place, they started to select dogs in very basic ways for different functions and jobs. Through this period, we started to differentiate dogs for different purposes. To start with, most of this would have just been by selecting for size, colour and behavioural traits — what could be seen and observed. One study of dogs suggests that by 8000 years ago, three different-sized dogs were identified in the villages in Norway. These may have been breeds. It is speculated that the larger dogs were possibly hauling dogs, the middle-sized ones hunters, and the smaller size hunters and/or companions.

By 5000 years ago, breeding was much more deliberate, and we start to see the ancient breeds emerging, groups or 'basal' (base from which others came) breeds. Some of the ancient breeds include: Basenji (Africa) and Salukis Afgans (North Africa), both of which are sight hounds or plains hunters (dogs that hunt primarily by sight rather than scent); Akita, Chow Chow, Sharpei and Telomian (Asia), the guard and food dogs; the Dingo and singing dogs of New Guinea (originally from Asia, but which moved south to Australia and New Guinea); and Huskies and Malamutes (the Spitz type, from the Arctic). Genetics now shows that these ancient breeds are the most closely related to the early ancestral wolves (they share more genes).

Fast-forward around 2000–3000 years ago, into the homes and castles of the élite in Europe (and in China even earlier), and we see the emergence of companion dogs and small lap-dogs. However, they were still an exception, with most dogs still bred to serve a function.

Over the next 1500 years, further specialisation and the raising of many different types of dog occurred. For example, in Medieval Europe deerhounds, wolfhounds, foxhounds and others started to emerge. By 400–500 years ago, dogs entered an even more speciality phase, and played an important role in society for various reasons.

Cross-breeding or hybridisation still occurred all the time; evident in the amount of flexibility and variation we see in dogs. Hybrid vigour (i.e. healthy genetic variation) was maintained, resulting in dogs staying healthy and vigorous, with survival high. However, the special traits weren't as predictable.

Further genetic separation of breeds came about from us selecting for specialised attributes and variations. Initially, it would have been very utilitarian — the breeds would have been bred for practical reasons — sheep dogs, sled dogs, guard dogs, scent hunters and sight hunters, etc. It wasn't until we started to control breeding in a more direct way, by organising and limiting mating, that we truly took control and so were able to standardise breed types more.

To create breeds, we mated dogs with similar traits, and to our best ability separated them from other dogs so they couldn't inter-breed. Initially, this was only moderately successful, as fencing was limited, so genetic variability would have been maintained. Natural selection and survival of the fittest still had a dominant influence, even though we had started to intervene. However, even doing this roughly, we could still achieve broad breed types. Different breeds started to emerge, such as the herding dogs versus the livestock guard breeds, and later the pointer (that points) or retriever (that retrieves), the guard dog (that guards) or the sled dog (that pulls).

Von Holdt and his colleagues in their 2010 research clarify the breeds into ten breed classes: the ancients and Spitz types, spaniels, scent hounds, working dogs, Mastiff-like dogs, small terriers, retrievers, herding dogs, sight hounds, and toy dogs. For the purposes of behaviour, training and simplicity, I place these in five related groups. I find this is more helpful from a behavioural perspective as it classifies them according to their behavioural predispositions.

1. The Basal breeds are genetically closest to the wolves, for example the Basenji (maybe the oldest of the ancient breeds), the Chow Chow, Akita, Sharpei and Telomian (the blue-tongued dogs), the Spitz types (the Huskies and Malamutes), and the sight-hound types the Salukis. They are defined by being less trainable, less human-focused and less socialised. Later breeding and hybridisation led to other breeds from them. Although also ancient breeds, because of their significance I have seperated the Spitz and sight hounds into their own group.

2. Spitz group: This group derived from the ancients with the curly tails, such as the Malamutes, Husky types, Elkhounds, the American Eskimo dogs and Samoyeds. They are possibly influenced by the northern, cold-weather wolves. Behaviourally, they are characterised by being pack, sled or pulling-type dogs; they are stubborn and predatory, recall and obedience are hard to train, and they are quite dominant but good in the harness.

3. Scent-focused hunters: These were probably influenced by the forest-hunting wolves, who also have a scent focus that may have contributed to the working dogs, Mastiff types, scent hounds, Spaniels, Retrievers and Terriers — generally, hunting dogs. Except for the working dogs in this class, the rest of the scent-focused hunters are characterised by being highly distracted by their scent (nose) and their hunting drive when it comes to trainability. They also tend to have a higher level of gaminess (arousal to hunt and aggression).

4. Sight-dominant hounds: Dogs in this group are likely to have

Spitz class of breeds.

been influenced by the plains-hunting wolves, which led to the Saluki and Basenji types, and later to the other sight hounds, such as Greyhounds, Whippets, Irish Wolfhounds, Borzois and the like. These are the slim, fast, Greyhound-shaped dogs that hunt by sight. These sight hounds are very prey-driven by movement, are hard to train (especially a recall), are self-workers, fast, lean and good for coursing dogs.

5.   Herding dogs: These dogs are closely related to the sight hounds above, with a strong sight focus, too — dogs such as the Border Collies, Corgis, Shetland Sheepdogs and Australian Shepherds. Due to their herding function, they have developed a greater level of cooperativity with the handler and so trainability is good to high. They have high energy and are reactive to movement.

Of course hybridisation of these groups into breeds is how breeds came about, and there is likely to be lots of variation, but certainly from a behavioural point of view breeds do have relatively clear traits. As a trainer I rely on this knowledge, and it is very helpful, although not unfailing due to variability caused by hybridisation.

Line breeding (pure breeding under strict control to ensure that breed criteria are maintained) as a generalised practice is only about 150 years old. This now provides us with near complete control of breed selection. Effective fencing meant we could isolate breeds for the first time, and so could create very specific forms or breeds. The formation of breed clubs for working and hunting dogs, then the kennel clubs with records and competitions, really accelerated dog selection. Not only did we get an improved working dog due to sheepdog and hunting trials, but we also created more dog fanciers, with the look of the dog becoming a major selection criterion. However, as we 'in-breed' we start to see 'in-breeding depression': that is, negative, recessive traits combining to create harmful traits and lowered breeding success and survival — congenital diseases increase, as do defects. Hybrid vigour can be something we miss in our line breeding of today.

With complete breeding control, we now have an extraordinary level of control around the dog. However, eugenics — the strict and fanciful selection of appearance traits — may be contributing to the loss of the functional purpose of owning a dog. With a strong focus on looks, this is starting to compromise the dog. Once function, health and behaviour lose their priority to appearance as the most important traits, we enter a worrying time for the dog's health and wellbeing.

We are now seeing inbreeding depression manifesting as physiological and behavioural aberrations infiltrating breed genetics, to the point that some breeds are almost completely dysfunctional. This can manifest in heart, eye, hip, joint and nasal problems, cancers and much more. Problems can also manifest behaviourally, such as genetic fearfulness, hyper-aggressiveness to other dogs and/or people and excessive gaminess.

These faults are a result of aberrant human choices, and they are threatening the central place of dogs as man's best friend. We must not let this happen. By far the most important priorities in our selection criteria should be docility and responsiveness to humans, and dogs' health and welfare. Anything else invites back the wolf's worst aggressive attributes.

With the full control over the genetics of dogs that we have today, these are the very real ethical and welfare challenges we face. Alongside the functional roles dogs play, our relationship is what counts: family co-operativity, play, joy and docility, and a healthy, happy bond.

Many of the wolf's skills and qualities were critical in the evolution of the dog. The key attributes the wolf contributes to the dog include:

- anatomy, sensory capacities and key functions, like retrieve, hunt and much more
- intelligence and plasticity, especially the ability to learn
- social brain and sociability
- helper function/inclination
- formative period
- peer-to-peer social communication system of signals, intonations and pheromones
- ability to form a social bond to the mother, and later the pack, and also to move to another pack later and bond again
- some cross-fostering potential in the formative period
- adaptable genome from early canids.

The key attributes the proto-dog and later the pariah/village dog contributed to the dog include:

- docility and juvenilisation — the wolf became a pup again to become a dog

O extended and delayed formative period — more time to socialise and adapt to a human world

O tolerance of other non-related dogs — no need to defend territories

O human focused — the core of our relationship; we control the resources and the love

O ability to bond with humans similar to our own attachment relationship — this, as with human infants, affords an extended time in family care to investigate and adapt to the world

O focus on caregiver (mentor) in a special way — wolves did this both as the original helper bond but also by moving from the familial to the breeding pack; growing up from helper to parent

O cross foster on to other domestic species, e.g. cats, sheep, birds, fowl, and most importantly, humans. This ability is one of the defining features of the dog

O heightened confidence and ability to habituate to novel stimulus — like an extended den phase

O ability to switch into a learning state more easily and stay in it longer. This is the critical difference between the dog and the wolf. It's not so much that dogs can learn better than wolves, it's that they can be switched into a learning state more easily and maintain it.

In conclusion

The dog's long journey beside us as we evolved out of the trees onto the plains as hunter-gatherers is unique in the animal world. How extraordinary that our parallel evolution saw us both develop complex social brains that enabled us first to hunt, then live in packs, bands and villages. This desire and ability to bond has been one of the key enablers of our 400-century-long relationship and collaboration.

How remarkable it is that the beloved, docile being in our lounge is 99.96 per cent wolf, and yet also just how much a difference that 0.04 per cent makes in distinguishing a dog from a wolf — who is not in our lounge! The wolf, and later its successors the proto-dog and the pariah/village dog, have given much to the dog we love today, and it is these attributes we look at next to guide how we bond with our dogs. Together we live happily in one big family, collaborating in so many ways. Truly man and woman's best friend.

Inside the dog's mind

In this chapter we will look closely at how dogs perceive their world, sometimes known as their Umwelt. 'Umwelt' describes how the world is experienced by a particular organism.

It was first coined by Jakob von Uexküll in the early 20th century when describing the world of a deer tick. Uexküll identified only four things that are important in the deer tick's life, so you can imagine that its life is simple and its senses and perception of the world is very different from ours!

World view is influenced by our species' drivers, perceptual apparatus (the means by which we perceive the world — our nose, eyes, ears, etc), capabilities and intellect; and each species is very different. All species have a different perception of the world, whether a flea on a dog or the

Marlow from Pound Pups TV series has life, intelligence and joy re-found.

actual dog! What is important to us predetermines our intelligence and focus in the world.

Dogs, like all beings, have their own unique perception of the world, their own culture and cultural view (Umwelt), and it is of course different from ours. We understandably have an anthropomorphic or human-centric perspective, and can often only see dogs through our own eyes and experiences. This can sometimes create real suffering for a dog. While dogs have co-evolved to understand us, they still view us from *their* point of view, reading us in wolf and dog terms. There are many differences in our perception of their world that cause misunderstandings, and that lead us to misunderstand and exacerbate problem behaviours.

A good example of this miscommunication is submissive urination, where we might punish a dog for urinating, when in this context the dog is actually using this behaviour to prevent punishment. It is saying: 'I give up!' Particularly with a young female pup, Dad — who from a small pup's perspective is very big — comes home and greets her with a big friendly 'Hello!' while reaching over her to pat her and looking fondly straight into her eyes. Reaching over a pup and staring can be construed as threat signals, so now the poor pup is thinking that she has done something wrong: she crumbles to the ground and rolls over in 'recumbent submission', as if to say 'I give up!' Dad reaches even further over her to pat her tummy, at which point she involuntarily pees as a further communication, saying: 'Seriously, Dad, I really give up!' Dad is not happy, so his voice drops and he possibly emits anger pheromones she can smell. He grabs her by the collar (thus grabbing the ritualised threat area of a dog) to take her out, so she pees some more, all the way outside. Dad repeats a growly 'No!' and puts her out, thinking that will fix that the next time. But when next time comes, and before he even gets close, the pup rolls over and pees straightaway, or scuttles away fearfully. And so it goes on: the Catch 22! A dog doesn't know that a carpet is important — carpet means nothing to a dog — but submissive urination means 'I give up!'

Sadly, this is a miscommunication between two worlds, two cultures that love each other but don't understand how each is communicating. It is a perfect example of species-specific behaviour conveying different messages to each other. This shows the paradoxes that can complicate the human-dog relationship. (However, please don't panic if this is all too familiar to you: the Excessive Submission chapter in Part D will help you with this highly treatable issue.)

Ultimately we must ask ourselves: what is it I must do to be in an effective and loving relationship with my dog? Dogs can't change their perception of the world, so it is up to us to understand theirs, know how it is different to ours, and through that create a shared language. Understanding their world and treating them accordingly: love is understanding.

In this chapter we seek to do this by understanding what is inside the dog's mind and world. We look at:

O How do dogs experience and so perceive the world?

O What motivates a dog?

O What does it mean to be in relationship with a dog?

O What makes dogs so intelligent, and how do they learn?

By exploring these questions, we hope to deeply understand our dogs, and through that be in a loving relationship with them, and so love them in the way they need to be loved.

3.1 SENSES – HOW A DOG EXPERIENCES THE WORLD

Dogs view the world through very different senses and sense capabilities than we do. Dogs have inherited most of their sensory apparatus from the wolf and earlier canids. Therefore, most of their senses are designed for hunting prey, living in groups and sexual reproduction. Some are also influenced by climate and other environmental influences.

PADDY: FROM RESCUED TO RESCUER OF TREES

Paddy was a rescue dog on our TV show *Pound Pups to Dog Stars*. A four-year-old Labrador cross, Paddy was rescued from a hoarder, who had him chained in a filthy back room full of faeces. Paddy had the saddest face I'd ever seen on a dog and knew nothing of life, but we soon discovered his beautiful, loving nature and that he had quite the nose! Slowly but surely, with Dog Zen we built a beautiful bond with him and resolved his issues — mainly food aggression from years of starvation.

To show that rescue dogs are smart dogs, we wanted to give him a purpose in his life. That's when we came across the 'kauri dieback'

Paddy before.

Paddy after.

programme run by Auckland Council — fighting a soil-based disease attacking our iconic national tree. There is no cure yet, so finding and isolating the infected trees is critical. The disease is undetectable by the human nose, and the council wanted to investigate whether a dog could detect it. Using scent-detection techniques, we trained Paddy to become the first kauri dieback detector dog in the world, able to discriminate and detect the disease a metre or more under the ground in the roots of a tree. Not bad for a dog so recently abandoned in a back room.

Smell — the dog's super sense

Dogs sense the world very differently to us. If you were to choose the dog's greatest sense, it is undoubtedly his immense sense of smell. Dogs have between a 100,000 and 2 million times better sense of smell than us, with 200 million to 300 million olfactory neurons (depending on the breed) — we have only 6 million!

The dog's nose is directly wired to his brain, and is the most rapid of the dog's senses. The olfactory bulb is massive, one-eighth of the dog's brain and relatively bigger than our visual cortex (with sight being our dominant sense). Dog's have a highly specialised vacuum-like system in their nose, which sucks in air and spits it out when fully vetted in a way that doesn't interrupt the air coming in. They also have a special organ in their upper palette called the vomeronasal organ (also known as Jacobson's organ), which is a unique taste-smell organ that allows them to detect pheromonal and other chemical information that we have no hope of perceiving. When using it, they sometimes chatter their teeth (known as the flehmen response), especially when a bitch in heat leaves scents and pheromones. It is because of this organ that dogs have a wet nose, as the fluid carries the taste-scent information. Relatively speaking, we might consider ourselves scent-blind, or near enough, in comparison!

Dogs smell us through the chemical mix of the different fatty acids we leave behind. They can detect minuscule changes in the mix down to a microgram or so. Because they can detect these subtle changes, they can, for example, tell by smelling footsteps and analysing their composition which way you travelled and how long ago you were there, even if it was a number of days ago. When you consider that dogs can smell you or prey several kilometres upwind, you might say that, in a way, they can know the future. If something is travelling their way, they can intercept that person or animal, ambush the animal if it is prey, or greet the person if it's their owner. Have you ever noticed how your dog's demeanour changes as you are nearing home? We believe that dogs create a kind of four-dimensional image that includes time.

Dogs can also smell pheromones and other scents that inform them of not only what we have been doing, but also how we are feeling. They can detect moods that are shaped by hormones, such as fear and anxiety. This is critical to understand when you are training, because if you are feeling anxious (which is not uncommon if you are dealing with a difficult dog), it is likely that your dog will sense it. Your dog is guided by you, so if you are anxious it will influence him. I know it's hard to control, but it is something to be mindful of. However, you can override this olfactory information with appropriate postural communication — so fake it until you make it! (See the Shared Language chapter.)

It's extraordinary the range and variety of ways that dogs assist us thanks to this powerful sense of smell. The dog's sense of smell has created a whole range of jobs highly valued in the human world.

These jobs include detecting things like explosives, drugs, fruit, cancer, epilepsy, landmines, environmental contaminants and even lost people, to name a few. This, together with their desire to help the family, makes dogs an invaluable asset to humans, as these jobs can save lives.

Dogs find it difficult to identify individuals without movement, so in my experience dogs often rely on scent recognition if they are at all unsure visually. I find fearful dogs take more time to identify people and their 'negativity bias' is greater, so they tend to react fearfully or aggressively in situations they don't have time to assess with scent. I am conscious of this when I think my dog might need the time to sniff something to gain clarity.

In terms of general training, scent is most relevant as an obstacle that will limit our ability to communicate with our dogs. When a dog is on a scent (tracking a scent), most owners describe it like their dog 'doesn't have any ears' — they aren't listening and won't come back to them. Your dog has been captured by a scent, a very high driver in a lot of dogs. She is in a high-arousal, non-learning state, focused on her scent world and where it is taking her, and therefore ignoring you!

A strong bond with your dog is critical to override her scent focus. It is a very strong natural driver and, when linked to a strong predatory drive, it can be very difficult to override. The higher the scent drive in a dog (like scent hounds — you Beagle owners know what I'm talking about!), the more challenging this will be. The earlier you start on bonding and recall (getting your dog to come to you on request) with your puppy, the better. A key is to know your dog's signals, which will let you know she's about to focus on a strong scent, because then you can intervene early to get your dog's focus back on you.

It is, however, very important to let your dog experience her scent world (under control, of course). It is a fundamental part of your dog's world, and so a key part of our dogs having a fulfilling life.

Sight

Of course it can't all be so extraordinary!

Dogs don't have as good a sense of colour vision as we do; we are trichromatic (with three base-colour receptors — red, green and blue) and they are only dichromatic (two base-colour receptors — yellow and blue). A human with full colour vision sees red, orange, yellow, green, blue and violet; a dog sees greyish brown, dark yellow, light yellow, greyish yellow, light blue and dark blue. Imagine what the world looks like with only yellow lights on, and the red-green fades out.

Dogs also have poorer binocular vision and depth perception up close than we do, although the short-muzzled dogs with big eyes in the front, like Boxers and Boston Terriers, do see better than other breeds in this regard. However, those with side-mounted eyes see a broader field of vision. Animals with side-mounted eyes find it hard to discriminate between us close up, especially if we are not moving. If we move, such as to throw a ball, they see us better; that's why moving hand signals are my preference when teaching commands.

Dogs can detect contrast and brightness variations, and other indicators that help them discriminate between things. As they have evolved to see prey moving from a long way away, they see movement better than we do, and see in the dark much better than us, as they have adapted to hunt at dusk and dawn, and even at night at times. Their visual acuity and depth of field isn't as good as ours, because our eyes are more at the front of our head, but they have a greater field of vision to detect predators and threats from behind and the side.

Dogs have a high degree of sensitivity to the orientation of a person or dog. We know they can tell if you are looking at them, and if they don't know you, they may feel threatened if you stand direct on, stare at them, approach them, hold something up (stick-like), or are wearing unusual clothing. They are reading and relating to us in dog postural terms, accounting for our height, size and familiarity. In other dogs, they look at the ears, face, muzzle, tail, uprightness and the direction and duration of eye contact. They look to see whether or not the other dog is moving toward them, and for indicators of relative dominance or threat.

Dogs are different from wolves in that they look at us. They have special neurons for this, similar to those humans have. They are looking at our face for information, reassurance, guidance, for the location of food or to read our emotions — so much is held in a human face. We have a highly evolved and complex set of behaviour and mood signals that we display with varied facial expressions. These tend to be very accurate, honest and ritualised, and dogs have learnt to read these. This is a co-evolved trait that we believe we favoured in selection, as we naturally look closely and intimately at our family members, which stimulates the release of oxytocin and other bonding hormones.

This is Reggie's classic ball pantomime — encouraging me to throw him the ball.

REGGIE: THE EYES HAVE IT

Reggie, my closest dog, looks intimately and deeply into my face and eyes, searching for what I want. He also has a classic pantomime with his ball that virtually assures it will be thrown: eyes down to his ball placed strategically between us, then back to my eyes (yes, Dad's noticed), then back to his ball. This is combined with his tail wag, which moves as if driven by a rheostat; the more I move toward the ball, the more it goes. His eyebrows seem to wink at me to encourage me, too. The intensity of his stare is like a magnet that subconsciously sucks my hand onto the ball to throw it into the distance — I am putty in his paws.

Looking up to us and holding eye contact is an important part of training in Dog Zen to reinforce the bond. I encourage eye contact and the dog looking to me for direction. I call this 'contact', simulating and reinforcing the following response (the pup's natural instinct is to follow Mum and later the mentor). I'll talk more about this in the Creating the Bond chapter.

Hearing

Dogs have a much better sense of hearing in the upper frequencies than we do. They can hear as high as 35,000-40,000 cycles per second (cps) — up into the ultrasonic range where many rodents and some insects communicate, so they can hear mice in the walls. We are lucky to hear up to 20,000 cps. This means that high-frequency whistles can be used to communicate with dogs in training. Note, though, that they don't hear quite as well as us in the very-low-frequency range. Their discrimination of subtle intonation is also highly acute — they use it to read our emotions, and fMRI (functional magnetic resonance imaging) carried out in Japan reveals that parts of their brain, similar to ours, are dedicated to this function.

Dogs hear long before we do. As we live down a long, forested driveway, it is my dogs that first pick up on anyone entering the property. As I sit on the deck, I can see the change in Tommy's alertness. He goes from blissed-out nap to full alertness in a split second; head raised, turning toward the driveway, alert for danger, ready to respond if Dad needs him. (Did I mention that at all of 6 kilograms he thinks he's the biggest dog in our pack? Terriers punch way above their weight class!)

Intonation is a big part of verbal training cues. Using high-pitched tones when training your dog says 'Good boy, I am pleased'; low-pitched intonations mean you are not happy. As you'll see in the How Dogs Learn chapter, we all learn by contrast, so it's best to make a clear difference between the two.

Often we use tone automatically, so it can be hard to fool our dogs! The intonation most often will tell your dog more than the command itself, and certainly the intonation can override the command if they are in conflict (e.g. if you say 'good boy' in a growling voice, your dog will be confused but will likely think he's done something wrong). Keep words and intonations simple and clear.

It's best when first training a behaviour to start with hand cues only, and then introduce verbal cues once the behaviour is somewhat established. This is because dogs' language is largely non-verbal and we know dogs observe our gestures closely.

Taste

I won't go into dogs' taste much, as it's not very significant in rearing and training. The key thing to mention is in relation to training food. Generally, we need to use high-value food — that is, highly palatable food that they love, so that it will motivate them to work for it.

With dogs who have too high a food drive, we sometimes will lower the palatability of the food so they don't get over-aroused and therefore can't learn. Some dogs are picky eaters, so we have to build their appetite to take advantage of it in training. Most dogs do or can be taught to love their food, though a level of management might be required. When training, make sure you manage their food intake, including the training amount in their diet.

When training, we provide a mix of food types to ensure novelty and again motivation. We grade the food types from high value to low value, generally starting with the lower value. We use the treat-like food for training (for example cheese, chicken or dog roll) and simpler food for general feeding (for example dry dog biscuits).

Touch

Dogs (like wolves) are very tactile toward their pack. Dogs and humans share this innate drive for contact and touch — both of us enjoy it and are calmed by physical contact. It is a common activity that people seek in their relationship with their dogs.

Touch is an important aspect of bonding, and you often see more-bonded dogs near or touching their owners. I love how my dogs solicit me by placing their paws on my arms or legs. In terms of rearing and training your dog, touching and handling is an important part of your relationship, and is covered in the Shared Language chapter.

In conclusion

With an incredible ability to sense threats with their acute scent and hearing capabilities, it isn't hard to see why early humans valued dogs right from the beginning. Having a large, protective, alert predator with acute senses around would have been a relief and a huge evolutionary advantage. Maybe this is why our cousins the Neanderthals didn't survive: no dogs!

Dogs are significantly non-verbal, and so their sense world — watching, smelling, touching, hearing and tasting — is a big part of their perception of the world. They can discriminate so much using their senses — your race, age, sex, whether they know you or not, how close you are socially, and how you are feeling. Their sensory capability is vastly different from ours. It allows them to access a world we can't imagine.

3.2 DRIVERS – WHAT MOTIVATES A DOG

There are a number of key drivers in a dog's life, and these can help or hinder us with our training, depending on how we understand their impacts. Drivers can be used as motivators (rewards) in training, but we can also inadvertently use drivers to train inappropriate behaviours. An example of the latter is letting your dog inside and near you (contact with you is a driver) when he is barking at the door: you have positively reinforced and rewarded the barking behaviour. We can often give dogs what they want without realising it, and so reinforce the exact behaviours we don't want. Those are the days we end up wondering just who is training who!

Drivers can also be described as resources sought by a dog — the things your dog needs or wants. Whoever controls the resources in your dog's life is her mentor(s). Resources or drivers can include food, social contact, play, freedom, walks and many more things. When you are providing your dog access to these resources, you are providing a reward. In day-to-day life (that is, when you are not formally training your dog), it can be easy to inadvertently reward your dog without thinking or knowing that you are doing so.

So in reality you are training all the time, a training technique I call 'Nothing in Life is Free'; that is, the dogs must 'work' for their reward/ resource. Whatever behaviour your dog is doing just before he gets those resources will be the behaviour you are training/shaping. Make sure you pay attention and observe what you are doing just before your dog gets what he wants, and ensure you reward your dog for appropriate behaviour. For example, if you let your dog barge through the door to go for a walk (a resource), then you are teaching your dog to barge, not wait. Instead, ask for a sit (appropriate behaviour), then release him with an 'OK' to let him out the door for a walk (reward).

The following are a few of a dog's key drivers:

Food

Food is one of the most important drivers for dogs, as it directly affects survival. As dogs became domesticated, we became the controller of food, so we took on a central focus for dogs. Food became the most important resource we could control, so it has become paramount in training. Dog Zen utilises the dog's orientation toward the human to solicit and acquire this important resource.

Eating is linked strongly to learning state. Anxiety, fear and hyper-excitability inhibit appetite. The fight-or-flight state (sympathetic arousal) inhibits appetite. In this state, the body redirects all of the blood and energy to the muscles so that they can *act*! The primitive brain short-circuits thinking and learning so that it can act. Therefore, one of sympathetic arousal's primary identifiers is a lack of food drive (a very handy clue in training, which we will discuss in detail later). The peak training state — learning state, also called the rest and digest state — is marked by the desire to eat (go to the Learning State chapter for more details).

The food drive is so strong in dogs that it can lead to a number of problem behaviours, including food resource guarding, which can lead to dominance; pica (eating inappropriate objects — a particular problem with retrievers and Labradors); anorexia (an unnatural, inhibited appetite that is either physically or psychologically based) and hyperphagia (excessive eating). Some eating disorders are physiological and require vet advice. This is always a necessary first step for these issues.

The methods we use in training (especially clicker training) will help to develop healthy appetites and relationships to food. (The clicker is a small hand-held tool that has a button or strip of metal on it that makes a distinctive click sound.) Administering your training food in a controlled training context will train your dog to have appropriate eating habits and entrain a healthy relationship with food. Training creates a purpose for the dog.

Predatory or prey drive

In hunting canids and herding dogs, adrenalin and related hormones are heightened up to four-fold when confronted with prey or herding stimuli. Learning when in a predatory state is greatly inhibited, because the dog is in a state of high-level sympathetic arousal (a non-learning state), which makes it a difficult behaviour to treat. Generally, the best way to limit this drive or avoid the dog chasing stock, etc, is through correct exposure and cross-fostering in the formative period, as well as good recall training and breed choice. Early contrast training is important too.

Ball-chasing is a mock prey-chasing behaviour, so is highly motivated, too. Although some people reward with a play item, in my experience it often interferes with learning. Like any prey-related behaviour, it gets the dog too aroused and out of a learning state. Instead, I use ball play for rewarding my dog after a sequence of learning. You can also use this to exercise and give a mental outlet for dogs.

Sex drive

This can, and does, easily interfere with training, and can lead to many behaviour problems in dogs. The influence of pheromones and hormones can be a major driver in behaviour and behaviour problems, including roaming, hypersexual behaviour, dominance, dog–dog aggression, and micturition (marking with urine). The use of de-sexing and therapeutic hormones can play a significant role in treating sexually motivated problem behaviour. This is discussed in part D.

Social contact

Sometimes your dog's driver is contact with you, other dogs or family members. Generally, the drive is warmth, connection, calming and contact. Being close to you, such as in the car (if your dog likes travel) or house, especially the bedroom, bed or couch (the closer to you the better), is a very sought-after resource. However, an over-dependent bond causes both you and your dog anxiety; therefore, developing a healthy bond is critical. Separation distress can be the result of an over-dependent bond, so see the chapter on Separation Distress if you suspect it is a problem.

Freedom

Running free is often important to a dog, especially one that leads a restricted life. Again, using this freedom as a reward is powerful when done properly, and can be dangerous when not controlled.

Working

Working is often a modified hunting behaviour, and so prey drive is the motivator; this means that for working dogs, engaging in their natural working behaviours is very self-rewarding.

Play

Many dogs love the water, and for those dogs access to water can be a reward. Play itself is often a motivator for a dog.

It is important to understand what motivates your dog, as it will be the doorway to successful training for you both. For the first four to six weeks when I train a dog, I identify his drivers and manage them carefully, rewarding him for appropriate behaviour to help shape our shared language.

All dogs are different, so assume nothing — get to understand what motivates your dog.

3.3 EMOTIONS — OUR BOND AND ITS SIGNIFICANCE

Dogs are born to live in relationships; their intelligence is augmented by sociability. Dogs love us and we love them, and that is science, too!

HERCULES: A LOVE OF HERCULEAN PROPORTIONS

I think many of us can recount extraordinary tales of the special bond we have had with a dog. I have been lucky enough to have many special relationships, though one in particular stands out: my bond with Hercules, the famous 'Bugger Dog'. (You might remember the infamous Toyota 'Bugger' advertisement. It won 15 international awards, and Hercules even won Australian Dog of the Year!) Hercules was trained to respond to over 145 commands, and starred in hundreds of movies and TV commercials. My partner calls him my dog soulmate. He was my dearest mate, and although he died in 2004 (known and loved by many, with 2000 attending his funeral as he lay in state), he will always hold a very special place in my heart.

My son Bodhi and I raised Hercules from a pup, a handsome Huntaway (sheepdog)-Rottweiler cross. We started training him early (at eight weeks old) to be Hercules' dog on the *Hercules* TV series, and he proved to be an extraordinary talent. As he grew alongside my own young family, he was ever alert to any threats to them, and used to shepherd the kids away from strangers he wasn't sure about. He would pick up my bag if I left it somewhere, and I could ask him to get virtually anything — the TV remote, car keys, a beer out of the fridge. He even mowed the lawns (on a film set, that is). Even if I was in the bath, he would push through the door to come in, though he was polite enough to close the door behind him! The bond I had with him was exceptional. Oh, how I loved that dog. It broke my heart when he died.

The good news is that relationship is also central to our dogs. Their ability to bond has developed over millennia, with first the wolf and then the proto-dog providing the dog with a social brain and sociability. The importance of relationships has shaped dogs throughout their evolution, so to understand dogs we have to understand their need and drive for relationship. If we do that, then we can determine what it takes to be in relationship with them and love them in the way they need us to.

This chapter explores how dogs experience relationship, by asking:
O What enables a dog to be in a relationship?
O What is a relationship for a dog?
O How do they behave in a relationship?

What enables a dog to be in a relationship?

Imagine yourself back in those ancient times, with the evolutionary drivers that were shaping the proto-dog as it moved from hunter to scavenger. Its food resources are now found in one place (scavenging from tribal surrounds and village dumps), which means that Mum and Dad don't have to move around anymore, so the pups can look after themselves much earlier. They know it's those two-legged beings that supply the goods. Mum, Dad and the siblings are about, but those humans hold all the cards. The pup has a preference to adopt humans, as they've got what it wants.

We are central to the dog's world, clear and simple. It can't be emphasised enough how significant the shift of their focus to humans was. Recent research shows just how highly attuned to humans dogs are; they even prioritised us over their connection to their own kind. Dogs' sociability originally came from the wolf, but their human focus came from self-domestication and domestication. They need a sense of place and a role in their relationship. Contact is vital for them, and you can see that in how often you find your dog wanting to be close to you or have some part of him be in contact with you. Connection is central to their life and survival.

If exposed to it in their formative period, dogs are able to adjust seamlessly to family life because of their attentiveness and sensitivity to human communication, emotions and behaviour. Dogs have a great ability to understand us. They are sensitive to human communication and can read our gestures (like nodding), as well as follow facial

Hercules the 'Bugger Dog' may be the greatest film dog of all time. But most of all my best mate.

gestures, eye movements and pointing, and can even mimic our behaviours. They can smell our pheromones, and know when we are anxious, fearful or happy.

Dogs themselves use intonation and subtle signalling to convey emotions, and a parallel development in similar areas in the brain to the human brain helps them recognise our vocalisations and intonations.

We know that dogs are sensitive, and we often attribute human feelings or emotions to them, such as jealousy, guilt, shame and empathy. Science has distanced itself from some of these human-centric feeling descriptors, though there is now more agreement that dogs feel the more 'simple' emotions of fear, love and happiness. Emotional stimuli are processed in the right hemisphere of dogs' brains, so they turn their heads to the left when emoting.

A key feature of our relationship with dogs is that they are attentive to us. Dogs find human contact very rewarding, and are motivated to please us. Dogs look at us for direction, to recruit help, for reassurance and information, for direction to important resources, especially food, and just to connect to us. They know that we are in control of the key resources of their life (food, contact, freedom, etc), and that they need to engage with us to stay a part of the family and gain access to their needs and wants.

Dogs are very aware of where we look, what we are doing and where our attention is. The interesting thing is that not only do dogs watch our gaze, but they also gaze back and are aware that we are attentive to them. Studies have shown that dogs know if we are reading a book, for example; and if we appear distracted, then they will do what they want to do. However, if they know that we are attentive to them, they will stay connected to us and look to please us.

As dogs became more human-focused, they became very good at recruiting help from us. They understand that we can help them get to their end goals — namely, access to some form of resource. This attentiveness and seeking help from us is a useful mechanism for training; however, care needs to be taken that your dog doesn't end up training you!

Dogs have an ability to look us in the eyes. This is an unusual behaviour in the animal world, where staring is often a threat gesture. If you stare at a wolf it will feel threatened by you, as it is a ritualised form of threat in their social communications. Intense and/or sustained staring means that to dogs and to us, too; however, when a bond is established this changes. Instead, for us and dogs, looking each other in the eyes has become a defining feature of a healthy bond.

With this in mind, you can now understand why looking up to us and holding eye contact is an important part of training in Dog Zen. I encourage eye contact and looking to me for direction. I call this 'contact', reinforcing the following response I expect them to have toward their mentor: a combination of looking to me (it doesn't need to be continuous), moving with me, sitting and lying when I stop, then moving off when I move off. This is subtly reminding the dog to stay engaged with me; in a similar way the pup first follows his mum and then the mentors in his pack. (I call this Joining Up; see the Creating the Bond chapter in Part B.)

Eye contact has subtle nuances of duration, fixedness and force. You know just by holding a stare with someone on the street for a second too long how the other person disengages, or how a flirty stare may be held for a second or two longer than normal. A good trainer uses eye contact to manage and communicate subtly with a dog, firming up the eye to fix the dog in a stay or wait, and relaxing eye contact or turning it off for a recall (it's less of a threat, so draws the dog toward you).

Dogs follow our gestures, look at our faces, notice the things we touch, watch our hands for food, notice our postural signals, and much more. We need to be very conscious of how to use visual cues to our advantage (and also know when we are giving unintentional cues). Using changes in our body orientation, posture, hand signals and gesturing helps us sculpt our shared language with our dogs.

What they require in a relationship — the mentor

Research shows that the bond between dogs and humans closely resembles that of mothers and infants. The bond between a human baby and its human mother is important, as it allows the young to safely explore and learn about the world. The effect of this primary attachment relationship is called the secure base effect. For dogs and infant children, it is the safe person or place from which they can venture out and learn about the world. From studying wolves, we have learnt that as the pup transitions away from its mother in the whelping den toward the pack, it forms its first significant relationship (outside of Mum) with a helper wolf, or as I call for our purposes, the 'mentor'. The 'secure base attachment' shifts to this mentor as well.

In the wild, this mentor is normally an older sibling wolf. This mentor wolf shows the pup the ways of the pack and the world. It will teach it what it can and cannot do, what is safe and what is dangerous, and what its role and position is within the pack. It will provide clarity around the pup's place in the pack, and guidance around decisions.

This role requires attentiveness and flexibility to create new bonds, key attributes we utilise in our bonds with our dogs. For our dogs, we are that mentor as they move into their new packs (us and our families). It is our responsibility to guide the pup, then dog, through life. An adult dog still has a need for a secure base attachment, all the more so due to the juvenalisation effect of self-domestication.

By building this secure base, the pup is in a peak learning state. She has confidence to do things when the mentor is around which she might not be able to do when the mentor isn't there because she is too anxious. Research has shown that when dogs were tested to see whether they would play with a stranger, they would do so when the owner was present. However, when a dog's owner was absent, they didn't play with the stranger in most cases. Similar results have been seen with children.

A well-established secure base relationship will have your dog looking to you for confidence and direction. If a dog feels secure, then she can continue to be calm and stay in a learning state. A well-attached bond means that a dog will be a better learner and more readily able to adapt and respond to people, animals and events in our dynamic world. It means that your dog will stay connected to you as you go about your day, checking in to see where you are, what is needed and to get guidance if a new situation occurs, such as if she meets a new dog or person or there is an unexpected noise. This secure base also helps build resilience to stress.

Interestingly, this secure base can be transferred spatially to a place associated with the mentor, too. It is this that I call the 'den effect', which we rely on with the clip station and crate (see the Dog Zen Toolkit chapter), especially in separation distress cases.

The establishment of a sound mentor bond is a key aspect of Dog Zen. In Part B we will explore just how you go about establishing this bond through 'Joining Up'.

How dogs are in a relationship

Social competence

Humans and dogs are very different species, yet we have similar ways of engagement and conduct that allow us to be able to live harmoniously together. Both of us have intrinsic honesty and resultant trust that underpins our social orders. Ádám Miklósi, a colleague of mine and one of the leading canine cognitive scientists, says that 'dogs have a high level of social competence'. He says that 'social competence depends on a number of factors, including the ability to form attachments, control aggression, learn and follow family rules, and help and participate in group activities'. Psychologists define 'social competence' as the ability to harmonise our needs and expectations with those of the group.

Marc Bekoff, an early mentor of mine, says that 'both dogs and humans have relatively egalitarian societies that are "other regarding" (consider what each other needs), so members generally wish to help others. Dogs and canids have a suite of behaviours that cultivate and regulate social interactions in these terms. These include fairness, cooperation, altruism, patience, forgiveness, understanding and mutual benefit, all readily evident in the way wolves and dogs play with one another.'

Through their ability to follow our gestures and learn by observation, dogs can learn the family rules and synchronise their behaviours with ours. Dogs want to please us and have an ability to understand 'yes' and 'no' — both of these allow them to learn and follow the family rules.

This shared sense of fairness and cooperation, and the very similar attachment relationship, are the glue that makes the dog man's best friend — in fact, a family member who follows the family rules. The dog's helping culture in the family, and the mentor relationship, underpin the strength and significance of the bond.

Recent research in Japan demonstrated how dogs had a preference for those who were helpful. Given the choice to take food from a person who had helped the dog's trainer open a jar, or one who was unhelpful and didn't help open the jar, the dogs consistently chose the helpful person.

Play has a specific role in the relationship, as it allows dogs to learn and practise the family rules. They can build trusting, cooperative relationships, knowing that members know the rules and will follow them. We can see how dogs — if they break a rule — apologise through posture, showing submission through rolling over, showing their bellies and licking their jowls.

TOMMY: NEGOTIATING THE RULES OF ENGAGEMENT

Tommy, my Jack Russell, was a breeder's dog for the first three years of his life. He didn't do anything other than mate, so didn't see much of life outside his kennel. I had to teach him how to play, but he caught on fast! I am watching now as Tommy and Porter start playing. Tommy drops into a play bow which calls out 'Let's play!' Porter (a much larger SPCA mutt) engages with intensity — he is one full-on dog! Tommy launches his ferocious mock attack, chasing Porter at top speed, nipping at his heels in rapid circles. They disappear around the corner, but soon enough they are back. Tommy suddenly turns and grabs Porter's cheek. Porter rolls in a graceful kung fu roll onto his back, now he's the dog underneath; a kind of conscious handicapping, a role-reversal to show trust and vulnerability. Oops, suddenly Porter grabs too hard in his enthusiasm, and Tommy grabs him. Tommy makes his point, Porter learns his lesson and off they trot together, Porter forgiven. Mates again, they investigate an interesting smell in the flax bush by the pond. Not much later they are lying asleep beside each other.

It all seems merely fun and games; however, the play context allows two very different-sized dogs with different temperaments to interact at high intensity, rehearsing and alternating places in the relationship. This allows them to negotiate relations without escalating into real fighting. They communicate using signals with clear meaning, such as the play bow, which says 'Come play with me!' They rehearse roles and engage in conscious handicapping (the bigger dog lying under the smaller), taking turns in winning and mock wrestling. They are rehearsing behaviour action patterns such as social interaction, fighting, hunting and even mating, and in doing so they build trust, coordination and cohesiveness in the pack. If they bite too hard in play, they have means to reprimand each other (growling, muzzle-pinning, scruffing, biting) or apologise (through mouth-licking and submissive gesturing). This cultivates tolerance and the learning of boundaries, allows all members to be involved in the games and facilitates bonds within the whole pack.

Play, socially affiliative (friendly) behaviours and peer-to-peer social signals all rely on consistent, honest responses. We see in our own society that for social behaviours to be effective and serve the collective good, we need to have reliable signals (be honest). Like human social evolution, domestication in dogs seems to have driven selection toward the most transparent, honest dogs. Marc's research in juvenile coyotes showed that individuals that didn't follow the rules of play were driven from the pack and were therefore four times more likely to die.

This also reminds us to be reliable and trustworthy in our actions with dogs. Like us, they can detect deception, so it is important for signals to be honest. The reliable nature of this communication builds the trust needed in complex social groups. Dog's pick up inconsistencies, excessive and unfair assertiveness, or if you are trying to trick or lie to them. Don't trap a dog and punish it. Create boundaries using techniques that preserve your relationship, like contrast training and apparently natural consequences, which we will cover later on.

Interestingly, one study showed that dogs play with humans differently to how they play with dogs. Dog-to-dog play, say with a tug toy, is

Porter does the play bow: 'Come play'. Tommy: 'Bring it on shorty!' (He's the short one).

often punctuated with competitive behaviour, whereas with humans the play lasts longer and is more collaborative and sharing.

Building healthy bonds

The bond is the most critical element for raising and training your dog properly. When you become your dog's mentor, your dog should be highly attuned to you, follow you, look up to you regularly, study you and to some degree mimic you to build her understanding of appropriate behaviour. You are the centre of her world. The bond must be created in a healthy way so that your dog not only learns to depend on and trust you, but also stays confident, relaxed and calm. This type of relationship brings joy to your dog and you alike, as it is one that is not plagued by stress or trouble. You may have experienced for yourself the strong bond your pup or dog forms with you.

Through the formative period (1–4 months), puppies have a trust, openness and lack of fear that makes them ripe for learning and socialisation, so ideally the mentor bond will be built during this time. However, we also have techniques, which we will describe later, that can take your adult dog back to this formative time in the den to help re-create a healthy bond if it's been missed.

In Dog Zen, we rehearse cooperative activities that strengthen the bond. We are re-creating the following response (pup following Mum or mentor) that comes naturally in the dog-to-dog bond. This is best demonstrated in the Joining Up technique. This foundational technique shapes and rewards the watching and following response through basic behaviours, like 'heel', 'sit', 'down' and 'wait'. This creates a ritualised sequence, almost like a dance, that builds between you and your dog, reinforcing and entraining the bond. We cover how to do Joining Up in Part B.

Unhealthy bonds

Alternatively, a lack of appropriate socialisation, support when frightened or understanding and empathy can create a weak bond that leaves the dog uncertain of his place, role and safety in the world. Research shows behavioural issues can stem from a poorly established bond between the dog and his mentor.

A strong and balanced attachment relationship creates the secure base that helps a dog feel safe. However, this attachment relationship has a downside when the relationship is over-developed, in which case the dog can suffer separation distress. That is, the dog displays anxiety, whining, destructive and/or soiling behaviours and other symptoms when separated from his owner for any length of time. This can come about when a pup isn't taught to separate properly and spend time alone when young. (See Part C on how to do this properly.)

In your adult dog, you can re-create this early developmental time in order to take your dog psychologically back to the den, to re-establish this ability to separate and build a healthy relationship. It is important to do so, so that your dog trusts you and is conscious and attentive of you and what you want from him. This is talked about more in Part B.

In conclusion

When I talk about that ultimate bond, it is the one that most dog owners have had maybe only once in their lives if they are lucky — it is very special. However, it is possible to have this with any dog if you know how to create it or re-create it!

It is so important that we grow our awareness and understanding of the dogs that share our homes. Make sure you watch your dog, observe him and grow in understanding of him. Dogs are not machines — they are loveable, unique and by no means perfect. Like all relationships, we have to understand our dogs, love them and allow them their idiosyncrasies.

Like my dear rescue dogs. Reggie is smart-as (he can fly a plane!) and crazy-mad about his ball. You bring his ball out and nothing else exists, he's on the hunt! The good news is that when used wisely, it's the glue for our relationship. Used unwisely, it's a pain! With Monty, gifting is his forte. He diligently searches *every* time for a present to give to you, normally a shoe in his mouth (bad animal psychologist!). He is the happiest dog in the world, and I'm sure he is a reincarnated yogi from Tibet. Then there's Blue: he, too, is famous, with a CV as long as your arm. Serenely beautiful and so reliable — but, oh, that Huntaway character. He barks for joy — and oh, how he loves life, especially at the beach! I'm faced with wondering: what is the balance between saving my sanity and watching his joy at his freedom? Thank goodness for his 'quiet!' command; Reggie's 'leave it' or Monty's 'drop it'.

We all face choices like these within our relationship with our dogs. For me, it's not about training my dogs to the *n*th degree, but supporting them to joyfully navigate and live in our very odd and complex human world. Some will be easier than others; some trickier, whether they had a difficult start or just because they are! Guide them, mentor them, ensure they fit well into our lives so we are all happy *and* understand what their glorious, unique characters are, and allow and celebrate that, too. Please don't expect them to be perfect. Now *that* is a relationship!

Before we head to the next section, here's a quick summary of the key aspects of our relationship with our dogs. Understanding these will provide a very sound basis for building a bond with your dog, and ultimately help you succeed in your training together.

What enables dogs to be in a relationship?
- Dogs are very human-focused — they know we have the resources they want!
- We are their ultimate tool: they look to us for direction.
- They have an ability to bond with us and be in our families.
- They have an ability to read our gestures, understanding us.
- They are very attentive to us, and watch us to see what we want.

What is a relationship for them?
- A secure base — the attachment relationship is very important.
- They like to have a sense of place and role, and be able to trust this. Our bond mimics the helper (mentor) role.

How do they behave in a relationship?
- Social competence — the ability to understand the other.
- They can recognise and follow family rules.
- They use play to establish and practise relationship behaviours, among other things.

Building sound relationships
- The ideal time to do this is in the formative period, but if necessary we can re-create this in adult life through 'taking the dog back to the den'.
- 'Joining Up' is a key tool in establishing a sound bond.
- A poorly established bond can create behaviour issues including separation anxiety.

3.4 INTELLIGENCE

Do you ever look in your dog's eyes and see a glimpse of intelligence that amazes you? Do you ever really wonder just who is training who?

I'll never forget when my kids were very young. I was watching them from my office overlooking the pool when I saw Hercules pick up my son by his nappy and move him away from the edge of the pool. He was acting as a true family helper. But how did he know the edge of the pool was a threat? Had he imagined his own pups and water and the danger ahead? It blew my mind.

In this section we'll investigate dogs' intelligence and how they learn, to provide a foundation for how we train with our dogs.

There have been a number of experiments that have shown that dogs can learn quite complex things. Chaser the Border Collie has been described as remembering over 1100 objects. He was even shown to be able to put them into different piles that classified them into classes of objects — toys, non-toys, etc. All of this by three years old, so he was still learning — that is amazing to me.

REGGIE: SO JUST HOW INTELLIGENT CAN DOGS BE?

What a remarkable day it was when the film crew for the *Dogs might fly* series climbed into the plane for the first time with Reggie in the captain's seat of the Cessna 172B. There we were, ready to attempt a first in the history of man and dog — a dog flying a plane! Why not?

The expectation on the producer's and director's faces, with their expensive budgets at stake, was palpable. Months of training were hanging on this one moment. Maybe 100 behaviours shaped and or chained together into this flying sequence. Reggie, the rescue Labrador–German Shepherd cross from North England, the most relaxed of all, was strapped in like a scene from *Top Gun*. The producer turns to me and says, 'Take it away, Reggie and Mark.'

Reggie is relaxed. We check his signals that I use to talk to him from behind — left, right and centre lights and tones. This was the ultimate test of bond, trust and a complex shared language built up from the Dog Zen basics.

Flight school was gruelling for my trainers and me, but ultimate fun for the dogs! Just like you will learn to shape behaviours (though maybe a few less), Reggie had had to learn a huge number of tasks, like how to work the yoke with subtlety of pressure, hold it back a little, feel the turbulence and make 60-degree turns with their G forces. He had to be able to maneuver a figure of eight, look out of the plane not at me, watch his turns and so much more.

We are off. The co-pilot takes us up, as Reggie's not allowed to take off (who made those rules?). I hear the co-pilot say he's handing over to Reggie, and the dog takes control of the plane at over 600 metres. He looks out both ways as he was taught to do, checking for traffic (he actually might have been looking for high-flying tennis balls, I'm not sure — but he did what he was trained to do). Within 20 metres of us is a helicopter bristling with cameras, flown by the stunt pilot from *Mission Impossible* . . . sticking to us way too close for comfort! Reggie has a look but then gets on with the job at hand: flying a full 'by the compass' figure of eight, straight and level. I'm sweating, he's relaxed. The co-pilot keeps his hands on his head as Reggie's in charge — Captain Reggie to you.

Yahoo, we are doing it! The co-pilot calls for the first left bank to 180 degrees south. I press a signal to Reggie to initiate the turn and he looks to port then slams it into a 60-degree bank. The helicopter rolls over the top of us to maximise its view of the first dog in the world aerobatically pulling a bank to port! Reggie leans back and holds the bank for 20 seconds.

Reggie knows the call and slams the opposite yoke — delicately, mind you. The plane rights and rolls out into a starboard bank. Reggie, leaning left in the seat, turns to me rather happy. I give him the cue for straight. Once out, I click, and Reggie turns for a well-deserved reward: sausage first-class, then back on the job.

Marc from the helicopter screams out on the radio: 'That's it — the world's first dog flying a plane!' I'm stunned — we did it, after two years of planning and ten months of training and shooting! It's amazing. He flew the figure of eight like a master. We do a low-level fly over the team and film crew, a fitting finale to a job well done.

When we land and get out, the crew go crazy. An incredible world-first achieved! 18 October, 2015.

Together we flew three rescue dogs, with Reggie being the first, really demonstrating that rescue dogs really are smart dogs. What an extraordinary thing it was to be sitting in the back as Reggie piloted.

Yes, I was acting as Reggie's mentor, but to see him put together all those complex training sequences — it was beyond belief that he could learn, memorise and retain so much, with both confidence and panache!

How context shapes intelligence

An animal's intelligence and the way it understands the world is related to what it and its ancestors were adapted to do. Most of the dog's pre-domestication intelligence goes back to the wolf. The wolf was a predator, so its intelligence was centred around hunting — navigation, anticipation, cooperation, observation and problem-solving.

Hunting large prey in very diverse environments led to the development of cooperation, sociability and pack living. This required a high level of adaptability and learning ability to adjust to the different environments and social dynamics. Cooperative strategies and observational learning underpin this. Working together required an adaptive strategy: try something, learn, get feedback, succeed, or fail and adapt. We know that the ability of sheep dogs' and guide dogs to predict what's going to happen next and make a decision, take turns and cooperate, has likely been retained from the ancestral canids. This is from their ability to anticipate what their prey and other pack members might do, imagine some options, then choose a preferred action. If correct (and they gain a reward — catch prey, for example) the inference (thinking of different solutions and choosing) becomes insight (understanding). This anticipation can start to manifest as insight and predictive behaviour. When this is well developed, we consider this a good sign of intelligence.

The ability to make inferences has a strong survival value when you need to make decisions quickly (think hunting). This ability leads to a lot of flexibility (or plasticity). We know the dog has inherited a highly adaptable genotype from the wolf and other canids, driven by the need to adapt to many different prey types and environments.

Another key contributor to dogs' intelligence is the wolf's social brain. Originally, the untapped niche of large prey drove the wolf to hunt in a group and therefore form a social pack. This created the social brain. With the need to develop multiple relationships in a social pack, the brain requires more capacity, resulting in a more complex organ

Reggie focused on the controls in preflight rehearsal.

that has more neural connections. It is this social brain that allows for the dog's unique degree of social competence. What is interesting is that the same social evolutionary drivers that led to humans' immense neural plasticity and intelligence and adaptability have parallels in the dog's evolution. You can see how we became such good companions and the ultimate collaboration in Nature.

The twist in the intelligence tail

Cognitive tests of dogs' intelligence have often stumbled (or so it seemed, dogs stumbled). Often the results indicated that dogs were less intelligent in certain areas than wolves, which was surprising given that the basis of the dog's intelligence came from the wolf.

It turned out that many of the tests were misled by the fact that the dogs were looking to humans for direction. More specifically, the dogs' attention was focused on where the human attention was, what they touched and their smells, and this interfered with results. What was eventually figured out was that dogs were looking to the humans to help them out: the doggie equivalent of 'Come on, give me a clue' or maybe even more directly 'Pass the cookies, please'!

Dogs were factoring us in as intelligent tools to help them solve problems. Dogs knew that watching us or other dogs was the best short-cut to working out how to do something. This intelligence came about from being an animal that has lived with and depended on humans for so long. From ancient times, we have been the provider of so many resources and their focus has shifted to us. They have learnt to use us as this intelligent tool to help work things out and do things. Remember, they are good at working co-operatively, defining roles and sharing the load, so why not get those who know better than you to do those things you don't understand — that's smart! Dogs learnt long ago that the real gold wasn't just the resources in our dumps, but actually us and what we could do for them — something the likes of seagulls and rats haven't figured out, evident by their still being in the dumps and not our homes.

'Reading us', 'learning from us' and 'asking us' are powerful and intelligent strategies. It is this shift in focus to *us* that has become central to their intelligence, transforming it. The centre of dogs' intelligence is dogs' sociability and relatedness to us. It is this focus of their intelligence that we are able to utilise in our training with them. The more complex the world has got since hunter-gatherer days, the more risk there is to dogs. Now more than ever they have the need for us, their mentors to guide them.

As I am writing this book on dogs and relationships, and working hard making money to buy dog food and squeaky toys, I look over to Tommy lying on his bed, having yet another nap: you've got to wonder who was the one who really figured out the perfect life . . .

Dogs' capabilities and limitations

It is important to understand dogs' intelligence capabilities and limitations to ensure that we are training within these. There is a lot of research that has looked at this and several great books on this subject, so please go to the references at the back if you are interested in exploring further. For our purposes, I now summarise the attributes I think are most important in relation to how dogs learn and understand the world, and hence Dog Zen training. It is these attributes we will consider as we move into the training/mentoring sections of this book.

In relation to us, the following are important aspects of intelligence and learning. Dogs have the ability to:

O co-operate with us
O recruit human help — that is, use us to help them do things

o understand our communication, both postural and vocal, especially intonation

o read our moods and emotions — remember, they have similar parts of the brain to ours dedicated to this

o attend to our eye contact and face, and be aware of where we look and our body orientation — they have dedicated face-detection neurons for this

o be aware if we are not attentive or are distracted, e.g. if we are reading

o potentially experience empathy and perform consolation activities (the possibility is that dogs may have mirror neurons and a 'theory of mind', where an animal understands that the 'other' has a separate mind and a different view or opinion of the world)

o learn the meaning of words, including 'yes' and 'no'.

o discriminate objects and classes of object (thousands of them)

o make inferences when solving problems, and generalise to solve new problems

o mimic others and learn by observation

o have a fundamental understanding of simple problem-solving, like using simple tools (e.g. pull a piece of string to get a cookie), but not much more complex, as it's outside their natural range

o remember the things that are the most important to them, such as prey-related items (e.g. where they lost their ball, where the food cache is, where burrows are), and family members, and toys' names, etc.

Limitations

Here are some of the limitations of dogs' intelligence that we need to consider in terms of their learning and training capability:

o Our behaviour can interfere with and influence dogs, overriding their own senses at times — we need to be consistent and be aware of what they are watching.

o They can get confused by multiple words: keep it simple, with one-word commands.

o Dogs don't consider a long way ahead. Unless it's an issue of critical survival, they stay in the now — keep training simple and broken into small parts.

o Old memories and default behaviours can interfere with new ones, so we need to remove or replace inappropriate behaviours.

○ Dogs can't understand the physics of their world, such as gravity or things moving out of sight, so therefore are not good at puzzle-type activities unless trained.

○ Dogs are not as good as wolves at navigation without landmarks. (Often they can't find their way home unless experienced and rehearsed or there are clear landmarks.)

The role of play in intelligence

As mentioned earlier, play is also a significant factor of intelligence. Play helps grow a dog's ability to learn about the world, practise behaviours and, interestingly, grow his brain neurologically — 'what you fire, you wire!'

During the formative period (1-4 months), the pup is changing rapidly in so many ways. Seventy per cent of his brain connectedness develops during that time, and many of his social, foraging and sexual patterns develop. We now believe that during this period play is a way for a pup to develop and practise segments of behaviour patterns he will require later in life, such as the hunting, conflict resolution and avoidance functions. It is a great time to start training, and also self-rewarding and very fun!

We need to ensure that pups and adult dogs get opportunities to play, especially pups in their formative period. So often I have seen in my clinic dogs who have been isolated, given few opportunities to meet other pups or dogs or experience new situations and environments. The consequences for them are enormous, stunting their ability to learn and be in the world, resulting in low confidence, a limited ability to adapt to change and increased anxiety. They can appear closed-down and unengaged, often with little or no understanding of play. It is a very sad thing to see.

MARLOWE: REDISCOVERING THE PUPPY WITHIN

Marlowe is a beautiful Golden Retriever off my *Pound Pups to Dog Stars* TV series. He was very socially deprived — couldn't play or engage with anything, would just stand unmoving if a ball was thrown toward him, and was deeply fearful of water. He was completely closed-down, which is so unusual for this loveable and friendly breed. It made me very sad to think how abandoned to his own devices he must have been to be that withdrawn.

However, it is possible to teach old dogs new tricks. With lots of love and training through 'taking him back to the den', we rehabilitated Marlowe so that he learnt to play again and rediscovered the puppy inside him. It was beautiful to see him re-find that joy in himself. Have a look at Marlowe now: he has now become the ultimate water dog who loves his ball (page 84)!

3.5 HOW DOGS LEARN

When training dogs, it is helpful to understand how they learn, so that you train in such a way that your dog can actually learn! Here, we look at the importance of the formative period and learning state to learning, and the different ways dog learn.

The importance of the formative period in learning

The formative period (1-4 months of age) plays a huge part in a dog's ability to learn. It is a period of enormous brain growth and learning in the dog. It is the dog's optimal learning time, and so has a major impact on the dog's future intelligence.

Extensive gyrification (expansion of the white matter of the brain) occurs within the dog's formative period. Dogs have their full complement of neurons from approximately four weeks of age, but the number and complexity of the connections between these continues to grow rapidly. The puppy brain grows in volume from 8 cm³ to 80 cm³ in the first four months. This provides the dog with the capacity to learn, and therefore adapt to the very complex world we live in.

One of the results of domestication in the dog is an extended formative period (longer than that of the wolf). The longer the period, the longer the time dogs have to learn things. The formative period is an intensive period of learning. This intense learning state is in part due to the dog being in a less anxious state relative to the wolf, due to the evolution of smaller adrenals and less fight-flight reactivity. This makes dogs more confident and less prone to fear. If a dog is fearful and goes into a non-learning state, then the dog closes down, learning stops and development is compromised.

The formative period is critical in determining what and how dogs can learn (hence why it's called 'formative'). Their ability to learn about many things is predetermined by their exposure to those things at this time. Significantly, if they don't get exposed to things then they don't adapt to them. If they don't get exposed to stimuli e.g. trucks, other races of people, kids, ducks, old people, men, cats, etc (anything really), then they will either be aggressive towards or fearful of them. This lack of appropriate experience (mal-socialisation) is largely the basis of many behaviour issues and euthanasias'.

Pups' 1-4-month formative period establishes the critical foundational skills they need for their adult lives. There are a series of developmental stages they should go through, building one on top of the other. We call it 'cascading': a series of steps that the pup learns and grows through, related to his age and development stage. If one of these steps is missed out, it can create difficulties in the next stages as the necessary foundations haven't been built.

It is our role to ensure that our pups go through these necessary stages and build the skills they need. We need to make sure our pups have the right experiences at the right time (go to Part C for practical guidance on this).

Near the end of the formative period, the fear-imprint period heightens, around the last month. This fear-imprint period starts between 8 and 12 weeks in the wolf and between 12 and 16 weeks in the dog (reflecting the dog's extended formative period). This is the period when the sympathetic nervous system develops and the adrenals are activated, so fear responses heighten. The pup's fear sensitivity to novel stimulus increases through to the end of the formative period. This results in his socialisation ability and pervasive sponge-like learning state lessening (called the formative period offset). However, well-socialised pups exposed to a variety of general stimuli can extend even beyond this period. In fact, the ability to be open and learning continues into their first year in well-adjusted dogs.

The offset of the formative period relates to the heightened sensitivity to novel things. Fight–flight responses are established, and the pup is ready to deal with the threats of the big world. The wolf offset period is more strict, and the fear response is more heightened as the wolf goes out into the big, scary world to hunt. However, because dogs stay in a more stable environment, the dog's offset period is less defined. As a general safe guide, if you haven't started to socialise and broaden your pup's experience by at least 12 weeks of age, you will end

Marlowe at water play — what a transformation!

up with a mal-socialised dog and all the problems that go with that.

But here's the rub: exactly when the fear-imprint period will start depends in part on the experiences a puppy has. The earlier you start and the more varied the experiences you offer your pup, the longer and richer her formative period will be. Limit her experience early, and you limit her formative period. Experiences and habituation (natural learning to accept novel things — that is, by habit) build on each other: the more you do it, the more you grow your pup's, and ultimately your dog's, capacity for novel experiences. You can see why limiting your pup's experiences during this period is one of the most damaging things you can do. (See Part C to find out how to manage the conflict with the vaccination period.)

TOMMY: OPENING UP A CLOSED-DOWN WORLD

Tommy is a good example of what happens if a dog isn't exposed to varying environments in puppyhood. Tommy was a breeder's dog who was restricted to a very simple environment for his first three years, so had little opportunity to learn. At three years old, I had to teach him so much: how to play (with Blue as his mentor), how to go down steps, housetraining and what chickens and cats were. He hadn't learnt to learn, so was slow at learning new things and highly sensitive to novelty. He is now a great example of the benefits of being taken 'back to the den'.

Learning state

Learning state is a psycho-physiological state (the relationship between the mental and the physical) that is inherent in the formative period. It is the state your dog is in when she is able to learn. It is a foundation of Dog Zen, essential to any training you will do. Needless to say, it is essential when we are trying to teach our dogs new behaviours or modify undesirable ones.

The learning state is largely controlled by the autonomic nervous system, which has two sides: the 'parasympathetic nervous system' and the 'sympathetic nervous system'. The parasympathetic nervous system is also called the 'rest and digest' state, which is when the dog is calm, relaxed and non-fearful, so has the capacity to focus and, tellingly, is able to eat. Interestingly, humans have an ability to override this 'don't eat when stressed' function, so we often eat to help ourselves manage stress, which can result in problems like stomach ulcers and obesity. Dogs, however, can't override this function, so stopping eating is a very powerful indicator that they are out of the learning state.

When your dog is in a non-learning state, his sympathetic nervous system is switched on and he is in sympathetic arousal — the fight-flight state. Imagine a wolf has been threatened by a bear: adrenalin and the other stress hormones fire, and it gets ready to either fight the bear or flee. The wolf certainly won't be in the mood for eating or sitting nicely and learning something new!

Later on, in Part B, we will explore how to switch into and maintain your dog in a learning state for training purposes.

The different ways dogs learn

Outlined below is the key ways dogs learn: the critical ones for us being associative learning, reinforcement training, contrast training, inference and observation. I add a couple of others as well for interest. This may feel a bit heavy-going, but persevere, as understanding how dogs learn is the foundation from which we train them. Most importantly, grasp clicker training and the use of positive reinforcement. Maybe break it down into small parts, and click and reward yourself with walks with your dog!

Associative learning

Associative learning is one of the most fundamental forms of learning. All animals, including ourselves, learn by associations between events and positive stimuli (do more of) or negative stimuli (avoid). Pups from eight weeks old already have associative learning capacities.

A natural example of a positive association is a dog finding food in a rubbish bin. A few rewarding experiences/associations, where searching in rubbish bins equals finding food, will increase the frequency of the behaviour. The fact that it gets rewarded now and again (intermittent schedule of reward) maintains the behaviour, just like a gambler on a one-armed bandit!

Dogs learn also by negative association, such as getting pricked by a hedgehog and learning to avoid it. Investigative hedgehog-prodding behaviour correspondingly decreases in frequency. These negative associations can also be called punishers or corrections (in this case, a natural consequence).

Reinforcement training

I'm going to go into some depth in this section, as reinforcement is the main principle behind the clicker — the primary tool used in Dog Zen. Note the use of classical learning psychology and terminology that still underpins modern learning psychology. When you see such terminology as 'punishers', Dog Zen only uses it in the context of apparent natural consequences, if at all.

Reinforcement is an event that happens after the completion of a behaviour. The defining feature is that the behaviour and event follow each other immediately, and the behaviour seems to cause (engender) the reinforcement.

Reinforcers can be positive, such as food, a pat, praise or play, or they can be negative, such as a reprimanding check on the lead, a prickly plant in the nose or a raised voice. To be effective it needs to follow almost immediately and it needs to mean something to the individual. Not all reinforcers are meaningful to all: you may like chocolate but I may not; you may think a tickle is playful, I might think it is torture.

In training terms, a positive reinforcer is the offering of something your dog likes. If a dog does something like a successful sit, then you follow immediately with a pat or food if he likes those. A trainer will make sure the timing is immediate. The association of the behaviour and the event that subsequently happens increases the likelihood of that behaviour occurring again in the future. If your dog likes the positive reinforcer (food!) then the behaviour is likely to increase in frequency.

A negative reinforcer is the removal of something your dog dislikes, such as being locked outside or being away from you. The removal of the thing he dislikes increases the frequency of a behaviour. For example, if he is quiet you let him inside, so you are removing his separation from you and increasing the frequency of the behaviour (being quiet).

A punisher is the opposite of a reinforcer, in that it decreases the likelihood of a behaviour occurring. Positive punishment is when the behaviour decreases in frequency due to the delivery of something undesirable such as a raised voice or being put outside.

A negative punishment is the removal of a reward with the goal of decreasing the behaviour in the future. For example, when teaching a dog to heel, we initially give constant click and reward as the behaviour occurs. As the dog progresses, we withdraw click and reward if the dog is not making her best effort. That is, we negatively correct unwanted behaviour or poor performance, and positively reinforce personal best performances.

It is worth noting that the principles of learning by reinforcement are laws of Nature: all species learn this way, and they are in place whether you are aware of them or not. Think of the beeping sound in your car if you forget to put your safety belt on: the sound goes away when you put your belt on, therefore it is negatively reinforcing the likelihood of you putting your safety belt on each time, just to stop the noise.

The use of reinforcement or correction are natural and occur in Nature, setting boundaries and teaching dogs what is appropriate and inappropriate. What is important in Dog Zen is the humane and intelligent use of them, mimicking Nature as best as possible.

The most important thing in the case of corrections is where the dog sees the corrections to be coming from. The dog should generally experience them as external and remote from you as the mentor. Our goal is to build, not weaken, our bond with our dogs, while ensuring safe boundaries are established and our training is enriching not inhibiting. See contrast training later in this section for further details.

Conditioned secondary reinforcers

Now shake yourself off a bit and sit up straight, as this is important! A good example of a conditioned secondary reinforcer is my favourite tool of all time — the clicker (see next section).

A conditioned secondary reinforcer is a stimulus that is originally meaningless, but becomes associated with a primary positive reinforcer (the true reward) like food, a pat, praise or something else the dog likes. Examples of a conditioned secondary reinforcer (also known as a marker) can be a sound cue like a click or whistle, or a visual cue like a flag or hand signal.

An early example of the use of a conditioned secondary reinforcer is in dolphin and marine animal training. It was pioneered here because coercive techniques didn't work, and it was difficult to reinforce behaviours in the normal way, as giving food to the dolphin immediately after a desired behaviour was tricky because the dolphin was often out of reach. Instead, when a dolphin jumped and touched a ball, as it touched the ball (the desired behaviour) the trainer would blow a whistle (conditioned secondary reinforcer), so that the dolphin would come back to the trainer and get a fish reward (primary positive reinforcer). The whistle exactly marks the correct behaviour, and acts as a bridge to getting the food.

The conditioned secondary reinforcer or marker (in this case a whistle) can be almost anything, such as a click, a 'Yes!', or even a flag. A marker is any stimulus that can identify the right behaviour easily, and is immediate, discrete and difficult to confuse with others. It is best if the marker doesn't have any confusing emotional overtones or features, such as speech can have. A clicker is often the easiest and is my preferred marker, but a whistle or a 'Yes!' will do if you don't have a clicker on you.

In terms of your dog, the primary positive reinforcer needs to be motivating to the dog. Food is normally best (it is good to have different-value foods in terms of palatability), but other reinforcers can work depending on the dog, like praise, balls, etc. I prefer food as it is so strong and consistent a motivator in most dogs. However, it needs to be positively paired (associated) with the marker a few times to take effect.

Clicker training

Clicker training is a form of conditioned positive reinforcement, and is the most effective training tool I have come across in my 40 years of training. Another lesser-known but extremely important purpose of the clicker is as a 'switch conditioner': the click and food anticipation helps 'switch' the dog into a learning state. This makes it a brilliant aid to therapy. It also reinforces our relationship, building trust and confidence, because we get paired (associated) with the primary positive reinforcer (e.g. food) and so, in time, with the secondary reinforcer (the clicker).

The clicker is the conditioned secondary reinforcer, and the food (or whatever reward you choose) is the primary positive reinforcer. The click is a promise of a food reward, and must always be followed by food. I like to think of the clicker like a camera: you click immediately when you see the behaviour you want. You can imagine that you are trying to take a photo to show the exact moment your dog demonstrates the behaviour you want to train, and make the click the moment that happens. This immediacy is why the clicker is one of the most effective training tools: it's more precise at marking the behaviour, as the click is instant (voice and food rewards are slower, and are often mixed with confusing emotional messages due to tone and posture). Remember, dogs don't know what you want them to learn: the clicker makes this clear.

The number of times we click and reward is called the schedule of reinforcement. To start, we click each time we get the desired behaviour. This is called a continuous schedule of reward, and is what creates the initial and most important association — that's why we do it every time to start with.

Once the behaviour is established (approximately 90 per cent consistent), we move to an intermittent or random schedule of reinforcement. That is, we start to click and reward on every three or so successful attempts. Think of it like the gambler's 'one-armed bandit': what keeps the gambler there is the thought that the jackpot might be the next one or the next one . . . dogs keep performing the behaviour in the hope that this time they get the click and reward. Remember, it is the click that you are reducing: each time you click, you still reward with food. Slowly you reduce the frequency of the click and reward until you completely fade both for the behaviour you are training. When you are training a new behaviour, then you start from the beginning again.

The size of the reinforcer, if it's food, should be as small as possible while still being desirable. Especially with food, keep it small so that you can do more sessions and keep drive high.

Importantly, the clicker is only temporary. It is commonly thought that when you use a clicker you will need to keep using it. That's not true; quite the contrary. A clicker is only a training or shaping tool. Once the behaviour is fixed; you will fade it out. See the chapter on Proofing and Fading the Clicker.

Once your dog understands how the clicker works (and that it is always followed by a yummy treat!), she will learn faster each time you use it to train a new behaviour. Now that's encouraging. Clicker training can be very enriching for your dog (and you). You can start to treat it like a game, where your dog can start to chase the click and catch the reward. Go to the Dog Zen Toolkit chapter for instructions on how to use the clicker.

Contrast training

Driven by their desire to please us, dogs, unlike wolves, have an ability to understand 'yes' and 'no' from us — that is, they can distinguish what is wanted and what is not wanted. They have an inherent understanding that there are family rules of conduct, and they want to know them and follow them; they love to please us. They are inherently social beings. This allows us to guide the behaviours we need from them, hence their immense trainability and ability to be in our lives. All social groups require the establishment of, and adherence to, family rules to ensure social cohesion. The establishment of a shared language, rules or boundaries is an important dynamic of the social group.

All animals learn by contrast: we need to understand hot to understand cold, and vice versa. Contrast offers choice, and choice allows animals to make decisions and learn by them.

Contrast training is an effective tool to teach your dog the difference between right (with positive reinforcement) and wrong (through natural or apparent natural consequences). If there isn't enough contrast between behaviours a dog can't learn, because it is the contrast that facilitates the decision.

In training this means rewarding your dog for the behaviours you want her to do, while inappropriate decisions get redirected, replaced, ignored or corrected through mimicking natural consequences. This allows her to understand what is wanted (by reward) and not wanted (through natural consequence).

Dogs need the contrast between reward (click and rewarding the behaviour you want) and negative consequences (correcting against the behaviour you don't want). This allows the external world away from you to say 'Don't do that' (a correction that mimics natural consequences), paired with techniques that say 'Yes, I want you to do that' (click and reward). This is particularly important when you are modifying/changing existing behaviours you don't want, rather than shaping new behaviours you do want.

Note that the consequence is a mimic of natural consequences (which I call an 'apparent natural consequence'). In the wild, a dog would be growled at or have a lip raised (signal) at him before he would then be reprimanded by the other dog if he bit too hard in play; or a spiky plant might scratch him if he tried to eat it. These are consequences that occur in Nature which allow a dog to learn how to behave appropriately and stay safe. Remember the young coyote pups that got driven out of their pack for inappropriate play, or the dog that got pricked by the hedgehog? These behaviours have serious consequences in Nature that impinge on survival, and so naturally occuring consequences help shape adaptive learned responses.

The consequence should always come from outside of you, rarely from you, so that you maintain a strong relationship with your dog. The correction is remote from you, and is essentially teaching the dog that the item he is acting inappropriately toward (e.g. another dog or a plant or a chicken) is delivering the correction.

In Dog Zen we apply the consequence remotely from us through a check via a slip collar and a long-line or retractable lead. As the consequence is applied remotely (associated external to us), and the dog gets clicked and rewarded for returning to us, he will come back to us for safety. Thereby we don't get associated with the correction, we are just alerting the dog to the fact the consequence might happen (we become his ally). See Contrast Training in the Dog Zen Toolkit chapter on how you undertake this technique: it is a very important tool, particularly if you are trying to resolve behaviour problems.

There are two reasons why it is important that the item is offering the correction. Firstly, the dog associates the correction with the item, so if she sees a similar item again she will have learnt to avoid it or relate to it properly with or without you. Secondly, the dog will not associate the correction with you, which will preserve your all-important bond. This is an important effect that reinforces your positive status, because you are helping protect your dog from the world as a mentor does.

Conditioned aversive signals

As discussed above, it is important to have a technique where we can contrast between what is wanted and what is not wanted. To establish what is not wanted, we use a remote effective check (see the Dog Zen Toolkit chapter to learn how) to mimic natural consequences for inappropriate behaviours. However, before we apply these consequences we can teach our dogs a signal that indicates to them that a consequence for their behaviour is about to happen. This is called a conditioned aversive signal. This is a signal that says that something negative (a consequence) will happen unless you stop what you are doing. The signal gives your dog a chance to succeed first and avoid the consequence. This is a more effective way to learn than threats, as your dog has a chance to avoid the consequence. The opportunity to succeed increases the chances that the behaviours you want will increase in frequency and the ones you don't will fade away.

The conditioned aversive signal we use in Dog Zen is a 'no' command. (Go to Basic Commands in Part B to see how to establish a 'no' command.) Most corrections should come with a conditioned aversive signal, so that our dogs have an opportunity to succeed first and avoid the correction with a positive reinforcer to emphasise contrast and point the way to success. Mistakes are part of learning.

A non-reward signal

This is another technique that is used to shape new behaviours. It is a neutral signal, which is not associated with a marker (e.g. the clicker). It is a special case of a conditioned aversive signal. Saying 'wrong' (in a neutral tone) is a signal for 'Don't carry on on that pathway, give up: there is no reinforcer following [e.g. food].' It informs the dog that going down a certain track is not going to be reinforced (rewarded). It is said in a neutral tone so is neutral in nature, which is more helpful for training because it is not aversive at all. However, it is more for advanced trainers and dogs: if your dog is a new or an uncertain learner, don't use it as it might confuse him (as it is something extra for him to think about). This only works well for dogs who have been 'variably reinforced'; that is, have been taught and rewarded for actively searching for other ways to do something before. We call it 'throwing behaviours'.

Inference

Another way dogs learn is through inference or insight. This is when your dog can imagine different solutions or scenarios and choose between them. Until recently we didn't think dogs had a strong ability to do this compared with wolves, who need to do so for their survival: they are hunters, so need to understand their prey's behaviour, anticipate it and judge it to make rapid decisions. However, recent research shows that dogs have this ability as well; but, as noted earlier, it is oriented toward humans.

This is good news, as we can utilise this to strengthen the bond between us and our dogs, and build the dog's habit of looking to us for direction. In Dog Zen we shape looking up to our eyes and face during exercises, to facilitate the dog looking to us for direction.

Dogs can generalise an inference to help them solve problems, therefore learning from experience. An ability to problem-solve shows that they can generalise their learning and behaviour — that is, learn something in one context and move that learning to another. This means that we can teach them something in one context and they can apply it to a different context, which is very powerful in training. Most behaviours need to be generalised and broadened into other contexts. For example, when you first teach your dog to socialise with one or two dogs, you then need to generalise it to other breeds and age classes. This is also called proofing (see the Proofing and Fading the Clicker chapter later in the book).

Observation

Observation and mimicry are a major form of learning in dogs. Historically, wolves would look to their litter-mates and older wolves for guidance; now dogs look towards us, unless they haven't had human socialisation.

Often we don't want dogs to mimic us — eat off the table, sit in a chair or sleep on our bed — so it is good to teach dogs what to mimic and what not to, thus building understanding and love. We can teach dogs to mimic us in some ways, such as when chasing a ball, running around a tree or jumping up on a chair. This is called 'Do As I Do' and can be a game. It develops social coordination, and is fun play for your dog. It helps to shape behaviour through modelling and mimic.

BANDIT: OBSERVING AND MIMICKING THE PACK TO ESTABLISH A HUMAN BOND

Bandit, from our TV show, was a feral dog and had missed human socialisation, so he didn't orient to humans, and was scared to the point of learned helplessness and inhibition. He did, however, orient toward dogs, which means he must have had exposure to other dogs at a younger age. He showed observing mimicking behaviour toward dogs rather than humans. To bond with him, I had to build his socialisation to me through my pack: I let him play and interact with my dogs and me at the same time. Observing the way my dogs interacted with me as their mentor, he learnt to mimic that behaviour and accept me as his mentor, too. When he did, it was a profoundly joyful moment. It took some time for it to generalise to other humans, and it may never be as good as it is with a well-adjusted dog, but we were all amazed at what we achieved. From there, Bandit quickly learnt to observe and learn from me, too. Within weeks he was doing a commercial on TV with me, showcasing our new bond.

Dogs can learn by themselves

Because of their learning abilities around inference and observation, dogs are very capable of working things out for themselves. You have to be very careful that you don't inadvertently help your dog learn the wrong things, though. A good example is if your dog learns to escape from your backyard. He has learnt he can do it, so he will try harder the next time to find a way (even if you have blocked up that hole). So it's important to put up good fences straight away so your dog doesn't learn to just try harder (think Houdini).

A key driver for a dog is gaining access to various resources in her life, such as food, social contact, play, freedom and walks. You are the controller of the resources in your dog's life, and receiving these resources can be seen as a reward for your dog. So you need to be very aware of when you give these resources or rewards, and what behaviours you may be shaping. Whatever behaviour your dog is doing just before she gets those resources will be the behaviour you are training/ shaping, whether intentionally or unintentionally. For example, if you get to the park and your dog jumps out of the car without control, you have rewarded your dog for jumping out with freedom — a dangerous situation if you are near a busy road.

When we turn this around, we make it so that the dogs have to work for rewards, so that they learn appropriate rather than inappropriate behaviours. For example, when you get to the park and carefully open the car door, make sure you have the lead on your dog and ask for a wait, then click and reward the wait. Then give an 'out' or 'come' command, and click and reward. You are training a controlled exit of the car.

Be aware that dogs can train us. I'm sure we all suspect that our dogs are doing this at times. They can work out that if they bark at the door you'll open it — we don't want to teach that. They are learning that they can shape our behaviour, too.

I like to get dogs to work for these everyday rewards for the first few weeks in training (about 4-6 weeks or age). I call it 'Nothing in

Life is Free' — the dog needs to obey a simple command like 'sit' or 'wait' before getting any resources she is likely to want. This uses those everyday life situations for the benefit of training. A well-known example is the 'sit and wait' before you feed your dog. She is learning all the time.

We have just gone through the different ways dogs learn: the key ones for us being associative, reinforcement (positive and negative), contrast training through apparent natural consequences, inference and observation. Next we will look at the key training techniques I use, which are built on an understanding of these ways dogs learn.

Applying learning psychology to training

MONTY: STEPS FOR DRIVING TO SUCCESS

For months we had been training Monty to drive a car for a campaign we did for the SPCA. An SPCA rescue dog himself, Monty was chosen to show that 'rescue dogs are smart dogs!' We broke down the sequences of behaviour into small parts, taught him the parts separately through shaping, then built them up into complex sequences (chaining). Strangely, I kind of got inured to the idea of a dog driving a car. That is, until the day all the hard work came together: I'm actually tucked up next to the media in the back of the car while Monty is driving. He turns the car on, throws it into gear with one paw, then puts a paw on the wheel to steer, the other pressing the accelerator, and off Monty drives — with me and grinning journos in the back of the car. One of the media people turns to me and says (in slightly stronger language than I care to share): 'That dog is actually driving this car!' That's when it struck me as well: Monty is actually driving this car! It truly was a surreal experience; as if we were on another planet.

Your dog might not have to fly a plane or drive a car, but understanding the basic training processes and techniques we use is critical to establishing sound foundations in our training regime and to solving behaviour problems. What Monty shows is that it's not dogs that are the limitation — guess who is? But not with Dog Zen!

There are two overarching training processes we use when we train our dogs — we are either creating (shaping) new appropriate behaviours or modifying (changing) old inappropriate behaviours. This section will explain the theory behind both 'shaping' and 'modifying' behaviour so that you can apply these to:

O building the bond (Part B — shaping)
O creating a shared language (Part B — shaping)
O training puppies (Part C — shaping)
O solving behaviour issues in adult dogs (Part D — modifying and shaping).

Shaping behaviours

Shaping is the creation of new behaviours in a dog, rather than changing old behaviours. It is done by breaking the desired behaviour into small pieces or steps, in order to teach it in stages and then build it back into a sequence. Some of the simpler behaviours, like a 'sit' or a 'down', can be taught almost immediately, so you won't have to shape these in increments. However, for some slower learners you might have to break down these simple tasks.

Because you are teaching new behaviours, most of the training is focused on positive reinforcement, because we all learn best this way. Usually, the clicker and food are my preferred tools.

Shaping is the foundational training process I use in Part B (shaping bonding and shared language behaviours) and Part C (training puppies), so understanding its principles will help you implement those parts more effectively. It will also allow you to teach your dog more complicated behaviours if you wish to. Part D (solving behaviour problems) is concerned with modifying existing behaviours, so that is a separate process discussed next.

The core principles of shaping that are important for you to understand are:

O Use shaping to establish any new behaviour.
O Break behaviours into steps (some dogs may need smaller and smaller steps if they aren't good learners, have a learning block or aren't reward-focused).
O Outline the steps required to achieve the behaviour. In this book, I have created the steps for you, based on my experience, so you don't have to do this. However, it is important that you understand

how and why that list of steps was created, so that you can implement them effectively. When you do this yourself for other behaviours, it is worth writing down the steps so that you can think ahead.

○ I largely induce the behaviour through luring (drawing the dog into a desired behaviour). Classically, in shaping you wait for the behaviour to happen naturally and spontaneously (capturing the behaviour). However, I have found that luring using food and a clicker is effective, quicker and easier for the more novice trainer.

○ Starting with the first step, click and reward the behaviour that is close enough to the desired behaviour. Click and reward this a few times to consolidate. Then start successively rewarding behaviour that is progressively getting closer and closer to the desired behaviour (this is called successive approximation). You are getting closer and closer to the behaviour you want, rewarding the steps towards it. Make sure you consolidate the approximate behaviour sufficiently so that it sticks, but don't go backwards. (That is, don't reward earlier behaviour — you have moved on from that, so rewarding it will take your dog in the wrong direction.) The only time you might go back to an earlier position is when your dog is struggling and has gone backwards. If so, go back and quickly move through the stages again.

○ I sometimes use an intermediate or 'keep going' marker (for more-advanced dogs). Use a 'Yes' cue as a 'keep going' marker when you see behaviour generally heading in the right direction (communicating 'Yes, you are on the right track'). I don't reinforce it with a click and reward. When the behaviour step I want is actually achieved, I then do click and reward. This keeps the dog motivated. However, don't introduce intermediate markers with dogs that are new learners or are new to clicker training.

○ You can also use a neutral 'wrong': in a neutral tone that is not aversive say 'Wrong' if your dog is doing it wrong, so he knows that isn't the right way to go. (Don't click and reward, of course.) However, don't use this with new or compromised learners, as they will get confused: it becomes too much to think about. Dogs who are good learners and have done a lot of learning pick it up quickly, so it can be very powerful. You are building up trust in the process too.

Note: as you get better at training, you can shape behaviours without lures, instead relying on timing and your newly improved observation and understanding behaviour skills. What we are doing above with lures is technically successive approximation. If you use physical guidance, it is called 'modelling' — like the golf coach standing behind you physically guiding your stroke. But be careful when handling dogs as you teach behaviours, as in some dogs it can interfere with their learning.

The essential rules of shaping

Use these rules to help you implement Parts B and C.

Take small steps, and step up in increments

O Keep it simple, training one part of a behaviour at a time. Keep the increments do-able and fun. Put current trained behaviour on an intermittent schedule of reinforcement before raising the bar.

When training a new step, relax expectations on the old one

O When you make changes, newly learned behaviours can falter a bit, so don't expect too much and just get on with the new one. Relax on testing the previous behaviour until a bit later, and don't use correction for failure, or you will bring attention to the failure and can exaggerate it. Keep working on positive reinforcement on the behaviour you are trying to teach — let him work out what he needs to learn.

If a shaping step is not working, try something new — be creative

O Maybe break it in half or look again at how to do it. Is there a behaviour that your dog does naturally that would help him to understand the next small step?

Finish each step or session well, and stay focused on the dog

O Failing to reward your dog for the right thing can be as bad as a correction.

O I like to jackpot exceptional performances with about five to ten times the normal reward and lots of praise.

Try again

O If behaviour goes backwards, be prepared to go back a few steps until you find what your dog remembers, then work back up systematically.

Establishing

O Rehearse the steps as a sequence at intervals, so you can identify any steps they might have forgotten so you can re-establish.

O To establish things in long-term memory, we need to rehearse sequences normally at least three times.

O Don't change trainers once you have started on teaching a new behaviour. It's okay to change trainers if your dog is used to that, but not in the middle of a new behaviour or step.

Finishing

O Finish each session on a high note with a success. It is sometimes hard to finish on a good performance, as success will often stimulate you to go for one more, better performance! But be conservative and finish a bit early. Your dog will remember the first and the last thing best, and be left wanting to play again.

O I like to finish with a ball reward, but not as a reinforcer for shaping behaviour. I also like to clip the dog on a clip station or put him in his crate for 10 minutes so to allow quiet time to consolidate memories, then let him have a big play and run.

Behaviour modification

It doesn't always go as we hope, so we also focus on modifying behaviour problems — 'teaching old dogs new tricks'. This requires the changing of old habits (inappropriate behaviours) and replacing them with the new behaviours that you want. For example, with an aggressive dog who has poor meet-and-greet skills, you will first stop him rushing up and barking, then replace that behaviour with appropriate social greets. Behaviour modification is the focus of Part D.

There are a number of different techniques we can use to modify existing behaviour. Below are some of the techniques we use in Part D:

O **Redirection/change motivation:** This involves changing the focus of a behaviour. For example, when a dog wants to chase prey, instead give her a ball and redirect her onto that. Keep your dog on the long-line during training and cue her (give her a command like 'fetch!' or 'get it!'). We also use apparent natural consequence and contrast training for this behaviour if the dog is too strongly motivated.

O **Shape the absence of a behaviour you don't want:** For example, if your dog is jumping up on you, click and reward for four feet on the ground instead (using a flat hand signal). Use this pre-emptively; that is, as the dog walks up, click and reward. You can also reward any other behaviour than jumping up, including 'stand', 'sit' or

Monty learning to drive.

Mr Cool — just did a world-first live on TV3 with Jaz.

'down'. (See the Hyperactivity chapter for an example of this technique in use.)

○ **Cue unwanted behaviour:** Put the unwanted behaviour on cue (command), then never give the cue, or teach the opposite and give him that. For example, teach a 'speak' and a 'quiet' command for barking problems. Only use the 'speak' command when training, but use 'quiet' whenever necessary. (See the Barking chapter for an example of this technique in use.)

○ **Extinction:** This can be useful for attention-seeking behaviours and minor issues. Just ignore, don't reinforce with attention or any other rewards, and it will normally go away. However, with difficult and persistent behaviours, other techniques are more effective.

○ **Counter-conditioning:** Also called switch conditioning, this is any technique that will switch a dog out of sympathetic arousal (the non-learning state) into parasympathetic arousal (the learning state). The key purpose for this technique in Dog Zen is to enable you to switch into and maintain your dog in a learning state so that she can learn. (See the Learning State chapter in Part B.) This technique was developed in human clinical psychology, and there are a number of techniques to achieve this. In my experience, the most effective tool to do this in a dog is the clicker and food reward.

○ **Generalised desensitisation:** This is the ordering of fearful stimuli from the least fearful to the most, and systematically exposing your dog in a carefully ordered manner to help desensitise him while counter-conditioning (ideally with the clicker). The goal is to generalise into the everyday the situations related to what is fearful. (See the Phobias chapter and table for an example of this technique in use.)

○ **Flooding:** This is exposing dogs to a mass level of the aggravating stimuli, such as people at a party (for human aggression) or lots of dogs at a dog park (for dog–dog aggression). Due to the safety risks involved to both the dog and others, this technique should only be undertaken by trained professionals.

○ **Targeting:** This is when we shape the dog to touch her nose or paw onto a target. For example, we get fearful or slightly aggressive dogs to touch a visitor's hand while clicking and rewarding. We start with our own hand, click and reward, and then move to the

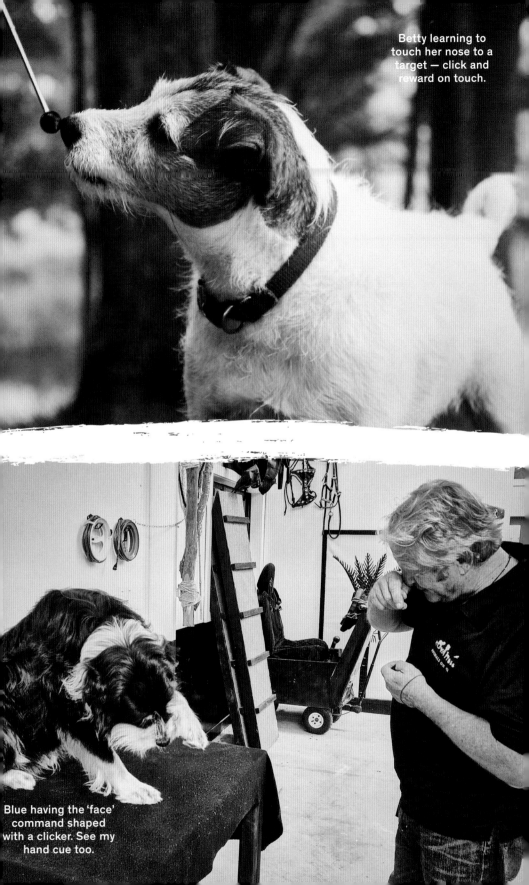

Betty learning to touch her nose to a target — click and reward on touch.

Blue having the 'face' command shaped with a clicker. See my hand cue too.

visitor's. (See the Human-oriented Aggression chapter for an example of this technique in use.)

In conclusion

I have taken up the challenge thrown down by a number of leading cognitive scientists and ethologists of today (such as Ádám Miklósi, Alexandra Horowitz, Brian Hare and John Bradshaw), to take their work and have it inform a comprehensive training methodology. What is needed to do this is an understanding of learning psychology and applied clinical psychology. Those of us who work and study in both fields, applying these in our work with complex training problems, can take this challenge up by developing training methodologies that are grounded in science and practical experience, and are effective and humane.

I began studying 40 years ago with the forerunners of these scientists: Professor Erich Klinghammer (a student of Konrad Lorenz and a great wolf ethologist), Professor John Paul Scott (the father of the dog's formative period), Michael Fox, Marc Bekoff and many more great minds. They assisted and inspired my original research into sheep dog behaviour and genetics. I continued to study developments in these fields, but ventured off into applied dog behaviour and clinical animal psychology, in which I treat behaviour problems, train high-level dog performances for TV and film, host my own TV shows, and produce a number of world-first behaviour performances with rescue dogs. I believe this combination has given me the skills and knowledge to take the current cognitive research, together with my applied experience and learnings, into Dog Zen and pick up the challenge.

Dog Zen is my dog behaviour and training philosophy, the shared language we create to both rear and train dogs. It firmly sits in the 'prevention is better than the cure' camp (doing the right thing at the right time), but also provides guidance on what to do if things go awry — yes, you can teach old dogs new tricks as well.

Dog Zen rests on the knowledge we have just explored in this section. We have explored multiple facets of dogs to build our understanding of them, so we can love more deeply and train with them more effectively. We have explored the defining features of dogs: their ability to bond

Charlie being worked, using the lead correctly with a clicker. His eye-line to his mentor is good.

with us; their extended formative period; and the importance of learning state. We looked at the need to develop a shared language so that we can bring our two disparate worlds together and understand each other.

We investigated how dogs perceive their world so that we can understand more fully how they see and engage with the world in order to connect with them in ways that support them (not hinder them, which we sometime inadvertently do). We have discovered the dog's defining focus on us, their ability to bond with us, and how this focus shapes their intelligence; how dogs look to us for direction, cues and assistance, and how we make use of that in our training. We explored how dogs learn and how we build on that understanding to develop our training methods to both shape new behaviours and modify old. And finally, we identified the central role of the clicker as a tool to shape behaviour, enhance our bond and most importantly to switch and maintain learning state.

From all of this we build the foundations of Dog Zen — ensuring that our training programme is grounded in understanding our dogs and how best to bond, love and train with them. This knowledge helps craft the five foundations that underpin Dog Zen, which we will explore in the next section:

O Building a powerful 'shared language' between us to create the family rules.

O Effective learning through the maintenance of 'learning state'.

O The creation of the 'bond' so we can both love and trust each other deeply and know our places and roles.

O 'Prevention is better than cure' — the importance of the pups' extended 'formative period' that allows them to socialise widely, cross-foster and learn extensively if exposed correctly, so they can live in our complex world.

O 'Old dogs, new tricks': it is possible to solve behaviour problems in adult dogs by re-creating the potent learning state of the formative period through 'taking them back to the den'.

Purina Pound Pups to Dog Stars team with rescue dogs.

Bandit — another Purina Pound Pups star.

The Training Foundations

This section covers the training foundations of Dog Zen that allow us to create a shared language for our dogs and ourselves. This enables us to communicate and bring these two disparate cultures together, so that our dogs can live in our complex human world safely and happily. To do this we need to know how to understand our dogs and how our dogs understand us. When dogs understand us they feel safer, happier and are more relaxed.

We explore the critical role of the learning state in effective training, how to recognise your dog's learning state and switch him into it. The essential rules of training are also outlined, so we can set up effective training sessions supportive of learning every time. We then build the Dog Zen Toolkit (tools and techniques) and the basic commands for successfully communicating with dogs. We will look at the purposes and meanings of these commands and tools, and what role they play to effectively build our relationship with and train our dogs. Even the simplest of tools in Dog Zen has a deeper purpose than we often understand.

We then bring all of these skills together to create the bond. The core focus of Dog Zen — a well-established and secure bond — will enable a trusting, loving relationship that will encourage our dogs to look to us for direction in any situation. We explore our role as their mentor using our unique method 'joining up' to solidify our 'bond'.

Together, these will build a rock-solid foundation for you to take into any training situation. Whether you are raising and training a pup (Part C), resolving behaviour issues in your adult dog (Part D) or further strengthening your bond and training relationship with your dog, these foundational principles will support you to build a harmonious, loving relationship and grow a happy, confident dog.

4

Shared language

Humans are from Earth, dogs are from Pluto!

We've all been there in our human relationships — when we're talking at each other but for the life of us we can't understand the other person's perspective at all. That can happen between two human beings who share the same language, culture and upbringings. So imagine what can go astray when we are talking about cross-species communications.

Dogs have a different culture, language and perspective of the world than we do, so we need to assist them to successfully live their lives as dogs in our human world. In order to do this, we need to create a way of communicating with our dogs that makes sense to them. We need to create a shared language, which we can use whenever we want to 'speak' to our dogs or understand why they are doing what they are doing or acting the way they are acting. Dogs can't change the way they are, so it is up to us to understand them and take the lead in creating our shared language.

In this chapter we will learn:

O how dogs communicate
O how dogs read us
O how to build a shared language together.

Why is creating a shared language important?

It isn't obvious to dogs why we do the things we do in our human world. Our requirements for a safe and happy life are often different from dogs' natural inclinations, which they get from their wolfish roots. There are many risks in the human world that dogs don't understand: cars are dangerous, aggression is largely inappropriate, killing stock and cats is unacceptable, and so on. These situations often come with death penalties to the dog and legal repercussions for owners. Having a shared language is critical to enable us to articulate to our dogs what it is we want from them, and how we will keep them safe. Through this they learn the family rules of conduct.

A quick note on dominance

As noted earlier, when I talk about dominance it's not in the old discredited 'Lupomorph model' of aggressive, dominant leaders of the pack. When I refer to dominance, I mean the sort of relationship that's based more on guidance, one a dog would have with a father, mother or older sibling — the mentor.

Dominance can be a gesture, signalling disapproval or 'don't do that', which prevents or averts actual aggression. This is the value of social dominance and subordinance signals: they remove the need for aggressive, violent action, by informing others rather than escalating to action.

4.1 UNDERSTANDING THE DOG'S SOCIAL SIGNALLING

Language is a two-way process, so the first step in developing a shared language is to understand the dog's language. Dogs understand our behaviour in dog terms, so we need to understand the way they perceive things so that we can adjust the way we communicate.

Dogs are communicating with you all the time: either intentionally seeking to communicate, or unintentionally signalling their internal state. This peer-to-peer social communication signalling is a slightly modified form of the system inherited from the wolves. Dogs show a less exaggerated form of these signals, and have more sociable gestures that are more friendly and affiliative.

Dog postural communication, like any language, is highly subtle and complex. Each component can have many nuances; for example, the stare can have many variations, from direct and active, to looking away, as well as a 'targeting' stare that is lining up the other dog or prey (which might include something as subtle as having one foot up, pointing). However, the basic postural components or shapes and their behavioural and emotional meanings are explained here to give you the important basics.

It is important to realise that the *time* between your dog alerting his behaviour and 'targeting' or fixing on the 'target' is critical for you to recognise, so you can intervene before the behaviour is initiated. Before your dog's adrenalin rises and the primitive brain kicks in, you have a window to make contact with your dog and get him focused on you, his mentor, so you can guide him in the right decision. Looking to you is the key: in most instances, as soon as he looks to you, you can intervene effectively.

Different breeds have differing drivers or motivations that are important to them. Understanding these drivers will help you antici-pate and interpret your dog's behaviours. For example, Terriers are self-driven hunters, so can be more aggressive and protective of objects. If they are staring, pay attention: they are more likely to chase! Herding dogs are driven by things moving and will want to herd them. Sled dogs run together and want to pull. Sight hounds see things and chase after them, scent hounds smell and follow their nose, Retrievers will retrieve and mouth. Guard breeds will be more territorial, Labradors and group hunters more accepting of a group and less competitive, and so on. We need to take these differences into account when reading dogs and understanding their predispositions and potential problems.

The basis of a dog's language is different from ours. Humans are highly verbal communicators, while dogs rely on a number of different attributes, primarily: posture; space; proximity; vocalisations including intonation which often indicates emotional content; and scent marks and pheromones.

Dogs are approximately 90 per cent postural communicators, so we need to learn how to read their postures to understand what they are saying or meaning. The main body parts you should look at to read a dog are the eyes, ears, lips, body, hackles and tail.

There are the six main behavioural states (and shapes) you need to be able to read. Remember that these are intrinsic (innate) so will be honest (true).

1. **Aggression/Dominance** — demonstrated through big postures which dogs use to make themselves look bigger and more dominant. Dogs almost always signal threat before an attack. This is the fight part of the fight–flight state.

O **Eyes** — staring directly and held longer than normal (a fixed stare), pupils dilated (enlarged).

O **Ears** — forward so able to pick up auditory information well.

O **Lips** — fully puckered forward into a full offensive snarl, or as fear increases retracted back (ventrally) into a smile-like gesture. A growl will often be paired with this gesture if it is dominance or offensive aggression: this is a signal that an attack is more likely. (Dogs add extra gestures as the threat escalates — giving you lots of warning.)

O **Body** — strutting and standing over the neck and shoulders of another dog. A dog on the verge of aggression may also stiffen up (standing-over tactics) or be directly in front.

O **Hackles** (the hair along the back of the dog's neck and back, even to the tail in some cases) raised (piloerection), which can indicate dominance or fear. (The difference is differentiated by back shape: see the fear section below). This really signals arousal, the adrenalin-induced fight–flight state.

O **Tail** — held up high or at least level (12 to 3 o'clock position). Most dogs don't wag the tail when they are aggressive, but some do, so don't rely on a wagging tail to identify a dog as friendly: look for other signals to confirm.

O **Tone** — deep growling, especially if the aggression is intensifying. Barking is a lower tone and occurs more behind barriers or on

Aggression/
Dominance.

Confident

the chain, as it indicates a level of conflict between approach and retreat, when dogs can't get fully away as they are contained.

O **Body orientation** — the more direct, the more threatening.

O **Approach** — the more direct, the more threatening. Circling behind shows an element of fear.

2. **Confidence** — demonstrated through upright and relaxed postures. This is the behaviour and posture we expect from calm, stable dogs, and is the state you would aim for your dog to be in most of the time.

O Eyes — looking at the other individual but not staring (the more sustained and direct the staring, the more threatening).

O Ears — upright, pointing forward and relaxed, not alerted.

O Lips — normal and relaxed.

O Body — upright, but not puffed-up or out, strutting or lowered.

O Hackles — not up, or if they are this can be just arousal level but with no other aggressive signals.

O Tail — normal, relaxed height (4 to 6 o'clock position), could be wagging slightly.

O Tone — normal to higher-pitched.

O Walk — calm, no strutting or no lowering of the body.

3. **Playfulness** — demonstrated by moving into play bows and play-soliciting behaviour. Dogs often use play to mediate and reduce conflict. Play behaviours are more often subordinate to the dominant dog, although dominants will initiate play to create safe interactions with subordinates and relieve the tension of a social interaction.

O Eyes — happy. Sometimes they will be staring in play threat when combined with a play bow. Note that the eyes convey many subtleties: open, wide open, squinted, pupils dilated, etc.

O Ears — relaxed, but can vary as dogs mimic other behaviours in play at times.

O Lips — the playful dog will approach, lick the jowls of the other dog (or human), then run away, approach and lick the jowls again, then run away.

O Body — play bows, soliciting play.

O Hackles — not raised unless a dog gets a fright, which could turn into a dominance interaction or an apology.

O Tail — wagging or relaxed.

Classic play bow
— come play
with me.

Submission,
belly reveal, ears
back, lips back,
submissive lick,
eyes squinting.

O Tone — an up intonation (a high-pitched bark or whining).

4. **Submission** demonstrated by a lowered positioning to make themselves smaller, but they stand still, slightly approach or roll over rather than withdraw (which we see in fear). The purpose of submissive posturing is to inhibit threat in another dog.

O Eyes — often not looking at the threat but actively looking away, although as the appeasement/solicit action element increases, the more the dog looks at the object.
O Ears — often back or flat.
O Lips — there might be a 'smile' on the dog's lips: the lips might be pulled back (called 'ventral retraction'). The dog can be licking the jowls of the dominant from underneath.
O Body — lowered. The back half might be lowering down towards the ground, or the dog might roll right over onto the back into recumbent submission. A submissive dog might also urinate.
O Approach — will approach the other party (whereas a fearful dog will avoid the other party).
O Hackles — not up unless very scared.
O Tail — often low, but out from the body (5 to 6 o'clock position).
O Tone — whining and solicitous.

5. **Affiliative (to associate)** — demonstrated through similar types of behaviours as submissive. However, submission is normally slower, more wary, with lower energy and precautionary. Affiliative state is more active, so you'll see more tail wagging, more licking and higher energy. The dog is more actively engaging of the recipient than when submissive. He is not fearful. You'll see it more in puppies, though adult dogs can exhibit it.

The purpose of these gestures is that your dog is trying to get something: for example, security, support, food, play, contact, etc. Affiliative greeting became ritualised in dogs' social evolution through rituals around the pack leaving for, and returning from, the hunt. When the pack heads out on hunts, the pups go through a hyper-excited departure routine and jump up over the adults, doing affiliative behaviours that build bonds plus excitement for the hunt. On the return of the pack, pups solicit pack members to regurgitate food, so they can feed.

Affiliative.

Fear.

6. Fear — demonstrated by lowered and arched positioning and/or withdrawal.

O Eyes — pupil dilation extreme.

O Ears — back or flat.

O Lips — a full gape and open mouth sometimes, but the lips will at least be pulled back like they are in submission.

O Mouth — open threat gape; snapping toward you in a defensive threat, in the hope you will back away (generally displayed only to ward you off). Only if you continue to encroach into their personal space might they defensively bite.

O Body — lowered, but normally in fear a dog will not roll over unless cornered, back often arched.

O Approach — the dog will be demonstrating extreme avoidance behaviour, trying to get out of the situation. He will not approach.

O Hackles — often up all the way down to the tail, not in threat. This is adrenalin-induced 'flight' in 'flight and fight'.

O Tail — down or tucked fully under the body between the legs (often the most obvious sign).

O Tone — quiet or high-pitched, whining or barking (often combined).

Note that a submissive dog is unlikely to bite whereas a fearful dog may bite if he is continued to be pressured beyond his ability to cope.

Threat displays from offensive to fear. Overleaf you will see the transition from full offensive aggression through to a conflicted state to fear-induced aggression. Note the varying ear, eye and lip/muzzle positions.

Intonation and barking

When you are reading your dog, posture is the most important thing to read, followed by intonation.

In general, a dog's intonation will be a high-pitched bark or whine if they are soliciting and happy, and maybe in fear; and low-pitched and growing in a full aggressive, threatening, dominance state. Sometimes the dog might be barking in a deep tone.

Barking in dogs is a mix of tones influenced by various environmental and emotional factors. Often dogs who bark are in conflict; that is, they are torn between a threat and a retreat. Normally they would probably prefer to retreat but if contained or tied up they can't, hence they are in

This sequence of photos shows a change from offensive to defensive fear-based threat.

1 Offensive aggression. Lips puckered, forward, direct stare, ears forward.

2 Offensive aggression, but some conflicted signals, turned side-on, ears back more.

3 Lips retracted back a bit more, eye contact less direct, ears back more.

4 More fear components, slight gape, lips back, ears flattened.

5 More fear seen by mouth gaping further, ears back.

6 Full fear gape, may snap if aggressor keeps pushing.

conflict. This is evident by the alternating frequency/tone of bark (from high to low, defensive to offensive). Dogs barking in yards, on chains and in houses are often conflicted, because if they were free they would stay silent and avoid the threat.

Understanding the motivation behind the barking is helpful so that you can either fulfil the dog's need or resolve the conflict. Below are described different types of barking and their motivations.

o Threat growl or low-pitched (low-frequency) bark — when the sender is aggressive and wants the hearer to withdraw: 'Back off!'

o High-pitched tonal signals, like a puppy whimper (whine, lost call, play bark), tend to be care-soliciting, appeasement or play-soliciting. The dog is not threatening, but encouraging and telling the receiver it's okay to come closer. Play barks solicit play interaction.

o Hunt or scent bark or yodel — typical of the hounds, like beagles, who produce a characteristic, loud, high-pitched and tonal cry: the 'scent bark'. The outcome of giving this tonal signal is that the whole pack, along with its companion human hunters, rallies together and draws close to each other and moves to follow the scent.

o Soliciting whine — high-pitched vocalisation that is calling you to pay attention or to come to the dog.

o Separation distress — can be a bark or a high-pitched tonal cry, even a howl. This is attempting to call the owner back home. Wolves use howling to regather the pack after the hunt, as the physical nature of the sound is easy to locate. It says 'I'm lonely' or 'I'm lost — come back to me'. We feel it! This is a great example of tonal information that moves you emotionally — your mirror neurons are firing!

o Fear-induced bark — this is paired with the fear postural signals and is conflicted. If the dog were free he would retreat, but since he cannot he gives a defensive threat bark that has predominantly high-pitched vocalisations.

o Retreat woof — wolves, feral and mal-socialised dogs do a single or a few low-tone woofs as signals of retreat: 'Let's get out of here'. A mal-socialised dog has not established an appropriate attachment relationship, normally because of a lack of exposure in the formative period, so its behaviour towards strangers can be inappropriate — fearful or aggressive.

o Stimulus-oriented barking — this varies depending on the stimulus.

Appeasement/
affiliative jowl lick
— can be soliciting
regurgitation.

Muzzle pin —
gently saying 'no'.

A cat on the fence can cause a cross between the hunt bark and the threat bark. Hard-to-identify objects will induce a conflicted threat bark ('What is out there?').

Recent studies show that humans and dogs use similar parts of the brain to read intonation and to understand the emotional content of the sounds. We, too, use low-frequency sounds for threat and higher-pitched sounds to greet, care and solicit. Often when we talk to pups and dogs with our baby talk we exaggerate this tonal sound, and as trainers we rely on this, too.

Generally, women are read by dogs as less threatening because of their inherent higher-pitched vocalisations and their less-threatening size and posture. Dogs often prefer females, though may follow what they see as the older male, as to them he is more dominant. They will generally avoid overly assertive males if they possibly can. How often have you seen the dog obey Dad and seek Mum for nurture and comfort?

4.2 HOW DOGS UNDERSTAND US

We need to be very aware of our posture and tone, as dogs are highly receptive to human cues. For example, they follow our pointing (so it's useful to use pointing, especially whole limbs!), they follow our eyes and where we are looking, and they watch our faces carefully, knowing whether we are distracted or not.

All that said, dogs still come from a very different culture, and the ancestral meanings of many of their behaviours are different. What you are doing doesn't necessarily mean what you think it means to your dog. Dogs read our behaviour and language largely in dog terms: they are using their language to interpret us.

Many of our social gestures can be opposite to what dogs would do. A prime example is if you hug a dog that doesn't know you. In your human mind, a hug is a warm and friendly greeting. However, to the dog it will normally be perceived as a threat (the neck is the ritualised threat area and where dogs bite), so it can be a stressful experience. Staring into a dog's eyes may be loving for a human, but to a dog who doesn't know you it can be a threat.

Relationship and context are important. If you are well bonded to your dog, she will experience these gestures differently; however, it is most important to remember these guidelines for dogs you don't know. Just like us really: running up to a stranger on the street and giving him a hug is probably not wise, but for a friend you know loves hugs, no problem! Building a shared language and bond is aligning the dog's understanding and interpretation to yours.

Because dogs translate your actions into dog language, they are looking for your postural indicators. Of course you don't have all the right appendages (such as big ears and a tail), so instead they will be noticing:

O your eye contact (direction, duration, degree of fixation of stare, squint/open pupil size)

O how you approach them, including speed and orientation (direct or slightly turned-off)

O your height and stiffness of posture (postural tone)

O how and where you handle them

O your vocal intonation

O the context (e.g. the meaning changes if the interaction is with someone they know, or if it's near the dog's territory or car)

O the degree of freedom they have: are you holding their lead, are they chained up, are they contained or in a kennel, etc? The more freedom dogs have, the more ability they have to avoid the situation.

Through these physical behaviours, you will be signalling threatening, neutral or friendly behaviours. Again, this is with new dogs; your own dog will become able to reinterpret some of your behaviours based on what you teach him they mean.

Eye contact

One of the major threat gestures to a dog is direct eye contact. If you have a good bond with your dog and you aren't excessively assertive with him, then looking at your dog and him looking back can be subtle and encouraging. However, like humans, dogs can tell if your look is a threat stare or encouraging contact. Don't stare in a fixed fashion, especially if you are approaching a dog and using lowered tones, otherwise he will feel threatened. Dogs that feel threatened may feel stressed or counter-threaten you.

Approach

Moving directly into a dog's personal space (within about 1 metre) can be a threat, so when you greet a new dog simply walking up to her can be interpreted as a threat. If you let the dog approach you instead, it is much less threatening. Consider your speed and height as you approach.

As a general rule, stop a couple of metres back, if comfortable crouch down, hold out the back of your hand (in a relaxed fashion) and allow the dog to approach. If comfortable, call the dog to you in a higher-pitched tone if need be. If you are approaching, approach from the side or three-quarters on, rather than walking toward the dog straight on.

Height and posture

Be aware that height is a threat to a dog: remember, dogs try to make themselves bigger when they want to communicate dominance. Standing over a dog is threatening, and the bigger you are, the more of a threat you are for the dog.

If you want to lower the threat, lower your height by crouching slightly. Again, turn yourself three-quarters on to the dog, because the squarer on to a dog you are, the more threatening you appear.

How you handle a dog — safe and unsafe areas

If you are going to handle a dog that doesn't know you, handle him in the chest/chin region (safe). Handling him on the neck, cheek, shoulder region, the feet, the tail or the back is likely to seem more threatening, as these are the dog's ritualised threat areas.

If the dog lies down and you handle him on the tummy, this is normally non-threatening; but most dogs won't let you access that area easily at the beginning, unless they are in recumbent submission.

Intonation

The next important thing is your intonation. If you use a high-pitched, happy, soliciting voice, dogs are going to be happier with you. If you are using low, growly, threatening tones and telling them off, they will feel threatened, and there is more risk of you being counter-threatened, or of them showing submission or fear reactions.

Threat-reducing behaviours

O Do not make direct eye contact, but instead look just off to the side or glance occasionally at the dog. Appear relaxed — even if you have to 'fake it until you make it'.

O Hold out the back of your hand and allow the dog to approach you first, or just stand, relaxed, if you feel too vulnerable.

O If you approach the dog, approach from three-quarters on, stop a couple of metres away from the dog and crouch down.

O Do not stand over the dog.

O Handle the dog only in the chin/chest region at first, as this is a safer, less-threatening area. (Not on the head or back of the neck.)

O Stay silent, but if you use an intonation, use a happy, high-toned voice to speak to the dog. Test one short comment first: for example, 'good boy' in a quiet tone. (Watch posture.)

Situations when we should try to appear as non-threatening to a dog as possible include:

O whenever we are meeting new dogs, especially if it is on that dog's own property, including a car

O when a dog is threatening you

O if your dog is submissive or fearful of you

O when entering a property, including doorways front and back

O when approaching a dog's owner

O when a dog is on a chain or contained — ensure you don't reach toward the dog.

If you have a dog with behavioural issues, such as excessive submission, fear, fear-induced aggression, protective aggression or defensive aggression, it is important that you communicate to people meeting and engaging with your dog how they can act in a non-threatening manner. If your dog is aggressive, muzzle him.

4.3 HOW TO ESTABLISH A SHARED LANGUAGE
Recognise your dog's behaviour and respond accordingly

Learn how to read your dog's behaviour, and respond to how your dog is feeling and behaving in an appropriate way. If you see that your dog is fearful, work to alleviate that fear. If you see your dog is aggressive, ensure you control the situation so that it doesn't result in any injury, and remove your dog from the situation. Know how to read your dog's behaviour so you know early what's going on and how to

Threatening posture. Upright, direct, staring, height, hand up.

Non-threatening posture. Lowered, relaxed, eyes turned away, hand subtly presented.

respond. Remember: the time between the dog alerting to something and targeting it is the window to get contact and control.

Understand your dog's trigger points: what are the early warning signs that he is going to behave inappropriately? Understand how these might accumulate: the final trigger might be small, but it has resulted from a number of other earlier steps that can 'stack up'.

Use posture and intonation to communicate to your dog

A dog is reading you at all times, so use your posture and intonation (and, where appropriate, your words) to communicate the right message to the dog. If you want your dog to be relaxed, don't exhibit threatening behaviours. Remain calm and confident. If you want your dog to stop what she is doing, use a gruff tone of voice and stand up straight as you say 'NO'. If using fixing commands (commands for your dog to stay put), turn toward her and fix eye contact for a bit, subtle but effective (don't stare harshly). If you want your dog to come to you (drawing commands), then relax your body, turn slightly three-quarters on the and use a smiling, upbeat tone: relax your posture so you are inviting 'Come to me!'

Your dog can read your emotions and state of mind, so be aware what you will also be communicating down the lead to her. This is particularly relevant when approaching other dogs or people, with your dog on a lead. Tension on the lead and pulling away are both communicating your anxiety and fear. When training, if you are very stressed or emotional, think about whether it is a good time for training. It might be best just to play or even rest.

Joining Up

Joining Up is the foundational technique that enables you to establish a trusting relationship with your dog. It will encourage your dog to look to you for direction on how to act in any situation and to follow you. These basic behaviours trigger latent co-operative and social tendencies in your dog, mimicking the follower response. You are also reinforcing contact, so your dog focuses on your signals and the communication of your shared language. (See Joining Up sequence in Chapter 8, Creating the Bond.)

Use a clicker

This little hand-held tool enables you to make a distinct 'click' noise, which you use to mark the behaviour you want from your dog, followed up by a food reward. It also helps switch dogs into a learning state, which is critical for effective training. It is effective because it marks the behaviour precisely: vocal commands and food are slower and less precise, so potentially confusing. The clicker establishes precisely what you want from your dog, hence building your shared language.

Basic commands

Teach your dog the basic Dog Zen commands or cue words so that you have some actual shared words in your shared language. See the Basic Commands chapter.

5

Learning state and the essential rules of training

5.1 LEARNING STATE

This section will enable you to understand what a learning state is, recognise whether your dog is or isn't in one, and learn how to switch your dog into learning state so you can progress with your training. We finish with outlining the essential rules of training to set up effective training sessions that are supportive of learning.

What is a learning state?

Learning state is the foundational psycho-physiological state (the relationship between the mental and the physical) inherent in the formative period. It is the state your dog is in when he is able to learn, which is critical when you are trying to teach your dog new behaviours or to correct undesirable ones. It is a foundation of Dog Zen, and essential to any training you will do.

Associated with your dog's parasympathetic nervous system (the 'rest and digest' state), when activated your dog is calm, relaxed and non-fearful so has the capacity to focus and learn. This state is also stress-free and conducive to good health.

Conversely, when the sympathetic nervous system is switched on, your dog is in sympathetic arousal. This is the state dogs are in when they are fearful (flight state), aggressive (fight state) or in a hyperactive state — none of which are conducive to learning.

Think about yourself: if you are calm and relaxed, you are more able to learn something new than if you are nervous, worried or frightened. This is what it's like for your dog: happy and calm is good, stressed and anxious is not. When working with your dog, you need to be in a calm state, too, as dogs can actually smell and see what state you are in — it's as plain as the nose on your face to your dog.

Recognising a learning state

Signs of a learning state:
O a calm, happy and focused disposition
O attentiveness to you
O eating if presented with food
O a normal pulse rate
O normal pupil size — no dilation (expansion) due to adrenalin
O relaxed body language: ears forward or relaxed (not back), tail relaxed or possibly wagging, an upright and relaxed posture, and a relaxed mouth
O 'happy' eyes.

Signs of a non-learning state — sympathetic arousal
O most critically, not eating food if offered
O a stressed, anxious, aggressive or hyperactive disposition
O dilated pupils, increased pulse rate, shaking or panting
O fear or avoidance behaviours, such as escape, submission, fear or hyperactivity
O hackles might be up
O ears often back or down
O tail is lowered, not wagging
O posture is often lowered
O showing displacement behaviours — that is, coping behaviours that seem out of context, such as licking, squinting eyes or

yawning, scratching (dogs do these, as they can't face the threat so distract themselves and signal non-threat or avoidance).

Your dog is definitely not in a learning state if he is:
O being aggressive
O suffering separation anxiety
O overly stimulated and hyperactive
O acting in a predatory manner (e.g. chasing or hunting cats and birds)
O hyper-aroused with a toy, which he might be treating as mock prey
O fearful, anxious or phobic
O subject to inappropriate punishment
O dominated excessively.

Learning state test

The easiest test is whether your dog is eating when she should be or normally would be. If not, then she's probably not in a learning state, and the other signs above will confirm it.

An important indicator that your dog is close to going into a non-learning state is if she starts to take food more aggressively and snaps or nibbles hard at it. This often happens when pressure starts coming on to your dog; for example, when she comes head to head with a new dog that she finds threatening. Observe and learn what situations might trigger your dog into a non-learning state so you can be prepared to prevent it.

How to switch your dog into a learning state

Food! Or at least this is the primary one.

I know it sounds counter-intuitive that when your dog is not interested in food, you need to use food to put him in a learning state — but if you do it the right way, it works.

As a primary resource in Nature, food is naturally one of the strongest drivers in a dog. Food anticipation pushes your dog into a learning state, with hormones and digestive enzymes further activating the switch.

We do this by using a clicker: when the dog does what we want, we click and follow it up with a food reward. In this way, the sound of the click becomes a promise to your dog that food is coming, and this 'anticipation' makes your dog focused and attentive.

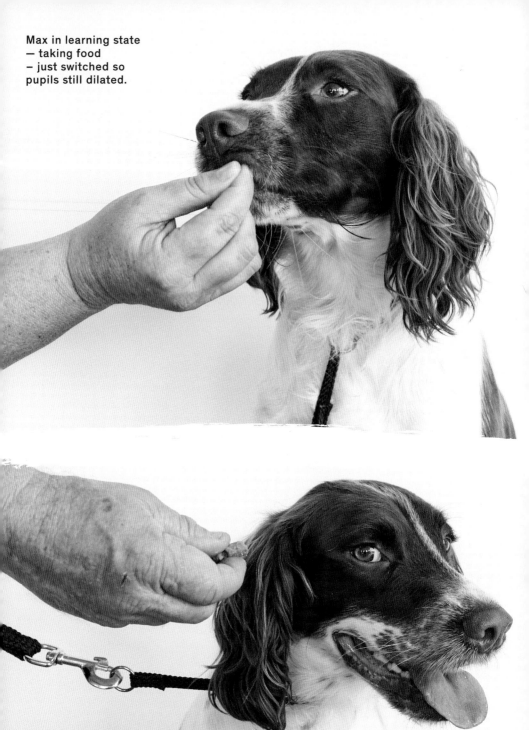

Max in learning state
— taking food
— just switched so
pupils still dilated.

Max in non-learning state
— refusing food
— panting
— pupils dilated.

Other switches

Basic commands can also be used to switch dogs into a learning state; for example, 'sit', 'down' or 'stay'. Once taught, these words act as a signal to your dog to pay attention as something is being asked of them. The more you use commands that have been associated with certain actions, the more they switch your dog into a learning state.

Initially, use these cues with the clicker: the familiar cue words indicate that you want your dog to do something, and the clicker brings anticipation of a food reward, so your dog becomes focused on you and ready to learn. That's why we begin training sessions by running through some well-known basic commands using the clicker.

If your dog is highly anxious or aggressive, simplify the environment you're working in, and take away as many stressors as possible so your dog isn't distracted.

Redirect into play before you start, i.e. change motivation — your pouch and pre-training routine help too.

How to maintain a learning state

Establishing a trusting relationship is critical: the safer your dog feels, the more her nervous system will remain calm and relaxed, keeping the dog focused. Make sure your dog feels happy, positive and loved; Joining Up and contact act as switches, too.

Other elements that help keep your dog in a learning state are:
- having training treats and a clicker with you — your dog will start anticipating these when seeing and smelling them, which acts as an early switch into a learning state
- managing food so that day food is for training and is high value, while less-palatable food is given at night
- a safe and simple environment
- a trusting, happy bond with you
- clarity and consistency of your communication
- you are focused, calm, alert and non-threatening
- when appropriate, another friendly dog present can provide social facilitation (potentially useful for fearful dogs)
- teaching your dog clear boundaries — what he can and cannot do.

Trying to train your dog when he is not in a learning state is one of the most common mistakes I see. Always check in with your dog first to see if he is ready to learn, and if not, help him switch into a learning state.

5.2 THE DOG ZEN ESSENTIAL RULES OF TRAINING

Here are the essential rules for all training sessions, whether shaping new or modifying old behaviours. These rules will establish a good learning environment, ensuring your training sessions are effective every time. They are based on modern learning theory and dog psychology.

Keep the environment simple

o Ensure that your training environment is set up in such a way that your dog can succeed. Be aware of extraneous olfactory, visual and auditory stimuli (smells, sights and sounds).

o You should be the most interesting thing in the area. There shouldn't be too much distraction or stimulation: we want your dog focused on you and what you are asking.

o Exercise your dog moderately before any training session, to blow off a bit of steam and help her to be calm.

Set up each training session

o Set up your training objective: know what you are training before you get started, and stick to it!

o Train one thing at a time so your dog doesn't get confused.

o Train simple tasks — break bigger goals down into small steps, teach each step and then build.

o Keep your training sessions short, approximately 10-15 minutes' duration, particularly when you are training new behaviours.

o Finish on a good note: make sure the first thing and the last thing your dog does is the right thing, as that's what she remembers best. It also means your dog has a positive memory of your training session.

o Finish a training session with a calm walk, then clip your dog up to rest the learning for a while so her brain gets an opportunity to consolidate.

Keep the environment simple.

Finish a successful session with play. It reinforces the session and eases any tension.

Your role is important

O Be patient, consistent, dependable and predictable.

O Don't rush. Sometimes repetition is necessary.

O Note your posture, intonations and mood — dogs read them easily.

O If you feel impatient or frustrated, either calm yourself or finish the session for the day.

O Take care to have only one trainer during the training phase. Different people have different styles, and this may confuse your dog while he is learning new things.

Have effective commands

O Don't introduce verbal commands too quickly. Dogs are essentially non-verbal, so train them non-verbally initially, to reduce the level of complexity.

O Keep commands (cues) simple: use one-word commands, and preferably one syllable.

O Check your timing: are you giving your dog the commands and using the clicker at the right time?

O Use your dog's name only to get her attention; don't use it as a command or a reprimand.

O Make sure you release your dog from the command. If you ask your dog to wait, make sure you let her know when you're finished.

Make training fun

O Praise regularly, but don't overstimulate and take your dog out of a learning state. Keep it positive but calm.

O Accept that neither you nor your dog is perfect, and that mistakes are part of learning.

O Dogs learn by trial and error.

O Reward your dog for a successful session with play.

Realise that you are training all the time

O Formal training sessions are an important time to establish new behaviours, but make sure you reinforce them outside of training. This is called proofing, essential to establish new behaviours.

O Remember that training sessions are a chance for contact and building your bond — so enjoy!

The correct lead position and clicker, shaping looking up to your contact.

6

The Dog Zen toolkit

Here I'll take you through all the tools and techniques you'll need to successfully complete my training programme. We'll look at the purposes of the tools, what role they have mimicking Nature, and how they come together to effectively build your relationship and train with your dog. The primary purpose of the tools we use is to help our dogs understand exactly what we want from them.

Our methods are based primarily around positive reinforcement and the use of natural or apparent natural consequences to shape the understanding of boundaries and build strong relationships. This enables us to establish a comprehensive shared language that allows our dogs to live happily and safely in our complex human world.

6.1 CLICKER

The clicker is a positive secondary reinforcement tool. It marks the right behaviour with the click, and is paired with a primary positive reinforcer (food) that reinforces the behaviour we are training.

O The clicker is a small hand-held tool that has a button (a strip of metal) on it which makes a distinctive click sound.

O The click acts as a marker (indicator) that tells your dog *exactly* what you want her to do (what is being reinforced).

O It's also a switch conditioner that switches your dog into a learning state.

O The click is a 'promise' to your dog that he will get a treat, so when you click the clicker, you must *always* reward your dog with a small piece of high-value food or other reward.

O It's more effective than just praise or verbal markers, because it has none of the confusing emotional messages your voice may contain. It is an unequivocal 'Yes, that's it!', because its sound is always consistent.

O A clicker is like a camera: you click immediately when you see the behaviour you want. Imagine you are trying to take a photo to show the exact moment your dog demonstrates the behaviour you want (make the click the moment that happens).

O Timing is everything. You must click the split-second your dog does the behaviour you want. That's why the clicker is one of the most effective training tools: it's completely precise at marking the behaviour, as the click is instant. (Voice and food rewards are slower).

O It is a temporary tool. You start clicking and rewarding each time, then intermittently, and finally you fade it out. It is only a training tool; don't use it forever. However, you can bring it back if you feel that your dog (or maybe you!) is relapsing, or you want to train a new behaviour.

Why do we use a clicker?

O It is the fastest way to create a shared language between you and your dog. Your dog doesn't know what you want, so you have to find a way to tell her — this is it!

O The clicker switches your dog into the learning state, so she is more open to learning new behaviours. This speeds up learning and helps even fearful, distracted dogs to focus and learn.

O Once your dog understands how the clicker works (and that it's always followed by a yummy treat), she will learn faster each time you use it to train a new behaviour.

O Training by the clicker builds affection and reinforces the bond between you and your dog, as you get associated with the clicker and therefore treats!

O It is a kind of game where your dog is trying to work out how to make you click. It's fun!

O It also becomes self-reinforcing: within a relatively short period of time, just the presence of your treat pouch and clicker — and of course your dog can smell the food — will be enough to switch your dog into a learning state. Look at your dog and you'll see she is eager to begin.

Learning to use a clicker

Equipment required:

O Clicker

O Pouch filled with high-value food (small pieces of cooked chicken or dog roll, for example)

O Hand-held lead

O Clip station

O Retractable lead or long-line

O Tennis ball

Preparation

O Set yourself up in a quiet space with minimum distractions; a corner works well for highly distractible dogs.

O Tie a wrist-band to the loop end of the clicker so you can access and use it easily. Elastic is best! Some use a lanyard.

O Secure the clicker to the wrist of your non-dominant hand (the left hand if you are right-handed, and vice versa) with the loop end closest to you. The length of the wrist band should allow the clicker to sit in your hand.

O Have a pouch with high-value food inside tied to your waist, accessible to your free hand. Cut the food into very small pieces so you can do lots of repetition — repetition is more important than the amount of food given each time.

Practise your timing

O Make sure your dog is not in hearing distance.
O With your clicker ready, take a tennis ball in your non-clicker hand and drop it from waist height.
O The instant the ball touches the ground, click.
O Practise this a few times, and once you are confident with your timing, start working with your dog. Remember that your dog will complicate things quickly, so make sure you are confident! Take your time to get it right. You will make some mistakes, and that's okay.

Getting your dog started

O Some dogs will be wary of the sound of the clicker initially, particularly if they are sensitive to noise. This will change quite quickly.
O As a precaution, start with your clicker behind your back. Click and throw the food reward on the floor. Watch your dog's reaction. If it is focused on the food and isn't reactive to the click sound, then all is good. Continue on with your clicker in front of you as normal. (Ensure you keep it away from your dog's head and ears to start with.)
O If your dog is at all reactive to the sound of the clicker when it is behind your back, wrap the clicker in a piece of material to muffle the level of the sound. Make sure the clicker is not too near your dog's head or ears, and work the clicker from the opposite side of your body from where your dog is.
O To start, spend time solely desensitising your dog to the volume of the clicker. Click and reward by throwing the food on the floor away from you, so that your dog moves away from you then comes back to you. By your dog moving, he will not be so intensely focused on the clicker, which will help to desensitise him. We are trying to get your dog focused on the food, not so much the clicker at this stage — so creating the positive association.
O Repeating this 10-20 times should be enough for a moderately sensitive dog. Watch for your dog relaxing through this time.
O For very sensitive dogs, the muffling material needs to be thicker. Try working the clicker from within your pocket. Don't let your dog get a fright from the clicker, so be conservative.

O Once your dog works out the food association with the clicker, he will love it!

O Keep your dog in a happy, upbeat state — don't let him get anxious. For example, if your dog likes the ball, maybe bring that out after a couple of clicks. Get him excited at the ball, then click and throw the ball. (The ball is the reward, rather than the food.)

Using the clicker to teach commands

Here is an example of how I use the clicker to mark the behaviour I am asking for when teaching a 'sit'.

Teaching a sit

O Set up in a simple, distraction-free environment and contain your dog at a clip station. Some dogs will be okay to be free, but work in a corner (a more-contained space).

O Place yourself in front of your dog, with a food lure in your hand.

O Get your dog to focus on the lure in your hand. You can do this by bringing the food lure close to the dog's nose to give her a sniff of it — just make sure she doesn't eat it!

O Lift your hand up 5 centimetres over the dog's head, twisting it like you are turning a key in a lock as you move it up.

O The dog should follow your hand with her nose, which should lead her into a sit position.

O If not, continue to lure your dog into the sit position with the food in your hand, lifting it up above her nose so that her head goes up and her bottom goes down.

O The instant your dog's bottom hits the ground, click and then follow up with a food reward.

O Timing is critical: try to make the click exactly as your dog's bottom hits the ground, then follow with the food reward as soon as possible afterward (within 1-3 seconds). The click is what marks the behaviour you desire, and tells your dog exactly what you want from her.

O Repeat and repeat, using some quiet praise following the clicking and rewarding.

Removing the click and food lure

O In your second or third training session, once the behaviour is

Rehearse timing and click.

Click exactly as the ball hits the ground.

consistent (after 20 or so successful repetitions), you can start introducing the verbal command 'sit'.

O Ask for the behaviour you want with your verbal command and hand signal. Once your dog is responding consistently for a few sessions, you can start to click and reward intermittently, not every time. This will make the behaviour more resistant to falling away (extinction) — remember the one-armed bandit of the gamblers: that's why they keep doing it!

O Click and reward less and less frequently, until you eventually fade the clicker completely.

O Once you get to the intermittent reinforcement stage on this behaviour you can move to the next behaviour (e.g. 'down').

O See the Proofing and Fading the Clicker chapter to proof (establish) this behaviour in more complex environments.

O Once your dog is performing the command consistently, the goal is to start removing the click and food lure, so that the behaviour becomes reliant on the hand signal alone.

Intermediate or keep-going marker

This is for more advanced dogs and trainers.

O I sometimes use a 'yes' command as a keep-going marker, which tells my dog he is on the right track when I see behaviour heading in the right direction. If you have used 'yes' as an alternative marker to the clicker, you will have to use another word for this.

O I don't reinforce it with a click, but when the behaviour is actually achieved I click and reward. This keeps the dog motivated.

O However, to avoid confusion don't introduce intermediate markers with dogs that are new to the clicker.

Trouble-shooting

Is the environment quiet?

O Move to where there are no distractions and you have control of the environment. Indoors is a good place to start, with no other people or dogs in the room.

Is your dog highly aroused or distractible?

O Try an even quieter environment and more containment; maybe a corner so you limit their options. Keep simplifying the environment.

Is your dog too distracted by the food reward?

O Clip him onto a clip station to contain his behaviour and use a lower-value food reward (e.g. just plain dog biscuits).

O Check that your timing is right. Are you rewarding the right behaviour?

O If your timing is too fast or slow, then you will be rewarding the wrong behaviour and confusing your dog. Go back and try the tennis ball practice exercise — maybe ask a friend to watch you and tell you if you are too fast or slow on the clicker.

Have you removed the click and food reward too quickly?

O Try going back a few steps and reinstating the food lure. Once consistency is achieved, begin to remove the food again.

Have you faded the food reward but are still using the clicker?

O Never fade food from the clicker: you must always reward with food after you click — the click is a promise of a food reward.

Once a behaviour is trained you can use the occasional food-only reward intermittently (that is, with no click). It is a good way to reinforce learned behaviours when you are out and about without the clicker but might have food on you.

How long will it take?

I recommend about two 10- to 15-minute training sessions most days while on-lead for four to six weeks; then another two sessions per day off-lead for three months. But each dog is different and some will learn and respond more quickly than others!

The clicker training game

- I have used this game plenty of times with my students over the years — it's fun and good practice! This game allows all the participants to practise the use of the clicker and learn the principles of learning: systematic approximation, timing, what works and what doesn't work.

- Choose one of the people in the group as the trainer, and another to be the animal. The trainer chooses a behaviour, but doesn't tell the 'animal'. It might be 'turn on light', 'stand on chair' or 'sit by somebody'.

- When the 'trainer' starts to shape the behaviour, we ask the 'animal' to move about the room. Nobody can talk. The 'animal' is asked to keep moving and try behaviours to see if he is doing something that will head him in right direction. The trainer reinforces by clicking anything close to the behaviour they want. It's a bit like hot and cold: if the 'animal' is heading in the direction you want, you click. If he heads in the wrong direction, you do nothing — the 'animal' has to try another behaviour until he gets a click (a clue he is on the right path). You'll be amazed at how quick some of us are and how slow others are!

6.2 LEADS

The lead is a tool that, when used with the clicker and the safety slip collar, helps create a psychological bond between you and your dog — it is an extension of you. In Nature, the wolf has this bond imprinted through pheromones, vocalisations and the primal drive to stay in close with the mother wolf or pack, which creates a following response

Nalu training a pup. Getting the lure — puppy watching.

Nalu's luring hand becomes her visual 'sit' cue. If a 3-year-old can do it, so can you.

— the desire for the wolf to follow its mentors in the pack. We don't have this natural bond, but we want our dogs to follow us and look to us for guidance, so the lead and clicker help shape and create this behaviour.

Hand-held lead

The hand-held lead acts as a physical connection between you and your dog, which stimulates a bond when used in Joining Up and umbilical training (see Chapter 8 — Creating the Bond), and provides control and boundaries.

A lead on a flat collar is not a training aid; it is just a restriction tool. In fact, it is like a harness: it teaches dogs to pull — not what we want. On its own, a hand-held lead doesn't offer learning information. Paired with a safety slip collar (see below), it serves as a kinesthetic tool that communicates different messages to your dog, and hence should cause different responses. For example:

O Pressure on: when the lead is pulling on a slip collar, it tells your dog 'Don't move away from safety' (that is, you).

O Pressure off: when the lead is loose, it tells your dog 'Good, stay in the safe zone' (that is, near you). When paired with a click and reward, it tells your dog 'Great, that's what I want.'

O Together, these two activities offer contrast: 'Yes, that is what I want' and 'No, that isn't what I want.'

O However, we initially try just using the clicker to shape the right behaviour, as that is enough for fast learners.

You are communicating at all times down the lead: each subtle movement gives your dog information about what you want or expect from her. Some trainers might say you are communicating energy. However, it's the kinesthetic messages along your arm into the lead, the subtle pressure on and off, and precise marking and rewarding that join you up and build a bond between you and your dog. You will see how this lead and the others that follow are used in the section on Joining Up. Certainly your postural and verbal tones are being read, as are your smell tones. As you grow in skill, you will learn to harmonise these — your growing confidence will help.

Umbilical lead

The umbilical lead is when you tie your hand-held lead to your belt to be hands-free. (You can get specially made belts with leads attached as well.)

This allows you to go about your day-to-day activities with your dog beside you and moving with you, further cultivating the following response.

It also gives you the opportunity to reinforce basic commands when you stop. Practise 'sit' any time you stop moving, and the 'down' and 'Zen down' when stopped for longer periods. This keeps your dog in a calm, non-reactive learning state when around you.

Using an umbilical lead encourages your dog to stay in your safe zone and move in relation to you while you go about your day — encouraging him to look to you for guidance and follow you, rather than ignore you or lead you. This practice will translate into any aspect of life; for example, when you're out on a walk and don't want your dog to pull on the lead away from you!

O Care needs to be taken with bigger dogs and hyperactive dogs, as they might throw you off balance, particularly if you are not steady on your feet. In this instance, this is probably not a good exercise for you.

O Care must be taken to match equipment to your dog's size and strength. For example, do not place a Mastiff on a thin hand-held lead and then attach it to a less-than-sufficient belt.

Long-line and retractable leads

Long-line and retractable leads allow you to train from a distance. They enable us to work and reinforce commands from a few metres away, which begins to simulate the off-lead relationship we want to eventually have. We don't want to have our dogs on short leads all of the time, after all! These leads allow you to maintain control and a connection with your dog, while allowing him to have a bit more freedom, so that you can test your training in different scenarios. They also allow a dog to move at his more natural speed, and smell and enjoy himself, without the sense of pulling.

Long-line lead

O The long-line lead is commonly around 7–10 metres; however, you

Umbilical lead
(staying in safety)
with loose line.

can use whatever length you prefer. You can also use it as a drag
lead, where it drags behind the dog so you can stand on and grab
it if your dog is not responding or coming when called.

O The long-line is great for practising recall. Once you have your dog
performing consistently inside, you can put the long-line on your
dog and head outdoors to a more distracting environment. With the
lead trailing on the ground, you can give your dog some freedom to
go out and explore. When you ask the dog to come, if you don't get a
response you can use the long-line and offer a 'no'. Click and reward
if she returns. If she doesn't, then repeat a 'no' and a check, and call
your dog back to you, reminding her that she is supposed to come to
you. When she arrives back, click and reward her. Ideally make sure
she is not looking at you when you check, so she doesn't associate it
with you. (It's a remote correction.)

O Sometimes I will hook my retractable lead to the end of the long-
line if the dog is still unpredictable. Do, however, take care with so
much line out.

Long lead to help proof behaviour.

Allows you to step on long lead if recall not effective.

Retractable lead

The retractable lead can extend up to several metres and has a hand-held braking system. Again, ensure the equipment matches the size and strength of your dog. (I like the Flexi make.)

You need to learn how to use the retractable lead properly for it to be effective. Some people don't like retractable leads, normally because they haven't learnt to use them well. Here are some tips:

O Don't grab the line. As it can retract and extend very fast, it can burn your hand.

O Don't tie a dog up on it, as a dog can chew through it.

O Take care not to get tangled; rehearse with it.

O Learn how to use the hand-brake effectively, on both lock and release.

O If it gets wrapped around your dog's body, let more line out, then lock the brake. Let the line lie on the ground as the dog walks out of it.

O The retractable lead is great for delivering an effective check from a distance. We use this with our conditioned aversive signal — our warning command signal 'no'. You'll learn more about this in the contrast training section.

6.3 SAFETY SLIP COLLAR

The safety slip collar, used appropriately, encourages the dog to stay in a position of safety — close to you. It is a nylon collar fitted with an 'O' ring at each end, like a nylon check collar.

To use, make a bend in the nylon rope and push it through one of the O rings. Pull the loop until you have made a 'P' shape. The dog's head can be placed through the loop, with the tail of the 'P' hanging under your dog's neck so that the slip is loosened when the lead is relaxed. Your lead is clipped to the O ring at the end of the P shape's tail. See photo page 156.

The safety slip collar is designed to put pressure on the dog when he's pulling away. Try the safety slip collar on your arm first, to test the impact it has on your dog: it isn't a major pressure, but it's enough to guide your dog to the right behaviour.

We use it in contrast training paired with a positive reinforcer. Pressure on (uncomfortable), pressure off (click and reward) — the contrast optimises learning.

O To get the right-sized safety slip collar, the minimum size should be the measure of the widest point of your dog's head (just in front of his ears), then add about a centimetre. It is too long if it can slip too

Reggie with safety slip collar on the correct way, making a 'P' if heeling on your left side.

easily over his head; it should be snug so that it can't come off easily.
o With dogs that are a little more advanced, or puppies or highly sensitive dogs, you can use a half-slip — a collar where only half of it slips.

6.4 GOING BACK TO THE DEN
What is it and why is it important?

Taking dogs back to the den is a foundational technique in Dog Zen for treating adult dogs. It is the re-creation of the psycho-physiological state (the learning state) inherent in the formative period. It allows your adult dog to return to this optimum learning state to help build a secure bond and re-establish behaviours she might have missed in her own formative period, as well as train new behaviours.

The clip station and the crate (described below) are the physical representation of taking a dog back to the den: that is, they are secure, contained spaces that allow a dog to be calm. This space will be associated with the mentor and inherit the mentor's safe influence. Joining Up is then used to strengthen the mentor bond and reinforce the 'secure base effect'.

It is the secure base that allows your dog to feel secure enough to adapt and learn. It re-creates the trust of having the mother or mentor (and her environment) around that gives your dog the confidence to learn and do new things.

6.5 THE CRATE
What is it and why is it important?

The crate is the physical representation of the den for your pup or dog: it is a small, safe, enclosed space that mimics the den in Nature. When you start using it early, your dog will love it. However, if you start it too late, your dog sometimes can become averse to containment, which means you'll need to train your dog to enjoy the crate, as it is a valuable tool.

It establishes safety and security for the pup, and therefore the growing dog. Slowly it evolves to being the sleeping site or mat as the dog grows. It is also an important aspect of house training, as dogs don't generally soil in the den (nest site soiling inhibition).

When you establish the crate early, it continues to be the place your dog can retreat to and find comfort, and you can re-create that space in the car, a café or friends' places. It will also be a haven for your dog when there's something potentially frightening happening, such as thunder and fireworks — an extension of the secure base effect.

Having a den space also decreases the risk of separation distress, as your dog will always have a safe place to go back to even when you are not there. This is an extremely useful tool when rehabilitating fear, territorial or human (visitor) aggression, by establishing a safe barrier (for visitor and dog) that allows the dog to remain in situ rather than having to avoid the perceived threat.

Make sure your dog learns to enjoy the crate. Click and reward, and feeding your dog in the crate help do this.

How do we use it?

○ As a rough guide, the most basic crate needs to be at least 30 per cent longer and 20 per cent higher than your dog, but not more than 50 per cent more, otherwise the nest site soiling inhibition disappears (they can soil at the other end of the crate).

○ Your dog should be able to stand up and turn around comfortably inside the crate. He should have a bed inside plus water and food bowls — that's about all the space you need. Dogs won't want any more room than that, as they like it to be snug, enclosed and 'den-like'.

○ When it's this size, it also inhibits any soiling, so it assists with house training.

○ When pups are young (2–3 months old), it's nice to have the crate largely covered to make it extra snug, like a natural den would be.

○ Make sure it's secure, so your dog can't pull it apart or drag it around.

○ The bottom should have a tray or some kind of waterproof base, just in case your dog spills water or toilets in there accidentally.

○ Within the crate, install a bed and paper — a different substrate from others on your home's floor (don't use lino or carpet).

○ Decide on where you want to put it in your home. Dogs love to be near us so in a living area is a good choice, or by a dog-door out to a fenced yard — ideally both.

○ Particularly when he's young, use it for all of your pup's naps and when you go out for an hour or two. Having access outside or into a puppy pen with an appropriate substrate is even better (see the House Training chapter).

Back to the den.
Reggie on a clip station
with a light chain.

Creating the secure
base. Reggie relaxed
in his safe place,
associated with me.

6.6 THE CLIP STATION
What is it and why is it important?

- The clip station is also a physical representation of the den for a pup or going back to the den for the adult dog. It is a lead clipped to the wall, with a mat or bed beside it. It helps re-create the concept of a den: it is a safe, contained place for the dog to retreat to.

- It is the next step beyond a crate. It mimics when in Nature the pup moves away from the den and transitions to the outside world. It gives your dog a sense of more freedom than the crate, but still with boundaries and control.

- It offers safety. To your dog, it's a controlled, quiet space. It provides physical control, which allows you to settle your dog down and complete training sessions. It is a starting point for separation, and is a place where she won't soil (unless desperate). It's a great place to facilitate house training, alongside the crate. It limits destructive behaviour, as the dog is secured.

- A clip station is also used at the beginning of contrast training, giving your dog her first experience of pressure on and pressure off. For fearful dogs, start the clip lead inside a crate so they don't panic when the pressure is on. This teaches them to deal with resistance. Keep it 20 centimetres short of the end of the crate.

- It teaches them separation from you, as you can leave your dog clipped at the clip station for periods of time while you are busy. Ideally, do this in a social part of your house first, such as the lounge. For outdoor dogs, use it by the back door or just inside the door, as it offers social simulation.

- It's a space you can re-create easily when out at other people's places or at a café: just attach a lead securely to a table, chair or even your own leg, though make sure your dog can't drag around what it's attached to.

- It's good to start your dog's training on the clip station early — the sooner the better, so he gets used to it and understands that it is a quiet, calm zone. For pups, start at around 3–4 months. Start with collar and lead training first. (Take care not to frighten them.)

- I like to have three or four of them around the house in all the main social areas. It also facilitates time-out if needed, but wait until it is well-established as a safe place.

O This is also an extremely useful tool when rehabilitating fear or territorial or human (visitor) aggression. For more-serious cases we use a crate.

How do you build it?

O Choose a location. It's good to have three or four clip stations around your home, all in social places as your dog loves to be near you.

O Secure a clip into the wall's baseplate ideally, or into heavy furniture. Ensure that it is anchored and secure.

O Attach a length of light chain or lead (if your dog doesn't chew) to the wall clip, with a dog clip at the other end.

O The chain or lead should be the length of your dog (0.7-1 metre long), no more.

O Place a comfortable mat or bed down beside it — you want it to be an appealing place.

O Leave a dog toy there (such as a rubber toy packed with food) to give your dog something to do and further make it a desirable space.

O You will use your clip station during many training sessions, and can have your dog on it from five minutes to three hours, depending on what you are doing.

6.7 THE MUZZLE

The muzzle is an important safety tool to use if you are treating aggression cases. It keeps your dog, other dogs or animals and people safe if your dog shows aggressive tendencies, and we strongly recommend that it's used in all aggression cases. You need to make a decision as to what level of risk your dog poses. We strongly advise that you are conservative in your judgement, though, and use a muzzle if in doubt. If unsure seek professional advice.

When choosing a muzzle, you will find that most brands indicate what breeds the muzzle is best used for, based on the average size of the breed. To be safe, though, it's best to take your dog along (keep him in the car) and try out different sizes to get the right fit.

If your dog exhibits aggression toward people or other dogs or animals you should follow these instructions and use a muzzle.

Here are my guidelines:

O Be careful putting a muzzle on dominant, aggressive dogs, as they could be aggressive toward you.

It's important to use a muzzle in aggressive cases.

- ○ Choose the right size and type of muzzle — it's important that it fits well.
- ○ Basket-type muzzles are good, as you can feed the dog treats through them, and they can regulate the dog's temperature.
- ○ A muzzle with a small cut in the front is good for training, so you are able to deliver food rewards.
- ○ When putting the muzzle on your dog, first put food into the muzzle before fitting it to your dog, so your dog creates good associations with it. Do this several times first.
- ○ Put the muzzle on your dog systematically and slowly, so she does not get a fright, as this can create an aversion to the muzzle very quickly. Slowly and surely is best.
- ○ Click and reward your dog when the muzzle is on.
- ○ To deliver food rewards, put the food in your cupped hand and push it through the muzzle while your dog's head is pushing downward. Allow your dog to work out how to retrieve the food from your hand without dropping it.
- ○ Have your dog in a safety slip collar and lead to stop them pulling the muzzle off. Click and reward them for accepting it.
- ○ When the muzzle first goes on and until she is used to it, keep your dog moving so that she is distracted. Keep walking and go through your basic commands.

O Keep a muzzle on only when training or when interacting with other dogs, animals and people.

O Make the muzzle positive by using the clicker and doing lots of clicking and rewarding. Dogs can get a learned aversion to wearing a muzzle if you don't make it a positive enough experience with the clicker and food rewards.

O Don't ever allow your dog to pull the muzzle off. Once she learns she can, it's very difficult to un-teach, and can ruin your muzzle training.

O Don't leave a muzzle on your dog unattended or overnight as a rule, or she will pull it off.

O Utilise click and reward to keep your dog in a learning state, taking her mind off the muzzle and helping her learn to accept it.

O Keep the muzzle on until you have consistent non-aggressive responses occurring.

O Fade out the muzzle as your dog demonstrates safe, non-aggressive behaviour improvements.

6.8 CONTRAST TRAINING

During that early period in a dog's life, you are shaping behaviour, so positive reinforcement techniques are the primary techniques used. However, if you are dealing with behaviour issues such as aggression, fear, hyperactivity, etc, then behaviour modification becomes necessary. These issues require the changing or eliminating of existing behaviours, as well as shaping new behaviours. To do this, we need contrast training. This involves rewarding your dog for behaviours you want him to do, and providing an apparent natural consequence for behaviours you don't want.

Contrast training is a natural method of learning for dogs that mimics natural consequences in the wild. Wild dogs and wolves are provided 'positive reinforcement' for good behaviour through social contact and access to resources such as food. Alternatively, they are given corrections for undesirable behaviour from other wolves/dogs and their environment. For example, if a wild dog tried to eat a poisonous plant, the plant's poison would cause the dog to be sick. If a wolf pup tried to bite its elder, it would receive a nip or pin to remind it that this is not appropriate behaviour. These are natural consequences resulting from undesirable behaviours, the kind of corrections we are imitating.

We normally apply correction remotely (from a distance via a long-line or retractable lead) so that it's associated with the thing we are trying to get the dog to avoid, so that the dog doesn't build a negative association with us. For example, if you want your dog to stop eating your shoes, you want the dog to associate the correction and negative experience with the shoe so he doesn't try to chew the shoe, whether you're around or not.

If you are teaching your dog to avoid an external object (site or object aversion) you do not use a verbal cue, otherwise he will associate the consequence with you. You need the dog to think that the correction is coming from the object only. Then he will avoid the object whether you are there or not, plus it doesn't impact on your relationship (you are still safety). We also try to offer our dogs a chance to avoid correction by using a conditioned aversive signal — that is, a warning signal to the dog that he is doing inappropriate behaviours and should stop before there are consequences. We use the 'no' (a warning signal) when we want our dogs to know we are their ally and are warning them of a consequence about to happen (we are safety). This allows dogs to avoid the consequence if they behave appropriately once offered the signal.

For example, say you don't want your dog to eat food off the table. You would click and reward your dog for leaving the food alone (providing a reward for the right behaviour). You would also give your dog an apparent natural consequence if he did try to eat the food (providing a remote correction for the wrong behaviour). This correction should appear to come from the food or table if applied correctly.

Why is contrast training important?
o Contrast training teaches your dog what to do and what not to do.
o It teaches safety and avoidance, as you show your dog what is safe and what to avoid.
o It helps shape behaviour quickly, as it uses both aspects of reward and natural consequences that mimic Nature, as well as an option to avoid a correction.
o Behaviours that are acceptable in the dog's world can be dangerous in the human world.

There are three key aspects of contrast training.

Firstly, 'safety and avoidance' training is designed to help your dog understand that you are safety, and that certain objects 'out there' should be avoided as they deliver consequences. You are the guide your dog should look to when deciding how to react in a situation; whether she should be near you or if she's allowed to play with other dogs at the park.

The pressure on, pressure off technique applied in Joining Up (see section 8.2) is useful in establishing safety and avoidance. The use of a nylon safety slip collar provides the contrast of: pressure off, paired with a click and reward, to provide comfort and a reward when your dog looks at you and follows your lead; and pressure on, which creates mild discomfort, and discourages your dog from straining away from you. In this way your dog learns that you represent safety and comfort, while 'out there' represents discomfort which should be avoided.

Secondly, positive reinforcement is provided by the click and reward. By marking and reinforcing the appropriate behaviours, our dogs are clear what is being asked of them.

Thirdly, an effective check (collar check) is my primary technique for delivering a correction for inappropriate behaviour. This is used when you need to tell your dog not to do something. This is done remotely where possible, initially with no verbal command so that it isn't associated with you. Later you can add a 'no' command as a warning signal to allow your dog to avoid a correction where appropriate.

To give an effective check, fit your dog with a safety slip collar attached to a lead. When she acts inappropriately, *quickly* snap the lead in a firm and swift upwards or sideways motion to briefly tighten the collar around the dog's neck, then release. Do not continue pulling on the lead and tightening the collar. We are not trying to harm the dog, but we are trying to create enough discomfort to *interrupt* the undesirable behaviour so that it stops. A check has been effective if it stops the dog's behaviour; if you are delivering a check and it is having no effect, you need to be firmer. Big, strong dogs will need a much firmer check than smaller or sensitive dogs. A check is ideally applied remotely (on a long-line or retractable lead) so that it's not associated with you.

A breakdown of contrast training
When teaching site or object aversion (avoidance)
- Use a safety slip collar and a long (or retractable) lead.
- When your dog is some distance from you and doing something you don't want (e.g. chewing on a shoe or eating food off the table),

without verbalising any command provide an effective check on the long-line. This is meant to mimic the natural consequences of the object correcting the dog.

O When your dog comes back to you to avoid the object and correction, you click and reward — rewarding your dog for returning to you and reinforcing that you are safety.

O This training is initially non-verbal so you don't get associated with the correction.

O Later, when your dog has learnt the association with the object, you can introduce the 'leave it' and 'no' commands. This will establish a conditioned aversive signal so you can warn your dog of the threat, allowing the dog to avoid the correction while seeing you as the ally.

When teaching you are safety (especially for recall)

O This technique requires you to use a safety slip collar and long (or retractable) lead, and have an established 'come' command.

O When your dog is some distance from you and you want him to come back to you (recall), try your 'come' command. If that doesn't work, say 'no' (warning signal to give them a chance to avoid a consequence). This is to say 'Watch out — something is out there. Come back to me, I'm safety.' Click and reward your dog when he comes back to you.

O If your dog doesn't come back, then say 'no' and apply an effective check on the long lead. (When you check, make sure your dog is looking away from you, so he doesn't associate the check with you.) Because you have not been associated with the check, your dog will come back to you for safety. Click and reward when he comes back. The more subtle you can be on delivering the check, the better.

Any form of correction, including citronella or even e-collars, needs to follow these rules or you will have problems. The use of these tools needs to be taught by experienced practitioners.

Right and wrong in our human world is not obvious to dogs, so they need the contrast to learn what is the right way for them to act. This makes it a lot quicker and easier for them to pick up what we want from them: what the family rules are, where the boundaries are and how to keep safe near you. Remember there are serious life-threatening hazards to a dog in the human world.

Basic commands – the foundation of our shared language

One of the most important things we can do for our dogs is equip them with a set of commands or words that enable us to keep them safe, and allow us to have a relaxed and stress-free life with them. These signals help us guide our dogs, and give them clarity about what we want from them. Having them makes all other aspects of dog training much easier. Dogs need to learn by association and positive reinforcement what we want them to know. The 'no' command is an exception, and needs to be associated with a remote apparent natural consequence.

Going back to training these regularly ensures that your dog stays strong on the basics, and it's a great way to spend time with your dog, build your bond and keep your dog motivated to learn and have fun.

See how this rescue pup starts to look to me for direction.

Any time spent with you is important to your dog, and he is getting treats, so he doesn't think about training the way we think about homework — food and clicker are fun!

Here's how to teach the 10 crucial basic commands — the basis of our shared language.

Tips to get you started

NON-VERBAL SIGNALS ARE IMPORTANT

O Dogs are significantly non-verbal — gestures and postures mean more to them than spoken words initially. This means that hand signals are important.

O Verbal signals (the actual word command such as 'sit') are secondary to the hand signal.

O Whistling (if you can) is a great tool to use for long-distance communication.

O When you are teaching a new command, start by using a food lure that becomes a hand signal. When your dog is performing consistently with the food lure and hand signal, then you introduce the spoken command on top of the hand signal. Starting with visual cues first, then the verbal later, this limits the number of things that might confuse your dog when he is starting out on a new command.

WORD COMMANDS SHOULD BE SIMPLE

O Commands should be single-syllable.

O Keep them simple and don't change them.

O Don't mix meanings: one command should have one meaning only.

YOUR DOG'S NAME IS NOT A COMMAND!

O Use your dog's name only to orient your dog to you.

O Keep names short, ideally one syllable (or use a nickname).

O Don't use your dog's name as a command. Don't yell 'Spot!' when you want Spot to come to you; instead, say 'Spot. Come!'

O The name just tells your dog who you are talking to (especially if you have other dogs); the command tells your dog what you want him to do.

YOUR BODY LANGUAGE IS IMPORTANT

For drawing commands (asking your dog to come toward you or be with you) — e.g. 'come' or 'heel' — you are being friendly and encouraging:

O Your body language should be inviting and non-threatening.

O Use happy, 'up' tones when speaking.

O Your body shouldn't be in a front square-on posture; instead, turn slightly three-quarters on to your dog.

O Bending or squatting down to lower your body can help you seem less assertive.

O No staring — smile and be encouraging.

Fixed commands

For fixed commands (when you want your dog to stay in one place) — e.g. 'sit', 'down', 'wait', 'stay' — you are asking your dog to stay put, maybe away from you:

O Use a slightly firmer tone of voice.

O Have your body square-on and make some eye contact which is slightly more assertive.

O Increase these if your dog isn't responding. Deepen your intonation slightly — but start out lightly.

O As your dog succeeds, ease the pressure. Again, you are offering contrast for the dog to learn. Work to neutral tones in the end.

7.1 SIT

Hand signal: Move your hand like you are turning a key in a lock

O Set up in a simple, distraction-free environment and contain your dog at a clip station if needed, or on a lead.

O Place yourself in front of your dog, with a food lure in your hand.

O Get your dog to focus on the lure in your hand. You can do this by bringing the food lure close to the dog's nose to give her a sniff of it.

O Lift your hand up 5 centimetres over the dog's head, twisting it like you are turning a key in a lock. Don't say 'sit' yet.

O Your dog should follow your hand with her nose, which should lead her into a sit position.

O If not, continue to lure her into the sit with the food in your hand,

1 Fixing command posture.

2 Drawing command posture.

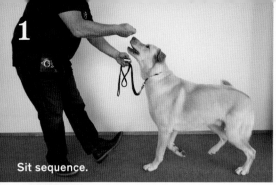
1

Sit sequence.

2

Note the position of my right hand lure.

3

Time the click!

4

Reward.

lifting it up above her nose so as her head goes up, her bottom goes down.

O The instant your dog's bottom hits the ground, click and follow up with a food reward.

O Timing is critical: try to make the click exactly as your dog's bottom hits the ground, then follow with the food reward as soon as possible afterward (within 1–3 seconds maximum).

O To repeat, throw a piece of food to get your dog standing up again and moving, then repeat the same technique.

O Repeat and repeat, using praise, but clicking and rewarding first.

O Once you are getting a consistent result, you can incorporate use of the verbal 'sit' command as you make the hand signal.

7.2 DOWN (LIE DOWN)

Hand signal: A downward movement of your hand with a downward pointed finger

O Start with your dog in a sit position.

O After making the 'down' hand signal, with a food lure run your hand in a motion down your dog's chest line (about 5 centimetres out from your dog's chest), then along the floor in front of him in a right-angle. Don't move the food any further than the distance your dog's legs will go when he's lying down. If it's too far, your dog will stand up; if it's too short, your dog won't go into a 'down'.

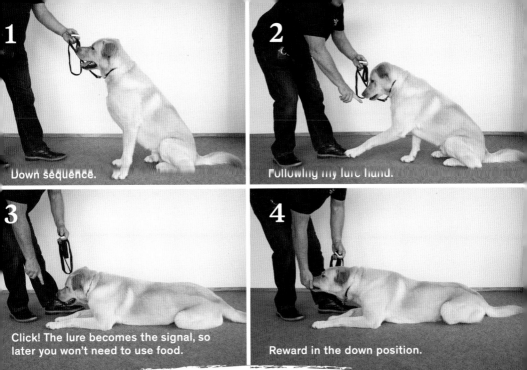

1. Down sequence.
2. Following my lure hand.
3. Click! The lure becomes the signal, so later you won't need to use food.
4. Reward in the down position.

- Do this slowly so that as your dog follows the food lure closely with his nose, he goes into a lying-down position. As he does, say the 'down' command (once the command is established — non-verbal first). Reward to mouth initially, later between legs.

- If your dog does not follow the food lure, put a little pressure between his shoulder blades. Push gently as you move the lure into the exact down position: one dog length plus 5 centimetres. Encourage your dog down; not too much pressure, nor too little. When he is down, release your pressure immediately. Avoid doing this too much, as touching your dog's body can inhibit training; only do it if you need to.

- As soon as your dog's chest hits the ground, click and reward. Throw the food reward between your dog's front legs so that he doesn't have to stand back up to get it from you. I like him to hold the 'down' for some time before allowing him to stand back up. To start he won't stay down long; that's okay; train this behaviour first. Once he is reliably going into a 'down', start extending the time he is down for, by extending the time you wait until you reward him — expect and reward longer and longer the time spent down. This will take place over a number of training sessions.

7.3 ZEN DOWN

Hand signal: Use the normal down ventrally, then in a continuous movement draw a semi-circle to the left toward your dog's groin area (parallel to the ground) so as to push her hip over and out.

The purpose of 'Zen down' is to encourage learning state. The 'Zen down' is an advanced lie-down position in which your dog rolls onto her hip into a relaxed, calm position — it's the position that will most effectively help you put your dog into a content and focused learning state. It's more curled than the traditional 'down' position. In it, both of your dog's legs will be on the same side of her body. It relaxes the dorsal muscles (the ones down the middle of your dog's back) and activates the vagus nervous system, which enhances learning and induces a state of calm. Once your dog has been trained to go into a 'Zen down', you may find she does it automatically whenever you ask for a 'down' — which is fantastic!

O Start in a 'down' position.

O With a food lure in your hand, work your hand from in front of your dog's nose to her side, so that as your dog's nose follows the lure, she curls around her front leg and flips over slightly onto her hip. If your dog doesn't seem to get it, use a finger to gently push the lower part of your dog's side to encourage her back legs to flip over so that she's lying semi-sideways (lower legs are laying on their side, but upper legs may still be lying straight).

O Click and reward as soon as your dog rolls onto her hip, dropping the food rearward between the dog's front legs to encourage her to remain down and relaxed.

O Continue to click and reward your dog while she remains in 'Zen down'. Encourage the extension of this position by clicking and rewarding your dog with food thrown between her paws at regular intervals. Delivering food to the ground like this encourages your dog to stay down longer, because it doesn't release your dog from the command.

7.4 WAIT AND STAY

Wait hand signal: Move your hand with a pointed finger in front of your dog's face from left to right, like you are drawing an invisible horizontal line in the air.

Stay hand signal: Showing your dog your flat hand (like a stop signal).

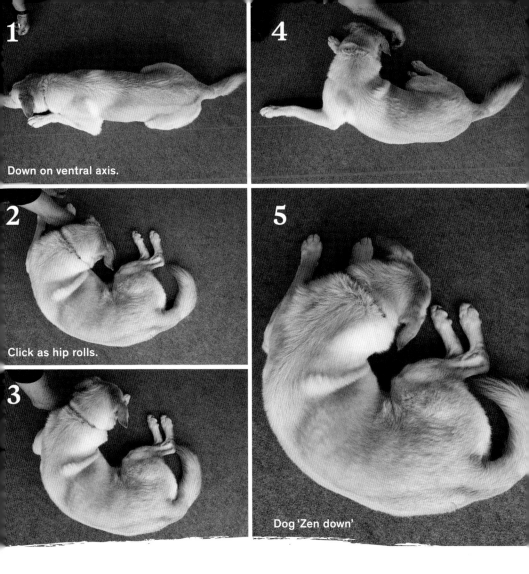

1 Down on ventral axis.

2 Click as hip rolls.

3

4

5 Dog 'Zen down'

Training the 'wait' and the 'stay' are very similar, so I have combined them here. Both 'wait' and 'stay' mean 'Wait in that spot until I release you'. The difference is that in the 'wait' you can release your dog from a distance, whereas with a 'stay' you must go back to release him. It is best to train the 'wait' first.

Both of these are fixing commands, so your body language is more upright, with a stronger eye and tone, to keep your dog in place. I like to virtually bomb-proof these commands, so that when I ask for them my dog stays there no matter what.

O Start with a 'sit', 'down', then 'Zen down'.
O Position yourself square-on to your dog, standing tall and giving a bit of eye contact.
O From the 'down' or 'Zen down' position, make the 'wait' hand

signal, then take one or two steps backwards (still facing your dog).

O Return straight away, then click and reward your dog for staying in the 'down' position. Reward your dog when you are really close to him, putting the treat between your dog's legs to prevent him from wanting to stand or sit up to take the treat from you.

O If your dog continues to get up, reduce your distance and come back faster — give him a chance to understand the process.

O Gradually extend the distance you move further and further away, until you can get the 'wait' or 'stay' from a longer distance and for longer times.

O At first, always walk backwards, still facing your dog, as you move away. You can repeat the command and hand signal as you walk backwards.

O Later, try turning around and walking away, not facing your dog.

O If your dog makes signs of getting up to move when you have asked for a wait or stay, say 'wrong' in a neutral tone (for advanced dogs only — if your dog is sensitive or difficult go to the back line explained next). Later, once the behaviour is trained, you can say 'no' if your dog breaks the wait or stay. (Take care with sensitive dogs.)

O If you are having difficulties getting your dog to 'wait', you can try the long or retractable back line set-up. This is when you have the dog on a long or retractable lead that goes through a loop in the wall before being attached to the collar, like a pulley system. This allows you to hold your dog in place from a short distance away.

O Go through the process above, and if your dog moves, say 'wrong'. You could hold your dog in position with the back lead. Click and reward if he waits. Try this about half a dozen times. If your dog is still moving say 'no'. Click and reward if he waits. After one go, if he is still moving say 'no' with an effective check on the lead. Click and reward a wait. Continuing practising this.

O When you do a 'wait' command, initially you can release it by walking back to your dog. Later, once established, release your dog by calling him to you from a distance using your 'come' command.

O Remember with a 'stay' you must go back to your dog to release him. I usually clap my hands and say 'okay' with an up intonation.

O Once well-established, try these commands in more distracting outdoor situations (proofing).

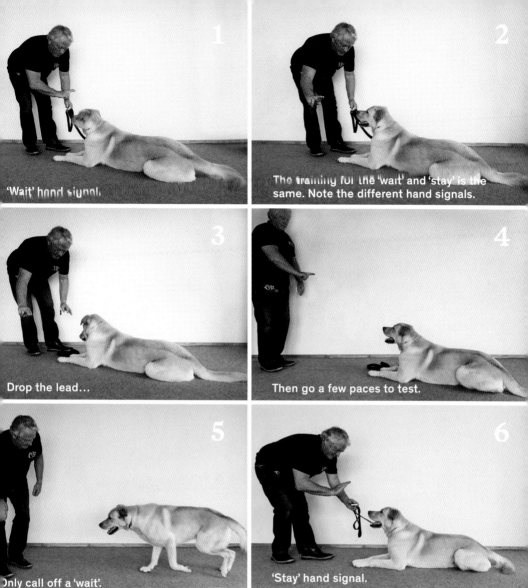

1 'Wait' hand signal.

2 The training for the 'wait' and 'stay' is the same. Note the different hand signals.

3 Drop the lead...

4 Then go a few paces to test.

5 Only call off a 'wait'.

6 'Stay' hand signal.

○ With the 'stay' command (once well-established) I like to really test it with my dogs. Do this by first putting your dog on a lead, put him in a 'stay' and, with your hand command still showing, slightly pull on your dog's lead to physically try to draw him away, while repeating the 'stay' command. Click and reward a stay, gradually increasing the level of your pull. This is a good exercise to strengthen your dog's resilience — that is, accepting there is conflict and thinking how to solve it. This training technique came from bomb-detection dogs whose need for a clear stay is evident.

7.5 WRONG (NO REWARD MARKER)

'Wrong' is a signal for 'don't carry on that track' ('Give up — there is no reinforcer following', e.g. food). It is said in a neutral tone, which is more helpful for training because it is not aversive. It is a signal we can use before we step up and use the 'no' command (which is more associated with a correction — although still a chance to avoid correction).

It is more for advanced trainers and dogs, and may confuse a new or uncertain learner.

Use it when you start training new behaviours, particularly when you are training in close to your dog such as for 'wait' and 'stay' commands.

Don't use the 'wrong' command when you are using a remote correction that you don't want associated with you.

Start teaching the 'wrong' command by saying 'wrong' when your dog is focused on you but doing the wrong behaviour — do not click and reward. Continue this until your dog does the behaviour or close to it, and then click and reward.

7.6 NO!

The 'no' command is a conditioned aversive signal taught remotely so that you are not associated with it. This is taught by using an effective check in conjunction with a 'no' command when your dog is doing something you don't want him to do. This quickly shows the dog that 'no' means 'stop immediately otherwise a consequence is coming'.

Here are some examples of how you can teach a 'no' command:

O On a long-line or retractable lead with a safety slip collar, ask your dog to come. If he doesn't, give a 'no' command. If he fails to come in a second or two, give him a second 'no' command and a check at the same time. (The first non-checked 'no' gives your dog an opportunity to succeed first before any correction — effectively becoming a warning signal.)

O Apply a check at the same time as saying 'no' in a firm tone. Then click and reward your dog on return to you.

O For example, if your dog barks and you don't want him to, say 'quiet', and click and reward quiet. If he doesn't stop, say 'no' (don't check), then click and reward quiet. If he continues to bark, say 'no' and apply an effective check. Click and reward quiet behaviour.

7.7 LEAVE IT

The 'leave it' command is taught by teaching your dog discrimination, so she knows she can do what you allow her to do, but must leave alone what you tell her to leave alone. This is incredibly important If you imagine a situation in which you see your dog about to eat something dangerous or poisonous, for example, and you can command 'leave it'.

- I prefer to start the first checks on the long-line or retractable lead. I don't use the command, but apply a remote correction, so initial checks get associated with the external enemy — I'm the dog's ally. Later I start the 'no' command.

- Once you are ready, mentally divide the room into two halves, with one half of the room for good treats and the other half for bad treats. Let's say the left half is for good treats, and the right half is for bad treats. Your dog is allowed the good treats, but not allowed the bad treats.

- Throw a treat into the left side of the room, and tell your dog to 'get it'. Click and reward your dog for getting the good treat.

- After about five repetitions of the above, throw a treat into the right side of the room, and tell your dog to 'leave it'. If she does, click and reward. If the dog doesn't immediately respond to 'leave it', by leaving the treat alone and returning to you, give her an effective check from a distance. Don't use a verbal 'no' command, so the correction appears to come from the item, not you.

- In the next session, if your dog persists after the check, say 'no' strongly at the same time as another check to reinforce the 'no' command, and to teach your dog that there is a negative consequence if she doesn't listen. Your 'no' is warning of a likely consequence, so you are acting as your dog's ally.

- When your dog leaves the treat and turns back to you, make a click then reward with a treat from your hand.

- Continue to practise, throwing treats at random either to the good treats or the bad treats side, using the same series of commands and rewards as listed above. (Take care with sensitive dogs.)

- When your dog is performing 100 per cent while in a distraction-free room, test your training in a different space with different items (such as toys) to proof the dog for other circumstances. The 'leave it' command is a very handy command if taught in this way, as you have an ability to command your dog away from anything dangerous or you need him to 'leave' something while outdoors.

7.8 HEEL

A 'heel' is when your dog is walking beside you, following you and sometimes looking up to you — it's an extension of our Joining Up activity (see section 8.2). The conventional heel position is having your dog on your left side, so his right shoulder is beside your left leg. (You can use the other side if it suits, but put the safety slip on the other way.)

O With your dog on a lead, walk around a room in circles and/or squares asking your dog to 'heel', and clicking and rewarding your dog when his right shoulder comes into line with your left leg.

O You should start walking slowly. Turn 90–180 degrees often.

O Use the principles of pressure on and pressure off to keep your dog in heel and focused on following you.

O Proof in lots of different situations, eventually trying the same technique off-lead.

7.9 COME (RECALL)

This is one of our most important commands: it's the one that will save your dog from getting run over, help you remove your dog from sticky situations, and prevent your dog from upsetting others who may not be so dog-friendly. Remember this is a drawing command, so you need inviting, friendly body language and tone. Stay three-quarters on to your dog, relax, smile and use an 'up' tone.

O Put your dog on a short lead and safety slip collar to begin with.

O Toss a bit of food away from you so your dog moves away from you. Once away, give the 'come' command, then click and reward your dog when she comes back to you.

O When you are achieving this consistently, move to a retractable lead or long-lead and repeat the technique, this time throwing the food further so your dog is further away from you and has a bigger distance to cover to return to you when you ask for a 'come'.

O If your dog ignores you and doesn't come immediately when asked, give her a 'no' command, and click and reward if she returns. If she doesn't return, say a second 'no' and give an effective check. Click and reward when she comes back to you.

O Click and reward every time your dog comes back to you.

O Master the 'come' command on lead in lots of different situations before you try off-lead — do this systematically, increasing the distractions (proofing). Go to the Proofing and Fading the Clicker chapter for guidance on this.

O Always click and reward, and praise your dog when she returns to you. Once you have faded the clicker and food reward, continue to give praise and a pat when your dog comes back to you.

O Reintroduce the clicker and food if failing.

7.10 NICELY

Later in the Meet and Greet section of the Creating the Bond chapter I will walk you through positive greeting routines for you to practise with your dog. These techniques are designed for well-socialised dogs (or puppies) that don't have any issues with aggression. If your dog does have issues, you should follow the techniques outlined in the chapters on aggression later in the book.

For now, I will teach you the all-important 'nicely' command. This is the command to use when your dog is greeting people or other dogs. It tells your dog that you are in control of this meeting situation, have noticed the new dog or person, and have judged them as okay, so your dog doesn't have to react. It tells him to be nice and not act aggressively.

O When teaching this command, start with friendly dogs you know or at the least judge as friendly. (Labradors, Golden Retrievers or small gentle breeds are a good bet!)

O When your dog is about to meet another dog and is close by to it, ask for a 'sit', then say 'nicely' and click and reward your dog for sitting nicely and calmly.

O Move closer and closer to the other dog, then allow the dogs to sniff each other's inguinal (groin) areas and rear ends (the dog handshake). Click and reward both dogs for doing this nicely.

O Click and reward both dogs throughout the interaction for having all four paws on the ground, not vocalising, and behaving sociably.

O Give praise to both dogs at the end of the meeting.

O You are always trying to teach 'nicely' through positive reinforcement — click and reward appropriate behaviour. If your dog makes threatening or inappropriate gestures (growl, stare, lips snarling), then head to the appropriate chapter on aggression in Part D to see how to address this.

8

Creating the bond

I remember when I looked after a client's dog called
Harry for two years while his owners went to France.
They were so tearful when they dropped him off; 'He'll
forget us,' they said. 'He won't remember who we are.'
I reassured them that he wouldn't forget his first, most
enduring bond. Two years later they called from the
airport, anxious again; I reassured them again. They
weren't convinced. When they got to my place he was,
from a distance, unsure. But then he smelt them (smell
holds their longest memories), and oh, how he went
loopy! For about 10 minutes, peeing on the ground,
jumping, circling, whining — you name it, he did it — and
how his owners loved it. He remembered them and still
cared, of course. We all smiled like crazy idiots. Dogs are
bonded to us for life — there really is no doubt.

When you create this kind of bond, you know it, and it can be one of the most joyful of your life, akin to coming home to your children after a long trip. Establishing this heartfelt relationship with your dog is fundamental to a harmonious life together. Hercules, Scott, Jess, Tyson, Tammy and Carlos — each of them moved me, touched me, changed and enriched my life. I remember whole epochs of my life by them: Scott raised me, Carlos and Tammy coached me through my university years, Herc and Tyson (Herc's film body-double) brought my family up, Jess was 22 years of my life from my farm days to working on *The Last Samurai* with Tom Cruise.

And now today I have Reggie, Monty, Blue, Tommy — each of them so special and having achieved such amazing things alongside me. Monty became world-famous and generated 100 million tweets as the world's first driving dog. Blue is a stalwart of film. Tommy's the spoilt one (it helps being cute and little). We rescued Reggie while creating a TV show in the UK and working alongside the likes of Ádám Miklósi, and taught Reggie how to fly, doing 60-degree banked turns — the pinnacle of my training career! I built a bond so special with Reggie that I brought him home with me to New Zealand: he brought me insights into the boundless power of that bond for life, where even the sky's not the limit!

Dogs and humans both live for relationships; however, it doesn't necessarily mean that we know how to do it together! We come from two very different worlds, so our relationship is firstly made up of understanding. Once we have an understanding of the dog's world, then we can look at the practical steps we can take to build our bond with dogs.

Here, we'll look at our role as mentor, then go through the foundational techniques I use to build a strong bond with a pup or adult dog — Joining Up. From there, we finish with understanding how dogs meet and greet new dogs and people. Dogs, just like us, have a formal way of greeting dogs and people, and if *not* taught that in the formative period dogs can grow up 'impolite' or, even worse, aggressive.

8.1 YOUR ROLE AS MENTOR

This section is about you and your role as your dog's closest friend and mentor. In the wild, wolves and dogs have helpers in the pack that support the pup as they move away from Mum. In our world, you are taking on this function. However, as you don't have the canine pheromones, taste, smells and behaviours that would entrain the follower response naturally, in Dog Zen we simulate these processes using subtle and effective replacements such as Joining Up.

When I think of this powerful relationship, I always think of my dog Hercules. The relationship I had with Hercules epitomises the mentor bond that I want you to grow with your dog. We were so attuned to each other: he was always near me, he could sense my mood and always knew what I wanted of him — the smallest gesture would be enough to inform him of my intent and desire. He was in complete synchrony with me.

What is the mentor role?

When you create this mentor bond, your dog will stay close to you, look to you for direction, study you and your behaviour. He will be attuned to what you want, look at your face and even into your eyes, knowing when you are attentive to him. He will have full trust in you; you will have proven trustworthy in dog terms.

Your role for your dog is to provide guidance. It is to expose him to the stimuli he needs to understand and adjust to, reassure him that you have things in hand, and provide a sense of safety, trust and reassurance of his place in the family. You will teach him appropriate behaviours, so he understands the family rules, like 'Don't pee on the carpet' or 'Come when called' and the like.

Next time you are on a walk, check to see how close your dog remains to you and how often your dog looks up to see where you are. This will give you a good idea how connected your dog is to you and therefore what work you might need to do to strengthen your bond.

Being your dog's mentor is not about being the dominant, totalitarian 'leader of the pack'. In wolf packs, dominance and subordinance are ritualised signals to replace aggression and maintain harmony in the pack. They are gestures to communicate social unity, roles and biological priority (elders often have priority to resources), rather than a pecking order. Dominance in this context is being assertive, influential and guiding, rather than overbearing, heavy-handed or authoritarian. Always remember *effective* is the operative word — not too much assertiveness, not too little. The amount needs to be moderated by the temperament of your dog. Some dogs are more sensitive than others, so soften up on those types; it won't take much. On the other hand, be

more assertive with the rough-and-tumble kind of dog.

A mentor relationship isn't just about providing a loving bond (though of course that is essential) it's also about providing guidance, setting boundaries and helping a dog navigate her way through this foreign human world. Many behavioural issues stem from a poorly established bond between the dog and her mentor, so it's worth putting in the time and effort to establish and maintain a sound, loving relationship. The cross-foster bond (with other species) needs developing early, too. Your dog must get contact and exposure during that formative period to those creatures you want her to have friendship with over her life or she will treat them as prey.

Where learning boundaries are necessary, you will see the ingenious means we use to create apparent natural consequences. I am always protecting or enhancing the sense of safety and trust in the bond with my dogs, so rarely if ever do I allow a negative experience to be associated with me or my family. I am the ally, not the enemy. This is a form of contrast training and creates safety (you) and avoidance (things they should be leaving alone).

Building your mentor bond

Think about your current relationship with your dog. Is it relaxed or stressed, in control or out of control? Does your dog look to you, or does your dog make his own decisions? If your dog is in contact with you, he will often check in to see where you are and what you might want him to do. If not well bonded, you'll find your dog is often away from you or looking away from you, and you will find yourself looking and calling for him. It seems that it is you doing the checking in — not your dog! To build a more connected bond, here are some areas to consider:

Time and contact

Establishing a 'secure base' is key to your mentor relationship with your dog. Time and contact are the foundation to establish the psychological secure base, and the crate and clip station (see section 10.2) reinforce the physical aspect of the secure base effect.

Make plenty of time for contact with your dog so that she gets used to looking to you for guidance. Make sure you (as the main mentor) are the one to feed your dog and take her walking. Make time to do fun things

Beautiful bond between Russo and Tuss (Tupac — *Hunt for the Wilderpeople*).

together: just like any relationship, the more you invest in it, the better it will be. Go to the park, play a game in the backyard, go for a swim, whatever you want. Give your dog lots of calm, soft physical contact — dogs love to be close to you, so rest your foot on your dog when you are sitting together, pat, massage and touch (remember that wolves touch on average six times an hour!). Massaging your dog's dorsal muscles each side of the spine encourages a calming response. All of these things will encourage your dog to see you as her mentor and beloved companion. Remember, though, only offer contact for appropriate or desired behaviours, not problem ones — contact is a reward.

Use a clip station to keep your dog secure and in your space when you are spending time at home. When your dog is misbehaving, you can also use the clip station as time-out. Your dog is allowed off the clip station for calm, relaxed behaviour — freedom is the reward. Just like any new behaviour during the training phase, don't use any negative reinforcer, so don't use the clip station in the early stages for time-out (generally at least not for the first month or so).

Make the crate or clip station a secure base where your dog is comfortable and happy, using lots of clicking and rewarding. The younger you do this the better, as the neo-natal nesting effect (love of the den) doesn't last long. If you haven't done any by 12 weeks, this will be harder to establish. With a pup, start with the crate, then from about 3-4 months introduce the clip station.

Your cues to your dog

Dogs are highly receptive to human cues, so your attitude, energy and posture are important — be patient, kind and consistent. Dogs will make subtle associations to negative experiences, which can inhibit learning and create training issues, so don't do training if you're stressed or in a bad mood — your dog will respond much better when you are calm and happy. Remember, your dog reads your mood through pheromones, postures and intonations. You need to be mindful and calm, with good situational awareness and confident posture, then your dog will look to you — fake it till you make it if necessary.

Also remember your dog is not a machine — dogs make mistakes, too, so have compassion and enjoy the process. Have an enquiring mind: studying your dog helps build an understanding of your dog's perspective on life and his individual idiosyncrasies.

Nothing in life is free (NILIF)

You are the mentor. You are in charge of access to what your dog wants or likes — food, attention, freedom, off-lead play, etc.

Reward your dog for appropriate behaviour by giving him access to these things. Don't give your dog free access to these things during the four- to six-week initial intensive training period — only reward when your dog is doing desired behaviours or commands, not if he is behaving inappropriately.

Training

To build your bond, do the training outlined in the following chapters:

O Joining Up (see chapter 8) — I recommend you do this regularly in the first two months of training, once or twice a day, then start fading it. You'll also find that when you are heeling your dog on a lead you are effectively doing Joining Up. Every now and then, top up with a training session. It's good bonding time, too.

O Basic commands (see chapter 7) — teaching the basics, particularly recall, is great for building a shared language and bonding with your dog.

O Clicker training (see chapter 6) — do plenty of repetitive training with small food rewards. Remember, the regular association with the clicker builds a bond, too — you are the switch and the 'bank' (food, of course!).

O Shared language (see chapter 4) — ensure you know what your dog is saying to you, and what you are saying back to your dog. A shared language is more than commands; it is a conversation or a dance of signals that are verbal, postural, body orientation, gestures and pheromones. It can be as subtle as a look or opening the door at the right time.

O For those who have more of a working relationship with their dogs, like shepherds or hunters, you may manage your dog a bit more at arm's length, but it doesn't change the fact that you need this bond. Dogs can and will adapt to kennel living, but to gain the real rapport that great working dogs have, you need to invest time in the bond, too. You can still love and respect your dog if she lives in a kennel, keeping her living space clean and enriching her life with bones or rubber toys as well as making sure she gets plenty of time out with you. Dogs love working, but the rules of training still

apply. A clip station in the truck or near your work space — the yard, shearing shed, wherever — helps build that bond. Carrying her own clip lead on her collar is a tried and true for shepherds.

8.2 JOINING UP

In my dog behaviour clinic, I often see owners with dogs that haven't bonded to them properly. Yes, their dogs may love them and are affectionate to them, but they haven't learned to be fully attentive and attuned to their owners; they don't listen to them, take their behavioural cues from them or pay much attention to what they ask them to do. One classic measure is whether or not they look at, and to, their owners often or at all — they need to.

Not having a strong enough bond creates myriad issues. If your dog doesn't look at you and to you for direction, then it's extremely difficult to get him to respond to your commands. He might run away from you while on walks and not come back, jump all over people or act aggressively toward other people and dogs — all of these things are symptoms of or exacerbated by a lack of bond between a dog and his owner. There are, however, exceptions; for example, some owners have a bond but no proper shared language that dogs need to navigate our world.

This section is about showing you how to change that. Even if you do feel that you have a good bond with your dog, I suggest you do the training anyway. It will set you up well for highly effective training sessions, it's a great way to spend time together, and is very enriching (stimulating) for your dog — dogs love spending the time with you!

What is Joining Up?

Joining Up is the natural process of bonding and cultivating the following and look-to response that Mum and the helpers inherit in the wild world, but that you need to create.

Joining Up is a training technique that helps you establish the fundamental relationship you need with your dog. It cements you as your dog's mentor: the person he looks up to for direction and guidance in all situations. If your dog is looking to you for guidance, it's far less likely that you are going to encounter behavioural issues or inappropriate decisions.

Usually puppies will learn to view their owners as their mentors, but you can re-create the opportunity with adult dogs by 'taking them back to the den', re-creating that time when a pup leaves the whelping den and bonds to a mentor. Dogs bond more specifically to certain individuals than wolves do, and will have preferential bonds based on who shares the most resources with them and who is the leading elder.

Here's a summary of the indicators that you are well joined up with your dog:

O You have close contact — your dog stays close to you and looks to you for direction.

O You have good eye contact with your dog. Staring is a threat in dogs, so if your dog can hold your eye contact (to a reasonable degree) it's a sign he trusts you, though note that some dogs find this hard.

O Your dog moves with, stops with and follows you regularly.

O A big test is recall (the command to come back to you): if you have a strong recall on your dog, then he is likely well connected with you. It means your dog feels that being near you is better than being 'out there'. Breed dispositions influence this.

A dog that is well joined up to you will be loyal, gentle and cooperative, learning and taking direction from you easily.

It's worth noting that at the other end of the spectrum are dogs that have become over-dependent on you. If you have a dog that can't bear to be apart from you, then he may be suffering from separation distress. See chapter 18 — Separation Distress before you move any further through your training, as we do Joining Up differently for dogs suffering this.

How to do Joining Up

Before you get started, you will need to familiarise yourself with the use of some essential tools — the clicker, clip station, leads and safety slip collar. You can learn about these in the Dog Zen Toolkit chapter.

Once you feel comfortable with these tools and have yourself set up with them. I recommend you do 5-15 minutes of training per session, ideally three or more times per day for about 3-6 weeks. It is fundamental. Once established and the bond is sound, I recommend you go back and practise this every 2-3 months just to keep the behaviours and your bond strong.

There are four stages to Joining Up:

O Stage one: Clip station to switch into a learning state.
O Stage two: Hand-held lead to create a following response.
O Stage three: Umbilical to extend hands-free into daily life.
O Stage four: Off-lead to achieve controlled freedom.

The stage two work is the critical part of Joining Up training, so I refer to this aspect of the training as Joining Up throughout the rest of the book.

Stage one: Clip station, including bed or mat

Use the clip station regularly when training your dog, as it keeps the dog contained and focused on what you are teaching. With regular use, it also simulates a den-like space for your dog, and can be a space that helps her settle, relax or even acts as time-out. Research shows that the secure base relationship can be associated with your personal spaces, so just being in these spaces (even without you) can help a dog maintain learning state (unless she suffers from separation distress).

The technique

O Establish a comfortable clip station, and place your dog on it until she is calm.

O Don't look very much at your dog. Wait for her to settle of her own accord, be patient. Give more contact and rewards once settled.

O Stay non-verbal; don't say anything to your dog. You can put your dog in a 'down' to begin the process, though.

O Subtly watch your dog (remember, staring is a threat and counterproductive), and click and reward her for calm behaviour. (Throw the food on the floor between her paws.)

O Once she is settled, she has likely moved into a learning state (see the Learning State chapter to see how to identify this).

O Use hand signals (stay non-verbal) to ask your dog for a 'sit' and then a 'down' position. Click and reward your dog each time she does a sit or down. Keep practising these commands throughout the session.

O Aim to get a 'Zen down', as this activates the vagus nervous system to further stimulate rest and digest or learning state.

O Leave your dog in a 'Zen down' after a while, with only intermittent click and reward.

O Move on to the next stage when your dog is relaxed and settled — leave her with a stuffed Kong brand toy, or similar.

Stage two: Hand-held lead

This technique develops the bond between you and your dog. It encourages your dog to want to be in your personal space, and teaches him that being close to you means safety, protection and an enjoyable experience, while pulling away from you is undesirable and unpleasant. We use a lead and contrast training to encourage the follower response. This teaches your dog who is in control of the resources, and where and what safety is. A lead and umbilical lead is of little use if it doesn't offer contrast to finding safety.

This training is done using a safety slip collar or half-slip and a lead. When the lead is pulling tightly on the collar, the dog feels pressure on his neck; when the lead is slack, the pressure comes off. The 'pressure on' is not harmful to the dog, but it does feel a bit uncomfortable. This basic discomfort of 'pressure on' versus the comfort of 'pressure off' is what forms the basis of how you use this contrast-training technique to guide your dog to the right behaviour.

However, here's the bonus: using the clicker and food with pressure off switches the dog into a learning state and enhances the contrast to the positive. This enables the dog to understand that you hold the resources and that proximity to you is the safe place.

Set up in a quiet, distraction-free room with your dog in a safety slip collar attached to a hand-held lead. I like to have the end of the lead looped around three fingers (from the little to the middle finger) on my left hand, leaving the forefinger and thumb free to hold the clicker in place. This leaves the right hand free to get food rewards from your pouch to give to your dog throughout training, and also means that your clicker is ready to be used instantaneously: this is really important, as it needs to mark the exact moment your dog does the behaviour you want.

The technique
Review and teach the 'sit', 'down' and 'Zen down' commands. You can start Joining Up without them initially if you like, but it's best to have them so that Joining Up becomes your go-to ritual when you are generally out and about.

O Start gently, using plenty of positive reinforcement. Click and reward your dog for good behaviour, such as looking at you or turning his head toward you.

O Walk slowly in circles or squares around the room, keeping a food reward in your hand, initially positioned to lure your dog ahead and beside you — your dog's right shoulder to your left leg approximately. (A loose line is the most important issue.)

O At intervals, also move your hand with the food lure in it so that it is positioned between the dog and your eyes to encourage your dog to keep looking past your hand to you (contact). Everything you do is communicating to your dog, so you need to be very relaxed, with no sustained tension on the lead if possible.

O Stay non-verbal initially, as it leaves less room for confusion for your dog.

O When your dog makes eye contact, looks up at you or is walking on the lead with no pressure on the line, click and reward (pressure off). This is the follower response happening, activating an ancient imprinting response.

O When your dog pulls and looks away from you, there is pressure on the lead: the lead is tight (pressure on — this discomfort is the consequence).

O As soon as your dog turns back towards you (safety) and gets in
   line with your walking, the pressure comes off the lead and you
   can click and reward your dog (pressure off). This teaches your
   dog that pulling away results in discomfort (pressure on), while
   turning toward you and walking nicely with you results in no
   discomfort and a click and a treat (pressure off). This is how dogs
   learn best — by contrast.

O Continue to walk in circles and/or squares around the room,
   ensuring there is pressure on whenever your dog is pulling away,
   and that you immediately click and reward your dog as soon as
   the pressure comes off the lead. You can click and reward your dog
   whenever it is walking beside you nicely and intermittently looking
   at you for guidance with the pressure off. Using corners to walk in
   squares offers up more contrast as you turn 90 degrees; a circle is
   gradual, so your dog might not notice it, whereas a square creates
   more distance between you as you corner, so the dog feels the
   contrast. A more advanced example is using 180-degree turns (walk
   in a straight line then turn right around and head back in the same
   direction). This provides very strong contrast as you completely
   change direction, so your dog has to keep alert and think — he will
   notice the contrast and will learn clearly. Start simply with the
   circle, then move to 90-degree turns, then 180-degree turns.

O If your dog continues to pull away, look away or is not focused on
   you, apply more pressure until he looks back at you. If your dog
   tries to jump up or paw at you, give an 'off' cue and a flat hand
   signal (this cue asks your dog to not jump up). Reward when four
   feet touch the ground, the dog returns his focus back to you and
   the pressure is off the lead.

O Keep moving if possible.

O Early on, stick to positive reinforcement only — click and reward
   pressure off.

O After a few sessions, if your dog is still pulling introduce a 'no'
   command, and click and reward pressure off. If this doesn't work,
   then on your second 'no' add an effective check. However, only use
   this if you have been unsuccessful in previous sessions.

This method teaches your dog to move when you move and to stop when
you stop, always keeping in your space and looking up to you for direction.

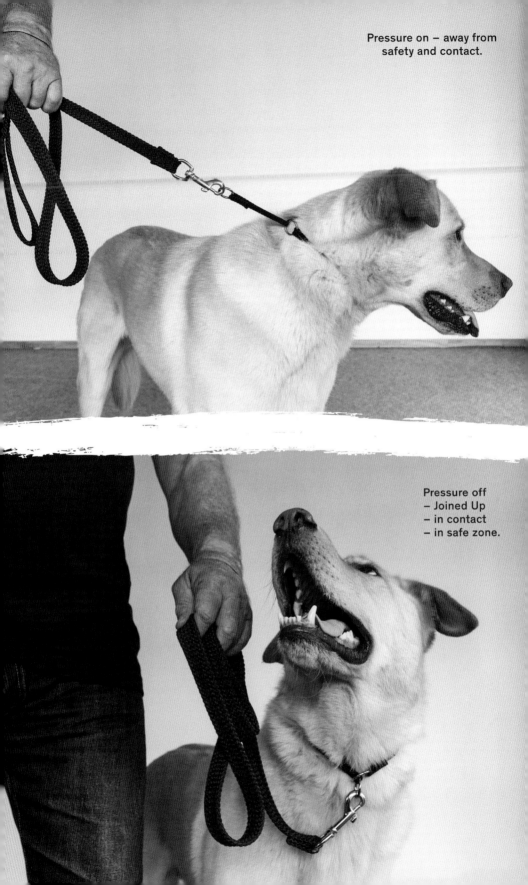

Pressure on – away from safety and contact.

Pressure off
– Joined Up
– in contact
– in safe zone.

Each time you stop, practise 'sit', 'down' and 'Zen down'. Eventually, you want your dog to automatically go into a sit for a short stop, and down for longer waits, whenever you stop moving. Use the 'sit' hand signal, click and reward for obeying, or when this happens naturally without the signal being used. Hand-reward a sit, and throw the food on the floor between your dog's front feet for 'down' or 'Zen down'.

Stage three: Umbilical

Umbilical training involves having your dog on a safety slip collar and a lead which is clipped to your waist (like an umbilical cord), moving with you as you go about your daily activities. It extends the behaviour you've cultivated on the lead, and brings it into your everyday life, hands-free, enabling your dog to get used to following you with less direct intervention than on the hand-held lead. Allow just enough lead to give your dog room for a 'down'.

Make sure you have progressed with stage two before you graduate to this stage, as you don't want to drag your dog around or vice versa. Bigger or more hyperactive dogs may require more work on the hand-held lead before they are ready for the umbilical. Be aware of any physical limitations you might have (particularly if you have a big, strong dog). Be careful that your dog doesn't pull you around or over. Ensure your equipment is appropriate to the size and strength of your dog.

The technique

O Clip your dog's lead to your belt (with your dog on her safety slip collar).

O Go about everyday tasks as per usual with your dog attached to you by the lead. Start slowly inside your house, having your dog tag along with you, and observe how she mimics your movement and relates to you and your space.

O Click and reward good following behaviour (when your dog is moving with you happily, and not resisting or pulling away from you). Click and reward pressure off.

O Give your dog a 'no' command if slow on the uptake of commands.

O If still not responding, give your dog a check on the second 'no'.

O Continue to uphold the principles of pressure on, pressure off. Later cue a 'heel' command for even better walking beside you.

For example, when you are about to walk through a door, ask your dog to sit and wait before you go through — you should always walk first through doors. If your dog obeys, click and reward the good behaviour. If your dog doesn't listen, say 'no' and click and reward good behaviour. If she persists, then on your second 'no' give an effective check by applying a quick and firm tug to the lead, then ask your dog to sit again. Repeat until you achieve the desired result: it is important to be consistent and insist on the right behaviour every time.

It's a bit of a hassle to begin with, but, believe me, it will pay off. Remember, it's the contrast you're after, not dominance. You are shaping the follower response. Dogs thrive on a clear sense of role and place in the family, with clear knowledge of who to look to, especially when confused.

Whenever you stop, ask for a 'sit', and reward your dog for stopping when you stop. If you stay in one place for any amount of time, go through your 'sit', 'down' and 'Zen down' commands, particularly rewarding a 'Zen down'.

When you move on, your dog's awareness of you should be such that she comes with you — it becomes second nature and a beautiful synergy develops. As you both get accustomed to this, you should be able to go about your daily activities with limited pressure on the lead. You are training your dog to move with you throughout your day. When released, your dog can relax and run free, but she should be checking in with you by staying in proximity; approximately a 20-metre vicinity is ideal. We call this the check-in boundary. I use a 'close' command for this. Say 'close', and if she turns toward you click and reward by tossing food toward her at intervals.

Stage four: Off-lead

Now we want to proof the training in real-world situations. Go through this series of steps to ensure that the bond you are building carries into real life.

The technique

o Start with low-arousal environments (e.g. inside the house or in your backyard). Click and reward your dog for moving with you.
o Once you have that established, start work on the long or retractable lead in more-stimulating environments.

O Remember to apply pressure on for behaviours you don't want, and click and reward pressure off when your dog is near you and looking at you.

O Once your dog is consistently staying near you and exhibiting pressure off behaviour, start taking your dog off the lead for periods of time — first in low-arousal environments, then increasing the stimulation (e.g. by moving to a dog park).

O Positively reinforce the sense of closeness and safety by clicking and rewarding your dog when he stays close. You want your dog to be aware and looking for you, to follow if you leave the area.

O Play hide-and-seek to make it fun. In safe environments, duck behind trees or bushes to have your dog get used to looking for you, and click and reward your dog for finding you.

O Once these behaviours are well established, your dog will be relaxed but aware of you and moving to your tune.

By practising these training techniques regularly, you will be able to build a close bond with your dog: he will know that he should stay close to you and look to you for direction. You will have become your dog's mentor, which will enable you to complete the rest of the training programme successfully, happily and easily.

8.3 MEET AND GREET

Dogs meeting new dogs or people need a formal greeting just like us. The way we are introduced to and meet other people forms the basis of our future relationship: if we have a warm handshake and a 'Hello, how are you?' with someone, we'd generally expect that the relationship is off to a good start. However, if someone were to stare meanly at us across the room, refuse to shake hands or say hello, then we would expect we weren't going to be the best of friends going forward. Similarly, with dogs, the nature of first introductions does set the tone for future relationships.

JOE: NOT OFF TO THE BEST START

I experienced a situation recently in which I was with a young dog called Joe. He was a rambunctious thing, and hadn't learnt how to greet older dogs respectfully. We encountered an issue when he ran up to meet my son's dog, Syd, who is an eight-year-old entire (non-neutered) male and more dominant. Joe jumped right on top of Syd's shoulders, and was all over him in a rough-and-tumble kind of way. It wasn't aggressive, but it wasn't appropriately respectful, especially when Syd's body language was communicating to Joe that he was not currently interested in playing. Syd was not happy! I could see his hackles go up and his body stiffen, so I quickly ran over to remove Joe from the situation before Syd had a chance to react any further and we had a nasty incident on our hands.

After this, Syd was guarded when Joe was around because of this negative first interaction. So I taught Joe the right way to greet other dogs in a nice way, and ensured he followed this greeting routine the next time he met Syd, rewarding both dogs throughout the process. Syd was then able to relax with Joe, and they were able to move forward in a friendly manner. Not all dogs, though, will be so forgiving: start well first-off with the 'dog handshake', it is the real answer!

This example shows the importance both of being able to read a dog's body language (like I did with Syd, when I noticed him stiffening and his hackles going up), so that you can react to ensure a situation doesn't become worse; and of establishing good greeting routines between dogs so that their relationships get off to a good start and you avoid unpleasant situations. This section teaches you how to create good meeting and greeting routines for your dog.

I will walk you through positive greeting routines for you to practise with your dog. These techniques are designed for reasonably well-socialised dogs (or puppies) that don't have any issues with aggression. If your dog does, you should follow the techniques outlined in the chapters on aggression later in the book.

Origins of dog greeting routines

Greeting routines in the ancestral wolf and dog worlds are very formalised and ritualised. Both greet each other by sniffing the inguinal and anogenital area: the groin and the area underneath the tail. This informs the dog about the sexual status, age and relative dominance of the other dog, and whether or not a female is in heat. After they have checked out all this crucial information, dogs will often greet and sniff at the face end, as there are pheromones there, too. When dogs

1 Joining up sequence.

Pressure off.

2

Pressure on.

3

Pressure off — click and reward.

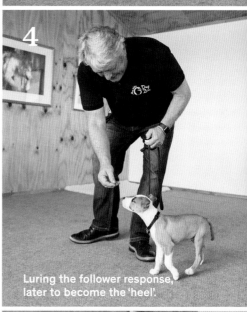

4

Luring the follower response, later to become the 'heel'.

5

Practising the 'sit'.

6

Click and reward 'sit' as the pup's bottom hits the ground.

7

Practising the 'down'.

8

9

If necessary, apply a little
pressure on the shoulder.

10

11

Practising the 'Zen down'.

12

Dog Zen down.

are doing this natural greeting, they use signals and postures that say 'Hello, I'm not going to fight'. Conversely, if dogs go head to head and are standing staring at each other, this forces them into a dominance gesture and can result in an aggressive interaction.

Dog body language

The most important thing to learn when cultivating good relationships between dogs and between your dog and other people is how to read your dog's body language. When you know what your dog is saying, you can react accordingly to ensure that you respond to the situation early. For example, if you know how your dog looks when she is feeling happy or playful, you will be able to recognise this behaviour when your dog meets other dogs and will know that they are friendly with each other and aren't going to be a problem together.

It is even more essential that you recognise when your dog is showing warning signs of annoyance, fear or aggression, so you can alleviate the situation immediately and reduce the risk of escalating aggression or a dog fight.

Check out the Shared Language chapter to learn about a few of the moods your dog might experience when meeting other dogs or people, and the signs to look out for — particularly dominant aggressive, fearful aggressive, playful, stressed, relaxed and approachable, and submissive.

The 'nicely' command

When I'm approaching a new dog, person or another animal, I use the 'nicely' command to tell my dog that 'Yes, I have seen this other dog or person, too, and I have judged her as safe and friendly.' This lets your dog know you are looking out for him and thinking about the situation so he doesn't need to. This helps encourage your dog to act in a sociable and friendly manner.

When paired with good greeting routine, the use of 'nicely' will also switch your dog into a learning state, rather than into fight-or-flight mode. This will help encourage positive interactions free from stress, fear or aggression. After some practise the use of 'nicely' and the clicker will induce a positive state.

Meeting new dogs

Dogs have a greeting routine they use to tell another dog that they are friendly. They do this by checking and sniffing other dogs in the groin and rear-end area — coming head-to-head is much more threatening for a dog. I call the check and sniff the 'dog handshake'.

Without correct exposure to other dogs in the formative period, that hard-wired knowledge of how to greet dogs properly doesn't get switched on. Being naïve about these intrinsic social signals means that dogs grow up 'limited', and it gets worse the longer they don't learn them. To rectify this, we must teach our dogs the meet and greet and the dog handshake.

When you are first practising this routine, start with friendly dogs with confident owners so you can limit the risk. If any offensive behaviour occurs while using this technique, it would suggest that the other dog is mal-socialised and didn't learn this dog greeting in earlier years. Be very mindful of the situation if this happens, and remove your dog as calmly and quickly as possible.

The technique

O When you first see a new dog, use your 'nicely' command to let your dog know that you have seen this new dog and have judged him as friendly. Use an 'up' tone.

O Approach the other dog calmly. The inexperienced dog is the one that should make the approach. If that is your dog you can ask the other dog's owner to hold their dog in place (quietly on the lead) if they have control, to present their dog's back end for your dog to greet (rear-present). You also should be able to do that with your dog, so you can approach the others and they can approach you.

O If a rear-present is not possible, try to approach from the side if you can, as this is less threatening than a direct face-on approach. Normally three-quarters-on is best, as it allows sniffing of the groin. Watch the posture and reactions of both dogs.

O Set up the interaction so that it is natural for your dog to go straight into an inguinal sniff of the other dog.

O Then make sure the other dog gets a chance to greet your dog. Do this by turning your dog so that his rear end is facing the other dog to minimise the likelihood of aggression — the other dog is very unlikely to be aggressive towards the rear end of your dog.

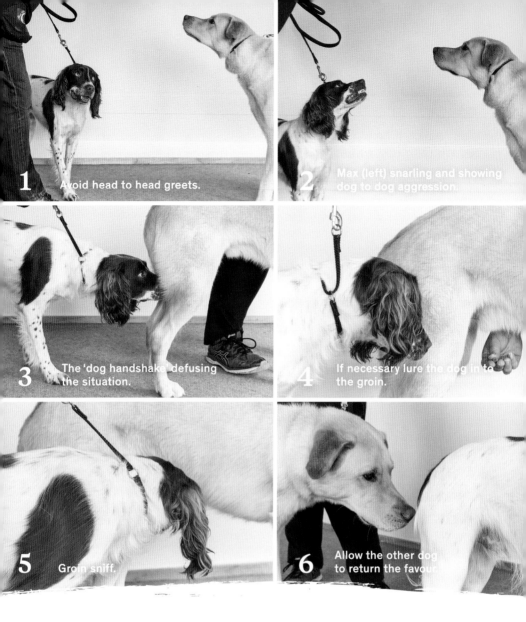

1 Avoid head to head greets.

2 Max (left) snarling and showing dog to dog aggression.

3 The 'dog handshake' defusing the situation.

4 If necessary lure the dog in to the groin.

5 Groin sniff.

6 Allow the other dog to return the favour.

We can often unwittingly set dogs up for negative interactions while we are out walking. Both dogs are likely to be on a lead beside their owners, so they are likely to meet face-to-face, which can be threatening. It's important that you give any dogs approaching you the opportunity to first sniff your dog's rear end before they approach the face. Do this by pulling your dog's head towards the front of your body so he is side-on in front of you (rather than face-forward beside you) or by stopping and moving your dog around so that his rear end is facing the approaching dog. In this way, you facilitate and orchestrate a better first interaction.

When the other dog approaches you and sniffs your dog's rear end, click and reward your dog for accepting being sniffed. It's also a good idea to get permission from the other dog's owner to click and reward their dog while it is sniffing, to further reduce the risk of an aggressive response. Then click and reward your dog for sniffing the other dog's rear end also. Be aware that both dogs will likely be more interested in each other than in your food and clicker — if it is all going well, don't interrupt them! As soon as you can, get onto the clicker to reinforce the behaviour. Sometimes you have to lure your dog into the engagement with a piece of food in your hand and draw him toward the other dog's groin.

If you take away one thing from this section, it is to remember to present dogs rear-end first if possible! Dogs won't attack the rear end in 99% of cases (take care with mal-socialised fighting breeds).

Meeting people

When it comes to meeting people, an appropriate routine obviously looks a little different. It's good to have a routine for people in place so that your dog knows how to act when meeting someone new. Use a muzzle if you think your dog might be aggressive.

The technique
- Practise first with known, confident people.
- When you first see the person you will be meeting, use your 'nicely' command.
- Ask the person you're meeting to stand still, then you can approach them with your dog so your dog can sniff them. A dog feels more comfortable approaching others than being approached, as a direct approach can seem threatening.
- If your dog is a bit wary or timid, have the person turn slightly side-on and lower their gaze so they are not staring as your dog approaches them. Alternatively, you could ask the person to crouch down or sit on a chair for the meeting to further reduce the threat level. It's important when your dog is first learning how to greet people appropriately that the people she is meeting don't demonstrate threatening behaviour such as staring, standing over, or handling the head, cheek or shoulder area of the dog.
- Click and reward your dog for positive social responses, including a wagging tail, sniffing the person's hand, having all four paws on

1 Good people meet and greets. Allow your dog to approach the person.

2 Click and reward a good response.

3 Shield the other person's hand first when offering treats.

4 Click and reward accepting treats.

the ground, not jumping up and friendly behaviour.

○ You can train and use a hand target with your dog. First teach your dog to touch your hand with her nose and click and reward her. Once established with you, you can then get visitors to do this as well. Encourage the new person to feed your dog treats as you click and reward your dog for her sociable response. First, have your and the new person's hands together with the treat — click and reward. Once the dog is comfortable, have the person give your dog a treat on their own — click and reward for sociable responses.

○ When your dog has greeted the person, ask for a 'sit', 'down' and 'Zen down'. This is what I encourage my dogs to do while I am chatting to people after they have met, so I click and reward them for sitting or lying down while I am talking.

O If you see *any* signal of aggressive behaviour, remove your dog from the situation. Go to the Human-oriented Aggression chapter for detailed instructions on what to do in this situation.

O Practise this greeting routine with adults and children alike; a cross-section of all different kinds of people is best.

Use similar principles as above for introducing your pup to other species during their formative period (see the Puppy Love chapter).

PART C

Puppy Love

Carlos — the first dog
I raised from a pup.

Tyson (a Pound Pups
rescue dog).

CARLOS: INVEST IN SUCCESS

Carlos is the first puppy who really sticks in my memory, maybe because I whelped and raised him, having rescued his mum Tammy while studying for my first university degree. She was a crazy, mal-socialised German Shepherd that reminded me of Scott, and since I was now studying zoology then surely the outcome must be different!

Carlos was to become my first well-adjusted, talented and easy dog. He was awesome. He saw me through university, into my animal behaviour consultancy, and became the very first of my film dogs. I was at uni when I got him, so he went everywhere with me — maybe by good luck rather than good management! He had farm, city and student experiences, so was very well adjusted. He showed me what it was like if you did the right things at the right time.

There's nothing more irresistible than the vulnerability, cuteness and playfulness of a puppy. Dogs are uniquely adapted to living with humans, producing the same 'love' hormones and feelings of emotional attachment as our own loved ones. With our bodies responding to dogs like children, it's understandable how we find ourselves treating them like children. And therein lies the greatest of our mistakes.

Dogs are dogs and need to be treated accordingly, and this is no truer than when they are puppies. They are not adapted for human life, so it is our critical role to act as a mentor to guide them. With an extended formative period, an ability to strongly attach to us and cross-foster to other species, dogs are very capable of adapting successfully to our world — if we offer them the opportunity to do so.

But — and here's the crux — those mechanisms of socialisation and adaption do not automatically turn on. They have to be deliberately 'switched on' during this period. If done correctly, it is simple and will set you and your dog on the path to a loving and harmonious relationship. Many studies show that the sooner you start a pup's socialisation, the easier it is and the better the results. If you haven't socialised your pup by 12 weeks of age then your dog will be in trouble, and by 16 weeks the formative period closes down. This is the most important message in this book: do the right thing at the right time.

Choosing the right pup for you

First things first, let's think about choosing the right pup for you. It's all about doing your homework! Choose carefully, it's for life — the dog's and a big portion of yours.

You'll need to consider which breed suits your lifestyle and personality, as well as how to pick the puppy that is best for you and your household from a litter — it's a relationship that will last 10-15 years, after all!

I met a very lovely woman recently who was in her seventies and had lost a lot of her mobility. She was a dog lover, but couldn't understand why her dog was so hyperactive and destructive. Having had dogs all her life, she had automatically adopted the same type of dog she'd always had: a young Border Collie pup, a notoriously high-energy breed with an extreme need for exercise and stimulation. It's no wonder the relationship was strained: the dog just wasn't a good match for her at this slower and calmer stage of her life.

To help avoid this situation yourself, here are some things to think about when you're next looking for a dog to join your family.

9.1 BREED

We've all been there: that reactive, emotional decision to immediately get that puppy, the cutest thing we've ever seen. I was in Australia recently when one of my team sent me a photo of a rescue pup with a cheeky suggestion that we should get him. He was the spitting image of my old boy Blue — same colouring, same look, even down to his quirky eyebrows. I was hooked and, with a rush of blood to my head, I responded with a very fast YES! Thankfully, my daughter staged an intervention with a kindly suggestion that a fifth dog probably wasn't what I needed right now. (Well, maybe not that kindly, given that I was in Australia and she was looking after my other four!)

Hopefully you'll have a steady head alongside you the next time you select a pup, so you don't make a quick, emotional decision. It is very tempting to simply choose the cutest puppy you can find, but you need to step back and look at the big picture.

There are over 400 different breeds of dog, and within them are thousands of lines of breeds that all have different character attributes and idiosyncrasies. Breeds are genetically different with different genetic markers and have been bred for different purposes, which creates behavioural differences. A Border Collie is very smart and wants to herd things, whereas a Saluki (a sight hound) will chase things by sight. Understanding these breed predispositions will help you determine if a particular dog is a good match. The choice comes down to combining your needs and wants from a dog with the attributes of various breeds and individuals (and therefore the dog's needs) to get the ideal match. The better suited you and your dog are, the more fun and happy your time together will be.

Below is outlined the various attributes you should consider. I give a few examples of dogs that display those attributes; however, do your own research and reflect deeply on what kind of dog will suit your life. The relationship you have with your dog does have a big impact on your life and your relationships, so it's worth taking the time.

Remember, too, that your lifestyle needs change across the course of your life, so the kind of dog you had in your teens might not be the kind of dog that you get when you have a young family or as you head into retirement. Think in 10–15 year spans.

Exercise level

It is important that your dog's activity level suits your own. How much can you exercise your dog? All dogs need some form of exercise, but the degree varies greatly from breed to breed. You don't want to deprive your dog of something as important as exercise or it may manifest into other issues: a well-exercised dog is a relaxed dog that's less likely to cause chaos! That doesn't mean you need to be a fitness junkie to have a dog; many breeds don't require as much activity, it's just a matter of finding the right fit. Note, too, that size doesn't always matter in regard to exercise requirements!

High-energy dogs that need a lot of exercise include most of the hunting and working breeds and many of the terriers. Some examples are the Australian Cattle Dog, Belgian Malinois, German Shepherd, Border Collie, Boxer, Boykin Spaniel, Dalmatian, Flat-Coated Retriever, Irish Setter, Jack Russell Terrier, Labradoodle, Pointer, Weimaraner, Siberian Husky and Doberman Pinscher.

Lower-energy dogs include the Basset Hound, Bulldog, Bull Mastiff, Cavalier King Charles Spaniel, Chow Chow, French Bulldog, Great Dane, Old English Sheepdog, Pekingese, Pug, Chihuahua, Maltese, Pomeranian and Saint Bernard.

Environment

Consider your family size, house size, land size, other animals on the property and whether you live in an urban or a rural area. Dogs need a contained environment as they are curious, prone to wandering and following scents (especially puppies and the hunter and scent-hound breeds who like to follow their noses). Obviously a larger area is better for a larger dog, and a small toy dog will be quite content with a smaller area. But that also relates to how often the dog gets to go walking or get out and about: a larger dog can cope in a smaller house if he is out exercising regularly during the day.

Size

This is generally a matter of personal preference, and is also relevant to your lifestyle. What suits you: a giant breed or a small toy breed?

Think about the size of the dog you think you'd like, then look at the characteristics of breeds to find one that also fits with the other considerations you're looking at. Remember that the range is from 1 kilogram to 100 kilograms or more, so consider the space you have, the size of your car, the cost of feeding a larger dog versus a smaller one, and certain breeds' predisposition to health issues, such as joint issues in a lot of the giant breeds. Also think about your ability to train a big, strong dog: Mastiffs, German Shepherds and other strong breeds can require a lot of strength to manage, so consider whether this is for you. I see this mismatch in my clinic a lot, so think carefully; it's not fun if it goes wrong.

Temperament

Do you want a very independent and self-sufficient dog, happy if she is at home while you are at work? Low-energy breeds like the Chow Chow, Miniature Schnauzer, Bulldog and Bichon Frise fit this bill. Or would you prefer a very affectionate and loving companion dog? Labradors, Golden Retrievers, Spaniels and the like fit this category. They love company, so be prepared to give it to them.

Do you want a dog that will be protective and alert you when people enter your property? Look to German Shepherds, Dobermans and Rottweilers. Or do you have a busy household with lots of comings and goings, which means it's better for you to have a quieter dog that doesn't make much of a fuss? In this case, perhaps consider a Pug, Bulldog or even a Scottish Terrier.

Some breeds used as guard dogs are the Bull Mastiff, Doberman Pinscher, Giant Schnauzer, Akita, German Shepherd, Staffordshire Bull Terrier, Rottweiler, Puli and Rhodesian Ridgeback. Make sure you socialise them well and teach them when to be a watch dog and when to greet in friendly fashion — teach positive meet and greets early. All need lots of exercise and stimulation.

Do you want a dog that isn't likely to chase other animals on your property? In that case, don't go for a hunting breed, Spitz breeds or terriers (or otherwise cross-foster them intensely onto these animals in the formative period). Or would you like a dog with some hunting drive? Setters, Pointers, Spaniels and other hunting breeds will do well here.

Some of the breeds that can make great family dogs for households with kids include the Basset Hound, Beagle, Bernese Mountain Dog,

Choosing the right pup for you is important.

Watch how they play – confident behaviour is good!

Boston Terrier, Cavalier King Charles Spaniel, Golden Retriever, Curly-Coated Retriever, Labrador and Irish Wolfhound. Dogs that are considered very gentle include the Pug, Golden Retriever, Labrador, Newfoundland, Cavalier King Charles Spaniel and Cocker Spaniel.

Whatever breed you do get, make sure you socialise your dog well in the formative period of 1–4 months with plenty of different ages and ethnicities, breeds of dogs and other species.

Trainability

Do you want to spend a lot of time training your dog in agility and obedience, or would you rather have a playful and cuddly dog? Do you want or need your dog to perform any specific tasks? Certain breeds are thought to be more eager to learn new things, and they are usually intelligent and high-energy dogs, which means you'll probably want to come up with new tricks and tasks on a regular basis to keep them stimulated and entertained. Trainable dog breeds won't usually settle for snoozing all day, so if training and being really active isn't your thing you may like to choose a different breed that's more relaxed. Many working-dog breeds are very trainable, but require lots of exercise and stimulation.

Because they have been selected to work cooperatively with their handlers, some breeds are more trainable. Examples are the Border Collie, Australian Shepherd, Border Terrier, German Shepherd, Papillion, Poodle, Shetland Sheepdog, Kelpie, Huntaway and many of the hybrids or crosses, especially if they have some of the above breeds in them!

Physical traits and defects

Do you want a dog with a woollen type coat for anyone in the house with allergies? Do you want a dog with a lovely long, silky coat for patting? Also consider any breed-specific ailments: certain breeds are prone to various congenital, medical and psychological problems, such as cleft palate, blindness, hip dysplasia, fearfulness and deafness, to name just a few. Do your research.

Pure-bred or hybrid

If you are choosing a pure-bred, it's important to choose an excellent breeder to ensure your dog doesn't have the congenital defects that can be associated with certain breeds. Inbreeding can cause negative recessive traits to be thrown up. A good breeder will begin house training and socialisation, be able to give you good nutritional advice and tell you more about the breed and its qualities.

Alternatively, choose a hybrid (cross-breed), where you will benefit from hybrid vigour (more genetic variability that enhances health). The advantage of hybrids is that you often get the best of both breeds. Out-crossing like this usually improves general health (called hybrid vigour), provides psychological benefits and can often result in higher levels of trainability, and is my personal preference.

If you have fighting breeds (pure-bred or mixed) included in the mix, make sure that your dog is very well socialised with children, other dogs and other animals. In my experience the 'gaminess' (desire to attack and kill things — prey initially, but in pit-fighting breeds it can be other dogs and, if mal-socialised, people) trait selected for in terriers and the predisposition to fight in fighting breeds means that if they are not very well socialised they may be more prone to aggression issues. Fighting breeds aren't inhibited from aggression by submissive signals, and their level of aggressiveness and ferocity of attack can be high. When paired with mal-socialisation it can make a deadly cocktail. Socialise them well early and de-sex them early. Hormones increase drive, dominance and dog/dog aggression.

Parent dogs

Remember, breeds aren't like a car, in that you don't get exactly the 'model' you ordered — there is considerable variability even amongst pure-breds. However, most pure-breds have been selected with certain looks and behavioural characteristics in mind, so it helps to think about what best suits you. It's also good to look closely at the dam and sire (mum and dad) to get the best idea of what your pup may be like when he grows up. If you give your pup the correct rearing at the right time, then you can expect your pup to be as good as, or better than, his parents.

Age

If you can, I'd recommend getting a puppy at 7–8 weeks old. This is the end of the neonatal period (the pup's primary period of socialising, focused on the dam and weaning), and the beginning of the secondary stage of socialisation, focused on the mentor and the pack (family) — the critical 'formative period' (2-4 months). It is the most important time in your dog's development and life. It is the time when pups naturally wean and leave the whelping den and start to meet the rest of the pack. You and your family are in essence the pack, and building that relationship during the formative period is essential to ensure a well-socialised, well-rounded dog. The most important point in this book!

Rescue dogs

With so many rescue dogs in need of a loving forever home, I always recommend that you adopt a dog from your local animal rescue shelter, especially a pup. If you want to rescue an adult dog, speak to the people at the rescue organisation to find out what the dog's personality is like, and if she has any behavioural issues you need to be aware of. I believe strongly in rescuing dogs, so I think this is a great route; you just need to consider whether you have the time and ability to train a dog if she has behavioural problems. This book is designed to help.

9.2 INDIVIDUAL (WHICH ONE TO CHOOSE)

Once you have decided what sorts of dog breed is going to suit your household and where you are going to find your new dog, you will need to make a choice about which puppy to choose from a litter. Whether you have chosen a hybrid or a pure-bred dog, there are some important things to look out for:

Confidence and activity level

When you first visit the litter, observe the pups' interaction with each other before you alert them to your presence. You should be looking for an outgoing pup that is neither excessively submissive nor dominant with the other pups (see the Shared Language chapter for guidance).

Sociability and temperament

When you first interact with the puppies, look for those that approach you with their heads held high and tails wagging. These are signs of confident, socially well-rounded pups that have had the right start in life.

From my experience, here are some tests you can do to check a pup's sociability:

O Pick up each of the pups and test their reactivity. They shouldn't struggle excessively or nip and vocalise, and they should settle relatively quickly in your arms.

O Gently manipulate their feet, tails and mouths to check that they are not overly reactive to being poked and prodded.

O Gently hold them down on their backs for 30 seconds. Initially, they won't like it, but they shouldn't bite or react too excessively, and should relax under your moderate pressure. This technique does take a little skill and confidence.

O Ideally the pup should want to be with you, follow you around and play with you when initiated. Take your children if you have any, and see how the pups react to them.

Unless you are experienced in raising and training pups, be careful not to choose the fearfully shy pup of the litter. We tend to fall for the underdog, but this fearfulness trait can be difficult to change. It is worth avoiding unless you have the skills to train the fearful pup effectively to give him confidence. Particularly avoid this if it is your first time raising a pup. Intensively socialise early if you do take a fearful pup.

Health

There's lots of information out there on this, but here's a quick list on what to look out for to make sure you are choosing a healthy puppy:

O The pups should be well-rounded and have a healthy, shiny coat (though rescues may not).

O They shouldn't be too skinny or too fat (though, again, rescues may be).

O Examine the pups physically and check that they don't have an under- or over-shot jaw.

O Check that eyes, ears and genitalia are clear, with no discharge or inflammation.

O Of the two or three pups you have narrowed it down to, take them aside independently to test their vision and hearing. This can be done by clicking, clapping or dropping something on the ground behind them to see if they respond. Also you can test their sight by putting a treat or toy on the ground near them and rolling it around, checking that they can see it and find it.

O Often you will know the one with the X-factor for you, but tick the boxes, too.

A good pure-breeder should have all the applicable papers proving the pups are of the highest quality. However, I would always recommend a quick vet check just to be sure in regard to health and medical concerns. Check any breed-specific weaknesses.

Good luck on the hunt to finding your new family member — it's so exciting when you do!

Most of these dogs were rescued and now live with family or friends.

10

Doing the right thing at the right time

'Give me the the child at seven, and I will give you the man.' (saying attributed to the Jesuits)

I say: 'Give me the pup at four months and I'll give you the dog.'

This is the crux of Dog Zen. Here, we look at the stages in a pup's development and what to do at what time. We will look at how to prepare for your pup, then what to do when you get the pup home and through his various developmental stages. You need to understand just how pivotal the formative period is to your dog's ability to live happily in your world. When it comes to dogs, 'prevention is better than cure'. Doing the right thing at the right time is what will set you up for a great relationship with your dog for life.

Recap: formative period (1-4 months)

We've already talked a lot about the formative period (also called the critical period for socialisation), but it is critical, so here's a bit of a recap in terms of raising your pup.

The formative period in a social species like the dog is designed to offer a nurturing environment for the young to learn social behaviours and environmental adaptability; that is, to learn how to adjust to novel and potentially frightening stimuli. It is also the start of hunting and reproductive behaviour often rehearsed as play.

It is now understood that puppies are like a different animal to dogs — like the caterpillar to the butterfly. The puppy has its own physiology, developmental stages, hormones, digestive system, etc. Juvenilising the wolf extended and delayed this period of puppyhood, giving dogs more time to socialise, get attached to others and adapt to a more variable changing world.

There are many intrinsic (innate) steps in a pup's development, and a huge number of switches that can lead in different directions, depending on the environment the pup ends up in: we call it 'cascading'. Think of each stage of development like a step down a waterfall. If the preceding step sends the water down to the next step, the flow stays on its course; but if a step has a hole in it, the water leaks out and is unable to make it to the next stage. Behaviour and even physiology drops through the hole, too, and goes in the wrong direction or even stops: each stage of development is necessary for the pup to move on to the next stage.

We need to know what's needed for the next stage to unfold. This chapter is about that, delineating the stimuli the pup needs exposure to in order to switch on the next step.

The formative period has a specific start (onset) and close-down period (offset): in dogs, it is the period of 1-4 months. Unless you whelp the pups yourself, the first month of the formative period (the pup's first 4-8 weeks) will be with a breeder, so choose wisely: early experiences do matter. The best time for you to get your pup is at around 7-8 weeks, when you become her mentor.

The reason the formative period is such a critical learning time for a pup is because her fight-or-flight nervous system doesn't complete its development until toward the end of this four-month period. The fear-imprint period kicks in properly after 3-4 months. A puppy cannot enter a learning state if she is in a state of fight or flight, so we need to take advantage of this early period and pack in as much learning and hardwiring as possible. They are like sponges at this stage.

Without fear, puppies are ripe for picking up new behaviours and adjusting to new situations. They are distractible, of course, but they are afraid of little, their nervous system is relaxed and they are ready to learn. Dogs are highly predisposed to adapt to many things, but they must be exposed them in the formative period. By the end of four months, their pack identity has been established and core behaviours have been acquired. Basically, this means that the base behaviours a pup has at four months are behaviours he will probably have for life, with responses maturing with age (unless there is intervention).

When you train your pup before four months of age, you are shaping behaviour rather than trying to change established behaviour and, believe me, that is much easier to do — hence why it's critical to take full advantage of this period. Reinforcing or shaping behaviours when they first appear is much easier, because you don't have to get rid of existing 'wiring' so to speak. They wire what they fire!

The key development stages

Right, let's get started. Below I will take you through the key development stages of your pup and what you need to do during each. I will compare each dog developmental stage to human ones to help you understand where your pup is at (as an approximate guide, seven dog years approximately equates to one human year). I adjust for size.

For each key development period we will look at the following features:

1. Social orientation — who is most important to your pup.
2. Major physical developments — key physical developments for your pup, e.g. eyes open, etc.
3. Learning focus and capability — how well your pup is learning, and what the learning focus is.
4. Developmental behaviour — what the key developmental behaviour going on is.
5. Training focus — what you should be doing for your pup.

10.1 NURSERY: PUP 0–6 WEEKS OLD (HUMAN 0–1.5 YEARS)

This period is all about the mother dog (the dam). At this time the priority is supporting her to look after her pups: keep her well, warm, happy and safe in a den-like space and ensure she is well fed. Vet visits are important at this time to ensure she remains healthy, as is allowing her to nest with some nesting material, helping to unfold natural maternal behaviours. The pups are mum-focused, bonding with the dam and forming their first attachment relationship, similar to human infants at this stage. The neonatal imprinting (bond) is with the mother. This bond is initiated by the familial (family-associated) scent and pheromones, as well as touch, vocalisations and suckling.

Consider carefully where you get your pup from: good contact with the pup's dam and litter helps establish a pup's socialisation, and significant learning occurs in these few weeks, so a good breeder and breeding environment is important. Most importantly, don't get the pup too late: the majority of the formative period should happen at your place.

Summary

○ Social orientation — Mum.
○ Major physical developments — eyes open at around 13 days; ears 19 days; teeth erupt 21 days; inhibition to soiling in the nest site begins around 4–6 weeks (though there is some breed variation).
○ Learning focus and capability — no extensive associative learning until near 6 weeks (so no point in doing much training before then, though socialisation with litter and Mum is important and with humans from 3–4 weeks is good): food interest kicks in around 4 weeks, weaning from 6–8 weeks. Pups need dog and human socialisation from 4–5 weeks at the breeder's place: beginning to meet other dogs is useful — ask your breeder to do this.
○ Developmental behaviour step — Mum, milk and warmth, then social interaction and play become important.

10.2 TRANSITION: PUP 6–8 WEEKS OLD (HUMAN 18 MONTHS– 2 YEARS)

7–8 weeks of age is the best time to get your pup. In Nature, this is the period when the pup starts to move away from Mum and pack-bonding begins (moving on to the helper or mentor, as discussed earlier). Puppies are at their most sensitive and able to transfer from Mum to pack at this time, so they are most open to separation and will be able to bond to you well. What you do now sets up you and your pup for optimal bonding.

Settling in

Firstly, as you transition your puppy from being under the care of his dog mother to your care, start preparing your house for your pup. Source the items you'll need, such as a crate, pen, bedding, food, bowls, collar, lead, toys, etc. Ensure you use the same food as your pup's breeders to prevent stomach upsets, or, if you are changing pup's diet, change it gradually by 20 per cent per day. Use age-specific food, as the digestive system is changing from milk to adult food. Dogs are very adaptable, as they evolved from scavengers; however, be conscious of pups that find digesting starches and grains difficult. This is a later genetic adaptation and some are better at it than others.

Travel

Critically, make sure the first travel journey is good, as this will set the scene for how your dog feels about travel in the future. Make sure the pup is kept secure and happy, and doesn't get stressed or have any frights. Break up the travel experience into bite-size chunks if necessary.

Bonding with you

This is the start of your bond for life. Those who do the most for their pup at this time will be the main mentor(s), and the pup will bond most strongly to them. Those in control of food, love and contact are especially important. Your pup will know your special smell signature, walk and intonation. The first couple of weeks' focus is on settling your pup into your home, helping him adjust to his new world and learning separation and house training.

House training

A no-brainer: you don't want excrement and urine on your carpet forever! Crate training is the most effective option for puppies, but there are three methods, depending on what suits you and your home. The rationale is based on a pup's natural inhibition to soil in his nest site and his substrate (surface) preference. We need to use this preference

Great house training set-up. Crate, pen and exit to fenced yard. A dog door would be even better.

A clip station (from 3 months on) with lots of stimulation. Short periods at first. Good for pup not soiling when not supervised. Teach gradually.

and expand the idea of the nest to the whole house. I cover how to do this in detail in the House Training chapter in Part D.

Teaching separation

This is your pup's first experience of separation. She has had Mum and siblings around fulltime until now, so she will be aware of their absence. She may get distressed and give distress vocalisations, so you need to ensure it goes well.

When you get your puppy home, it is important to set up a crate or a puppy pen area and start to teach separation. The den is a natural place of comfort and safety for pups, that's why they like holes, kennels, under tables, etc, as these places simulate their natural dens. Pups naturally associate you with the den, so you have a great opportunity to establish what their den is. The crate is a good option for this. Ensure the crate is associated with you and the social group for safety and comfort. The pup loses this association quickly, so it needs to be established in the key 6- to 12-week period.

Right from the start, give your puppy plenty of time with you *and* away from you during the day and at night. Start using the crate first (immediately), then the clip station soon after — from about 3 months.

If there is another pup, toys or anything you can put in the pen or crate for the pup to cuddle up to, that will help a lot with the separation, distracting her as you leave her alone for periods of time. If there's no other pup, put in a surrogate soft toy and/or something that smells of the pup's dam or litter. Anything that is warm and soft — a hot-water bottle wrapped in a towel or a heat lamp is good, as pups love warmth (just for the few days while she is getting used to her new environment). Start with periods of separation for an hour or two, and extend from there.

Also ensure that you separate the pup from her playmates for periods of time, so that she learns how to be alone and doesn't get overly dependent on other dogs either. The important thing is not to respond to vocalisations like whining. Allow your pup to get through it. Reward only quiet behaviours with your attention and presence. (See the Separation Distress chapter in Part D for further information on what to do if separation distress starts occurring.)

Remember, your pup is experiencing a lot of firsts during this period, so make sure your pup is supported and her firsts go well.

Transitional (6–8 weeks)

○ Social orientation — transitioning from Mum to pack and mentor (mimicking helper function)
○ Major physical developments — see above.
○ Learning focus and capability — associative learning capacity is complete by 8 weeks; that is, pups can learn from this point on. The earlier they start and more they are exposed to, the better they learn.
○ Developmental behaviour step — distress vocalising is decreasing.
○ Training focus — travel, settling into new home, establishing bond with you, teaching separation. House training should have started.

10.3 KINDERGARTEN (FORMATIVE PERIOD): PUP 2–4 MONTHS OLD (HUMAN 2–6 YEARS)

Righto, so roll up your sleeves, as this is where it all really begins to get interesting! This is the time when you absolutely need to expose your dog to new experiences and train him. It is when your pup is learning bite-inhibition, hunting, danger, aggression, dominance, hierarchy and — most importantly — social behaviour and order.

Continue with your house training (which you hope will be established by 3 months, but certainly by 4 months). This is your chance to mould your pup into the dog you want and need in your life. It is the time when your pup learns about your family's needs and wants (the family rules), so your pup needs intense immersion in your life and situation. Just like a child, this time is the pup's foundational months (years). The following are some key areas to cover:

Using the right training equipment

At this age you are using only a flat collar or half slip and lead — a long-line and/or retractable lead. Around 8 weeks is a good time to start your clicker training (but be conscious of whether your pup is wary of the noise). Do not use a slip collar or the clip station until 3-4 months, unless the pup is very robust. Make sure you are gentle and do it properly.

Socialisation

The most critical activity with a pup this age is to socialise, socialise, socialise. Pups need to learn who their family and village is, and the broader their experience, the better. For people, other dogs and other species they are likely to come across as an adult dog, get your pup out there and meeting them now! This teaches your dog that these things are not a threat to them and aren't prey items, but are extended members of their pack. Critically, this will help to ensure your dog does not act aggressively to any person or animal later on in life. If you don't do this, you risk raising a mal-socialised dog that grows up protective and/or wary of strangers, dogs or other animals, which can lead to fear-based issues, serious aggression or unacceptable prey drive.

You should socialise your pup extensively with people of all ages, races, gender, height and even fashion (such as people wearing hoodies, hi-vis vests, sunglasses, hats, etc — anything that might seem unusual or possibly threatening to a dog). Be aware of the types of people who are not often in your social circle, and make attempts to socialise your dog with them as well — it will prevent embarrassing or, worse, dangerous aggression issues later. Particularly make an effort to socialise your dogs with toddlers and children — there is nothing more distressing or difficult to treat as child-oriented aggression. Children act differently from adults (move fast, make high-pitched noises and are more unpredictable), so if dogs aren't exposed to them as a pup, they can see them as a completely alien species. Ensure that you socialise your pup with a range of ages, such as a toddler and a 10-year-old — dogs experience them differently.

Your pup should also be socialised with lots of other dogs of all different sizes and breeds, as well as cross-fostering onto different species of animals, such as cats, chicken, sheep, birds, cattle, etc — anything you think he is remotely likely to meet later as an adult dog.

To see how to best introduce your dogs to various people, dogs and other species, read the Meet and Greet section and see videos.

Vaccination period

Even though this time conflicts with your puppy's vaccination period, you still need to find ways to socialise your puppy in a safe manner, because if your puppy is isolated, he will have issues later on. Go to places that are less likely to have disease exposure, such as below the high-tide mark at beaches (it gets washed clean by the tide), friends' homes with vaccinated dogs, and reputable puppy classes. Take your disinfectant of choice (such as Virkon S) and spray surfaces beforehand. Avoid busy parks and other places where stray or unvaccinated dogs go.

Puppy: 10 weeks — cross fostering to chickens (clicker).

Pup and cat: 10 weeks — cross fostering with clicker (half slip on).

Novel experiences

While your pup doesn't have much fear, you want to expose him to a whole range of experiences that he may encounter throughout his lifetime. This is both to introduce him to these stimuli, and to get him used to novelty and change.

Your puppy is developing his important coping mechanisms and ability to deal with novelty as an adult dog, so he needs lots of different experiences to avoid becoming fearful of novelty later. Here's a non-exhaustive list of some stimuli you should expose your dog to: busy roads; fireworks, thunder and heavy rain (if none is forecast, play loud recordings of them); vehicles; vacuum cleaning; loud music; loud noises; wheelchairs; riding in cars; skateboards; motorbikes; sports games; children screaming and playing; people running around; big movements like kites, flags and umbrellas opening; puddles; water — anything you can think of!

Take care not to scare your pup: just give exposure, gradually and gently. Gun shots and cracker noises are particularly good to introduce early — around 6-12 weeks is ideal — but make sure you do it gradually. The best method is desensitisation: order the experiences from least to most frightening, and use a clicker and food rewards to expose your dog to them gradually (see the Phobias chapter for methods).

Continue to strengthen your bond

Start your basic Joining Up (see the Joining Up section) with your pup around 12 weeks, so you start cultivating their follower response. Use a standard flat collar, not a slip one, though you could use a half-slip. This will activate the attachment bond to you. At the beginning, do this for about 2-3 sessions of 10-15 minutes each day, slowly fading after 4 months. However, revisit this regularly throughout your dog's life, as a means of strengthening your bond and keeping him focused on you. Don't forget lots of play, cuddles and contact.

Resistance

You are teaching your pup not to panic when she experiences resistance, either on the end of a line or when tied up. I like to teach this using a flat collar and a retractable lead (but you can use a long-line), so the pup gets a gentle experience of resistance on the lead. Do it in a gentle,

It's important to socialise your pup with other dogs.

Puppy socialising at café.

systematic fashion. You are trying to give her a feel of resistance while you are in control. What you don't want to do is have her receive a strong pull on the lead, resulting in her panicking and accidentally flipping. Click and reward her when pressure is off.

Basic commands

A pup's associative learning capacity is developed by 6–8 weeks old (that is, his brain development is complete in terms of the number of neurons), but connectedness in the brain increases hugely with correct exposure. Take the opportunity to teach your pup all of his basic commands while he's ripe for learning (see the Basic Commands chapter). This continues to build brain connections, and with that comes an increased ability to learn. Practise as much as you can, so that these commands become second nature to your dog by the time he is older and has more independence. Make sure your recall is bomb-proof by then! This is also a great way to continue to strengthen your bond and have your dog look to you as his mentor. These basic commands are the foundation of your 'shared language'.

Continue establishing separation

As started during the transition period, don't spend every minute with your puppy or she may develop separation anxiety, which is highly stressful and difficult for a dog to deal with — a bit of tough love is required! You need to teach your pup how to gradually separate from you for longer and longer periods, starting with short stints of time away and slowly increasing this. It is fine to leave your puppy in her crate on her own for up to a couple of hours or more at a time so she will develop healthy separation. (See the Separation Distress chapter to see how to do this in an adult dog; it will also provide useful tips on how to do this with your puppy.)

Bite inhibition

Between 2 and 4 months old, biting is a natural behaviour, and occurs at the same time as chewing and destructive behaviour while pups are teething. This is seen naturally in the wild when pups play with each other — they are basically learning how to play and establish dominance order by play-fighting with each other. The adults in the pack teach the pups what is appropriate and what isn't by being

Desensitising 10-week-
old pup as truck goes
by (controlled).

Training starts early
in the Vette family for
all. Nalu and Meeko.

assertive back to the pups (typically by muzzle-grabbing or pinning) when they bite too hard. This is how pups learn bite inhibition.

For a young pup, this behaviour is very unlikely to be aggressively driven: it's just part of his learning to use his mouth and playing. Dogs use their mouth like we use our hands. However, it's essential at this time to clearly teach your puppy that mouthing and biting people is not acceptable: when they get bigger and stronger it is no longer cute or fun, so from the start it's important not to allow painful biting.

At home, we should teach them that it is fine to play and run around as much as they want, but they must not bite. To do this you need to take on the role of their litter-mates or older dogs. The lip roll and jaw pinch are two techniques I use to stop puppies from biting in the formative period, and both replicate the way pups would learn in the wild. These techniques are very simple to do and highly effective — you may start seeing results within the day! Please note that this is only suitable for puppies aged 2–4 months old; older dogs that are biting need a different approach (see aggression chapters).

The lip roll technique

When the pup approaches to mouth, bite or nip, you simply let your hand be enclosed by her jaw then roll her lip onto her teeth and press down slightly as she bites, until she pulls away. She is effectively biting herself, so experiencing what it feels like to be bitten, and so will stop.

The jaw pinch technique

For this technique, again let the pup approach to mouth or bite you. When he does, press your thumb on top of the puppy's tongue into the 'V' at the bottom of his mouth and pinch down against your forefinger on the underside of the jaw, again until he pulls away. It is not harmful to the pup.

You need to do this every time your pup tries to nip you, and use a firm 'no' command. It has to be effective: not too much and not too little. Some pups get testy at this, so you need to be quick and effective — be tentative and they'll beat you at the game. After a few successes, the 'no' alone should be effective (the pup will have learnt the association). Click and reward your pup when he stops biting.

Consistency is everything. It is important that you never encourage

Lip roll.

Jaw pinch.

biting of a person when you are playing with your pup (toys are fine!), and consistently respond to any inappropriate biting with one of these techniques. Doing it only a few times will not solve the problem. Keep going until your puppy learns and stops. Redirect his pulling and rough play onto toys if possible. Take care not to over-arouse him, though!

By doing this, you will teach your puppy quickly that biting people is not okay — a very important lesson to learn early in life.

Destructive behaviour

Puppies are teething during this 2-4 months old period, so during this time, they show a lot more interest in chewing, biting and mouthing. This is natural and expected in all puppies, but some are more inclined than others. They are learning to use the nose and sense of taste, along with how to use the mouth. They are also learning what they can and cannot eat or play with, so this is where we need to give them a bit of a nudge in the right direction.

The first thing we do around this age of teething is make sure our puppy has access to appropriate toys that she can play with and chew when she desires. However, it is very important that these toys do not resemble anything that is commonly found in the house: old shoes are a prime example of a bad chew toy, because once your dog realises she can chew shoes, you will have a hard time stopping her.

Select toys like rubber Kong toys, a rope or tennis balls, etc. We don't recommend soft teddy bears, blankets or pillows, as these will encourage puppies to chew cushions, couches and bedding. Don't leave your shoes, slippers or clothes around on the ground in the first few months of your pup's life, to remove temptations while she's young (everyone needs a helping hand!). See the chapter on Destructive Behaviour for more details.

Reward only the good — and be consistent!

Recognise when you are rewarding undesirable behaviour. If you pat or pick up your puppy when he's whining, you are rewarding that whining and building that habit for life. Same goes if you pat your puppy or speak to him in friendly tones when he jumps all over you: this tells your pup that you like that behaviour, so of course it continues!

The key to having a well-behaved dog for life is consistency from the beginning, and remembering not to unwittingly reward behaviour that you don't want to encourage. I know, the biggest challenge is that puppies are beyond cute, and at an age that they are likely to get away with almost anything! However, resist the urge — spoil them with lots of play and cuddles, but keep those boundaries clear.

Set boundaries

Don't allow your puppy to do anything you wouldn't let an adult dog do, such as jumping on the couch or sleeping on the bed (if you don't want them to), jumping on you or play-biting. Be consistent: it will be hard to change these behaviours once they're established, so nip them in the bud now.

Most family rules are conventions for your convenience and pleasure, so create the family rules together, write them down and ensure that all family members are consistent. Consistency is critical for a pup; it only takes one instance to undo all your good work. However, establish boundaries well in these two months and they will be rock-solid.

Sensitivity to correction

Pups are sensitive to correction, so be careful at this stage when setting boundaries and teaching the 'no' command. Use the 'no', but generally don't use a correction yet (except in bite inhibition, as it is required in this situation). The bite inhibition is a useful way to begin the 'No'. Generally, you use positive reinforcers like the clicker to shape desirable behaviours at this stage (e.g. click and reward four feet on the ground, instead of correcting the jumping up). Time-out in the crate can be used when pups need to be settled, but ensure they retain a positive association with it. It is good to redirect inappropriate behaviours onto play, otherwise at this stage ignore problematic behaviours or shape alternatives. You can use a remote correction with the half-slip (apparent natural consequence) for any major issues, but don't use the 'no' command so the check isn't associated with you. If you do, ensure that it is just effective, no more — be gentle. This technique might be particularly useful when you are desensitising to other species, like chickens. Make it appear like the chicken is biting back and winning.

A note on play

Play is prevalent in puppyhood, and another side-effect of the juvenil-isation effect of domestication. Play is said to facilitate the rehearsing

Click and reward pups with four feet on the ground, rather than correcting them when jumping up.

of truncated or cut-up parts of mature sequences of behaviour. This rehearsing grows brain connections, plasticity and learning, making dogs more intelligent with regard to living harmoniously with humans.

Play is an important opportunity for puppies to grow their brains and rehearse and practise behaviours for later in life. It is critical for complete balanced development, so make sure they get lots of play, both with you and with other dogs. It's also a great way for puppies to get lots of love and cuddles to strengthen their bond with you.

Hide-and-seek is a great game to play with your pup, to help him develop his orientation to and focus on you. Hide somewhere easy in a contained safe place (with no cars around) and click and reward your puppy when he finds you. Remember he is a pup, so make it easy on him!

Summary

O Social orientation — on the pack and the mentor (that's you), and independent of Mum.
O Major physical developments — second teeth, 60 per cent of adult size, brain connections increase 70 per cent.
O Learning focus and capability — sensitive to punishment, distractible, concentration span is short.
O Developmental behaviour step — formative period, cross-fostering, attachment, bite inhibition, separation from Mum, dominance hierarchy, play and cascading.
O Training focus — socialisation experiences, continue to strengthen your bond, basic commands, set boundaries, continue establishing separation, house training, bite inhibition, destructive behaviour, learn to learn, reward only the good and be consistent!

10.4 PRIMARY SCHOOL (JUVENILE PERIOD): PUP 4–6 MONTHS OLD (HUMAN 6–10 YEARS)

At this point, your puppy will be out of her vaccination period and will be fully out in the world. She begins to become independent, but is still very naïve and reliant on her family and mentor for guidance on how to live in the big, human world (which can be counter-intuitive to some of her natural instincts).

Continue to give your puppy lots of novel and new experiences. and socialisation with plenty of people, other species and dogs. Really consolidate socialisation as vaccinations are completed.

Continue your Joining Up training and start contrast training. Use natural consequences or apparent natural consequences so that you don't get associated with corrections (see Contrast Training in the Dog Zen Toolkit chapter). Do it sparingly, though: at this age we are shaping behaviour rather than correcting it, so there is much less need for checks and other corrections. We are mainly using the contrast of pressure on and pressure off to teach pups resistance and Joining Up. There is an emphasis on positive reinforcement.

As her independence builds, your pup will start to get very outward focused and may start running off, so work on your recall. Your pup will be easily distracted, so it's important to be patient with training sessions!

Summary

O Social orientation — outward focus, still mentor and family but distractible.
O Major physical developments — 70 per cent of adult size
O Learning focus and capability — distractible, particularly due to environment.
O Developmental behaviour step — investigating outside of territory, outer social relations.
O Training focus — socialisation, boundaries, recall, basic commands, contrast, maintain bond.

10.5 HIGH SCHOOL (PUBERTY): PUP 6–18 MONTHS OLD (HUMAN 10–20 YEARS)

Think hormones, hormones, hormones.

This is the time when our dogs go through puberty. Sex and dominance order can become their primary focus, but de-sexing can help this. I recommend de-sexing males by 6 months, before they start leg-raising and dominance issues appear: it's best not to let this start; also, the later you leave it, the bigger the operation. I recommend that bitches go through their first cycle, to allow them to become feminised (enhances their maturity more quickly) at 6 months, and de-sex after their first heat. In high-density dog living, sexual drivers often cause problems and stress, so unless you're breeding, it's easier on the dog and you to de-sex; as a general rule, de-sexed dogs are much easier to manage.

Start your pup early with the right toys.

Right toys and play (food-packed Kong toy).

If you keep your dog entire, be aware of some of the issues that might result. In males, for example, you might experience more marking, possible dominance and fighting, roaming and hypersexual behaviour, including mounting people and dogs. In females, you might experience heightened aggression toward other females when in estrous (heat) and toward people sometimes.

Between 12 and 18 months is the optimum time to finish off basic training for dogs, so that they grow into stable, well-rounded adults. Keep up your strong bond work with lots of Joining Up. Think of human teenagers aged 16-20 years old: they know how life goes and what to do, but are still learning their roles and place in the world. Dogs are the same: they will already know most behaviours and will now have some independence, but it's still good to give them guidance as they mature and keep them well bonded to you. They will possibly start to challenge the position of older dogs they are interacting with, and in difficult cases dominance aggression can develop. Their territorial imperative also grows through this time, so being broadly socialised helps. By 18-24 months some dogs will certainly be challenging (most likely males — particularly entire and more dominant males, especially in the bigger guard and powerful breeds e.g. German Shepherds, Rottweilers, Dobermans, etc).

It's good to continue to focus on recall at this stage, because if males are entire they start competing for bitches. Entire dogs are likely to be trying to roam, and will possibly fight more and become more dominant. A strong bond and good recall are critical to ensure they continue to look to you for guidance and de-sexing helps.

Summary

O Social orientation — pack, opposite sex, older competitors can be challenged.
O Major physical developments — secondary sexual characteristics developing, hormone levels rising, full adult size by 2-2.5 years (larger breeds)
O Learning focus and capability — trainability moderate to high, distracted by sexual hormones and territorial desires.
O Developmental behaviour step — sniffing, marking, opposite sex, mounting, mating.
O Training focus — firm up bond and basic commands, recall and sophisticated advanced training.

10.6 UNIVERSITY (SUB-ADULT DOG): 18–24 MONTHS OLD (HUMAN 20–24 YEARS)

Territory is more important now that dogs might be involved in guarding and protecting, as they are sub-adult and starting to take more responsibility in the pack. Recall can be a bit more challenging. Issues of dominance might start arising here, particularly in the bigger guard breeds like Rottweilers, pit fighters, big Terriers and Spitz types. Good generalised socialisation will help, as will a strong bond with the mentor who is keeping control of resources. Your dogs are at their prime at this time, so are eager to learn, fit, physically at their peak, and raring to go. This is when human athletes are at their peak in many sports, too!

Summary

- Social orientation — family and external stimuli, territory, family dynamics.
- Major physical developments — adult size at end of period.
- Learning focus and capability — trainability high, though previously learnt behaviours have influence (make sure they are good!), may challenge mentor a little at this stage.
- Developmental behaviour step — dominance, protection, sex if entire, family stabilising, taking more responsibility now.
- Training focus — good time to really advance training.

10.7 ADULT AND BEYOND: 25 MONTHS ON (HUMAN 25 YEARS PLUS)

By now you should have all the basics established for a mature, stable dog who is well connected and bonded to you. You know this if your dog is focused on you and keeps close, but is relaxed. Commands and shared language are now more of a conversation, and routines and rituals are established. Your dog has mature sensibilities and is able to read you and vice versa. The bond starts to synchronise and flourish.

If there are going to be dominance aggression issues toward family members and or other dogs they often start from 18 months onward, particularly for entire males and more-dominant breeds.

It is hoped that you and your dog have an outlet or purpose together — that is, something to stretch them and keep them learning (just like us!). This might be obedience, agility or some form of advanced training. Many of my dogs are film dogs: after a day on set, you can see that they have had a full day and look contented and happy.

A dog is always changing and learning, so it is important to keep reinforcing training with regular sessions, especially Joining Up and basic commands. This is also a good way to keep the bond strong between you, and keeping you connected and playing. It is great stimulation for your dog too — he will enjoy the time with you, the mental stimulation and of course food rewards.

Summary

- O Social orientation — family, taking responsibility, aware of external stimuli, mating if entire.
- O Major physical developments — generally complete.
- O Learning focus and capability — developed and mature.
- O Developmental behaviour step — stable adult, time to mate if entire, in charge biologically of their dog pack, mature in their decision-making.
- O Training focus — Joining Up, basic commands, continue to play, start consolidating some purposeful activity such as a sport or competition, otherwise ball play and other toys.

10.8 GERIATRIC STAGE

Domestic dogs live on average for about 10-12 years (depending on breed and size), although my dog Jess, a heading dog, lived until 22 years of age — that was exceptional! Here are some averages below:

- O small to medium dog: 10-14 years (human estimate 64-84 years old)
- O large dog: 9-12 years (human estimate 66-84 years)
- O extra-large dog: 7-10 years (human estimate 66-87 years).

By the time dogs are in the geriatric age class, they may be suffering similar health issues to humans, or they may be as fit as a fiddle. However, dementia and other ageing issues can come on pretty rapidly after about 10 years, though this can be younger in the bigger breeds. Behavioural issues can start to appear, as well as the onset of deafness and blindness and other sensory deterioration or organ failure and disease. It's a sad thing dogs don't live as long as us, but the joy is they live life to the fullest.

In conclusion

If you are getting a new puppy, I'm so glad you're reading this section. You have an opportunity to do the right things so that you have a wonderful friend for life: one who is attuned to you, has a great personality and isn't troubled by behaviour issues. Put in the work during this time and you will have an incredibly rewarding and happy life with your dog. This is true Dog Zen: doing things at the right time.

Of course, just like us, dogs can experience trauma at any time of their lives, which can disrupt their development and stability. This could be an attack by another dog, animal or person; an intruder entering the house; the owner suffering a trauma (injury or sickness); getting lost or left somewhere; or suffering a severe fright (such as a bad thunderstorm, close gunfire or being hit by a car). A dog with a powerful bond will deal with these traumas more easily, as he will have established coping mechanisms and resilience and look to you at the right time for help.

However, I see a lot of clients in my clinic who through no fault of their own, are dealing with the difficult results of traumatic incidents with their beloved dogs. Just like it would be with any member of our family, this is very distressing and I find it incredibly sad to see the difficulties some families and dogs end up in.

Just like us, trauma in dogs can be healed with time, love and commitment. Part D explores how we can address some of the most common behaviour issues I have seen in my clinic over the past 40 years. Whether the issues are caused by trauma or mal-socialisation, we look at how we can help our beloved dogs heal. If you have managed to build the Dog Zen shared language and that special bond, it will set you up to solve problems more easily. Follow my webinars for other problems, too.

Some problems are severe and require an expert behaviourist with the right tools and techniques to resolve the serious issues by consulting in-clinic help.

PART D

Old Dogs New Tricks

11

Getting started

Part D is for all of you out there struggling with unwanted behaviours in your dog. It can be very distressing, with enormous impacts on your life and relationships. This section will help you understand the issues you are facing and build a training programme to help you resolve them. It is also supported by our companion online programme dogzen.com — 30-plus step-by-step video guides that support the instructions below, as well as webinars dealing with other issues. We also have a Dog Zen online community and Facebook page to support you.

Behavioural issues occur when dogs develop inappropriate coping behaviours when they haven't developed or been taught appropriate behaviours at the right time. Most problems develop due to lack of

Mark in consultation
and training for
separation distress.

socialisation and habituation in the formative period, or through traumas, although some physiological origins can be a cause as well. When we treat behaviour issues we often need to modify (change) old, inappropriate behaviours and create new behaviours. Using a balance of positive reinforcement and contrast training is critical to ensure that your dog understands what is wanted *and* what is not wanted to make the change you need. Creating a strong bond and a healthy shared language provides sound foundations for solving problems.

To help resolve problem behaviours we'll first look at understanding the issues you are dealing with and your role in them. It takes two to tango! We'll then recap the critical training foundations needed to ensure success, and finally go through the therapy for the top 10 common problems I have seen in my clinic over the past 40 years.

Some other clinical animal psychology techniques, as well as coordination with your veterinary advisor, may also be advised, especially if drug or surgical support is required. I often act as a referral specialist to veterinary practitioners. Our approach is multidisciplinary, as all modern behaviour treatment should be: we are treating the whole dog.

Understanding the issues

You need to think of yourself as an animal behaviour therapist and imagine that you and your dog have just stepped into your clinic. Instead of me analysing the situation, let me help you (maybe with the aid of a family member or friend) go through the questions I would ask. We need a diagnosis, therapy plan and ideally a prognosis.

It's important you understand what both your dog and yourself (as your dog's mentor) are doing in the situation. Here are some questions to help you do this:

O What are the most important/urgent problems you are facing? Make a list of a maximum of five, and make sure you focus on one issue at a time when training or enacting therapy.

O What behaviours is your dog presenting around these problems? Write a list of your dog's problem behaviours (note 'behaviour', not your interpretation of your dog's emotions) that are worrying you (e.g. lunging forward, snapping at dogs, rushing up to dogs, pulling on the lead, pupils dilated, shaking, hiding behind you, excessive jumping up, running away). There is an example of a training diary at the end of chapter 23. It is most effective when diagnostic information is included. You will find it interesting when reviewing your progress.

O What are you doing about the issues? Describe the issues on paper if possible. Are you tense on the lead, pulling your dog back, not engaged at all? Are you avoiding situations? Are you convinced nothing is wrong, but your pesky family keeps suggesting there is an issue?

O How do you feel about this? Describe your feelings on paper. Are you anxious, wary, frightened, calm? This will help you recognise your role in the issue.

It's important that you (or a friend) describes the reality of the situation as honestly as possible. By understanding what is happening, you can determine its underlying causes and start resolving the issues. Observe and watch both your dog and yourself.

A lot of behavioural issues are self-evident (e.g. dog-to-dog aggression, barking or recall problems). However, you might be less familiar with others, like noise phobia, hyperactivity and separation anxiety. For these ones, read the following chapters to help you understand whether this is what your dog is suffering from.

Setting good training foundations

This is where doing your homework and laying the foundations of training are critical — part B is essential in this. You need to ensure that you:

O understand what a learning state is, and how to switch it on and maintain your dog in that state. It is very likely that your dog is not in a learning state when he is exhibiting problem behaviours.

O have built a good bond with your dog, so he is looking to you for direction (do lots of Joining Up).

O understand your dog. Can you read your dog? Do you understand how he behaves in the problem situations, understand what triggers him and how he will respond? What are his signals before

he does this behaviour (look at the Shared Language section for help with this)?
O have built a shared language through your basic commands.
O practise the key techniques, particularly the clicker, safety slip collar and leads, clip station, Joining Up and contrast training.
O follow the essential rules of training to build a simple, calm learning environment (see the Dog Zen Toolkit chapter).

Make sure you start each training session with Joining Up and basic commands in a simple, calm environment to 'warm up' you and your dog up, get your dog focused and attentive on you, and as always build your bond. In essence, you are 'taking your adult dog back to the den': re-creating that definitive learning state of the puppy in the formative period to help your dog resolve behavioural issues and re-establish appropriate behaviours. Remember cascading — how things missed in the unfolding flow of pup developmental behaviours destabilise their foundations when missed.

It might seem a lot for you to learn, but build it up over time and it will soon become second nature to you and your dog. Your dog will also find the routine that it creates a useful settling experience that he learns to trust as well. All of it will continue to build and strengthen your bond.

So let's begin. Take a deep breath, start at the beginning and slowly take one step at a time. Don't rush ahead with the outcome in mind, but just enjoy each moment. You'll be surprised how much you can achieve with consistent, diligent work and your own mindfulness. Remember: observe, watch and respond to both yourself and your dog. The rewards will be worth it for both of you. If you have an experienced handler or friend to support you, then definitely link up with them for training support. Also remember that this knowledge will guide you for a lifetime of dog companions.

Hyperactivity

Of all the dog behaviour issues I've come across in my time, there's none that causes quite so much internal conflict as hyperactivity. While a problem such as aggression is cut-and-dried undesirable behaviour we wish to quash immediately, with hyperactivity the line can become blurred. It can be very difficult to admonish your dog for over-excitable, exuberant behaviour — especially when he's greeting you!

But when you find yourself wearied by your dog's constant rampages, embarrassed by the way he jumps all over everything and everybody and are unsure how to deal with his excessive temperament, then I'm sure you'd like to know how to help your dog behave appropriately and relax.

'Hi! I can fly . . . bye!'
And this is just a hello.

CHARLIE: TOO MUCH BOUNCE AND NO REBOUND

Charlie is a black-and-white Springer Spaniel–Border Collie cross — a real beauty. So it was surprising to learn that he'd already been moved on from five homes, and was about to be put down. He was extremely hyperactive and aggressive to other dogs, and predatory. At 15 months old, Charlie was well into puberty, but hadn't gained any behavioural maturity with age. He was such a beautiful dog, it was hard to imagine what had gone so wrong for him.

Charlie would jump and scramble all over anyone who tried to greet him. When we put him on a lead, he lunged away from us with such force he was choking himself. If you removed his lead, he would run away immediately, with no intention of coming back. Water was his focus — a real spaniel drive! He'd spend what seemed like hours doing laps, trying to attack the water, splashing, yapping and making the most unbelievable racket. He showed no signs of tiring by the time I managed to get him out of the muddied water of my pond, not to mention my shredded lilies!

Charlie was simply unable to be still: he had no off switch. He was wriggling constantly, and couldn't even enjoy a treat and a pat in peace! With his fanatical disposition it was unlikely that Charlie was going to find a good home, despite the shelter's best efforts.

Charlie also didn't have much experience in meeting and socialising with other dogs, so he had no idea how to conduct himself with them. His stereotypic behaviours suggested a life led in institutions, having to look after himself with other maladjusted dogs, which I suspect had led to his mal-socialisation. It was very sad to see.

What is hyperactivity?

At its most basic definition, to be hyperactive is to be excessively active. With dogs, it can range from simply behaving with exuberance to showing constantly active, disruptive or frenzied behaviour. The actual clinical syndrome of hyperactivity — hyperkinesis — is quite rare in dogs, so for the purposes of this book when I refer to 'hyperactivity', I mean the behavioural version rather than medical condition. If you are concerned that your dog might have hyperkinesis, I suggest consulting a veterinarian as there are treatments that can help.

Hyperactivity is one of the most common behaviour issues I see in dogs. While it is a behaviour of degrees, I consider a dog to be hyperactive when it is exhibiting some of the following behaviours:

O pulling on the lead excessively, where checking or pulling back does nothing to interrupt the behaviour

O rushing up to other dogs and people

O jumping up on people

O seeming to be unable to sit still

O being over-excitable

O difficult to control and hard to train

O barking or yelping excessively

O constantly engaging in attention-seeking behaviours

O being destructive

O running in circles

O behaving obsessively.

If this sounds like your dog, you've come to the right place!

Why does hyperactivity occur?

Hyperactivity comes about as a result of a dog's natural play and soliciting behaviours, which evolved in ancestral wolves as an expression of each animal's desire to interact physically with its pack. The wolf's playful physical interactions and affiliative group behaviours stimulate the release of the bonding hormones oxytocin, vasopressin, serotonin and dopamine. These shape and reward amicable behaviours, and help build love, trust, co-operation and loyalty within the pack. Excessive behaviour is not tolerated by older dogs or wolves, so would have been nipped in the bud very quickly by muzzle-grabbing and standing over. Ancestral pariah or village dogs also show a high level of play and affiliative behaviours.

However, as humans and dogs have evolved together throughout the ages, the juvenilisation of the dog has increased the frequency of play compared with wolves. Both this and selective breeding for neotony (puppy-like traits) has increased the predisposition to hyperactivity.

This has meant that a dog's natural and healthy play and soliciting behaviours can at times go overboard. Also, our love for dogs can result in us unintentionally rewarding them for their hyperactive tendencies, and so exacerbating these.

An obvious sign of hyperactivity is when your dog jumps all over you as you enter the house. Wolf pups greet pack members coming back from a hunt in this way, by pawing, jumping up and licking their jowls to stimulate the elder to regurgitate its food. Wolves also show similar behaviour preceding the hunt: it gets them excited and encourages co-operation. These behaviours serve a useful purpose — they prevent pups from being forgotten after a hunt and left to starve, and helps bond the pack together. Later, proto-dogs and pariah dogs redirected this behaviour toward humans. However, without the natural ability to correct this behaviour as wolves and wild dogs do, it can get out of hand.

Hyperactive dogs show the same excited behaviours when they are going out (e.g. for a walk) or greeting you when you return home. If you were on all fours like a dog, your dog would be licking your jowls, but as your mouth is up high, your dog has to jump on you to try to get to them.

Those are the natural origins and purpose of your excitable pup's welcome; now let's go through some of the factors that influence why hyperactivity continues to occur in dogs that live with us in our human world and how we can make it worse.

Rewarding hyperactivity

We often accidentally reward and encourage hyperactive behaviours on a daily basis. Some ways you may be doing this are:

O by talking to or handling your dog when it behaves hyperactively

O by over-stimulating your dog when you come home with your own excitement at seeing her

O by giving your dog the outcome she desires when she's acting hyperactively, such as letting her out the door or off-lead (a natural reinforcer)

O by turning hyperactive tendencies into a game (if you want to play games with your hyperactive dog, make sure it is a clearly defined activity, so give the beginning and end of play a clear signal, and a dedicated toy that denotes that this is 'play').

A research wolf jumping up to jowl lick and test me a little... Notice my eyes 'off' and I'm relaxed.

Charlie day one, airborne as usual.

For example, if you lavish your dog with attention when you arrive home at the end of the day even if he has been jumping on you, you are giving him a highly positive reward for hyperactive behaviour. Or, if your dog pulls boisterously on the lead and you let him off, then you have rewarded the pulling, and the behaviour will continue.

Hyperactivity is a soliciting and affiliative behaviour: your dog is trying to solicit a reward from you, whether that be some of your attention, hearing your voice, feeling your touch, getting a treat or being let off a lead. We want to shape and reward calm, loving and affiliative behaviours, not high-energy hyperactive ones.

Contributing factors

LEARNING STATE (OR LACK THEREOF)
When dogs are in hyper-arousal, they are physiologically in a non-learning state and are unable to learn, so any attempts to modify their undesirable behaviour may be falling short. To train dogs out of hyperactive behaviour, we need to first switch them into a learning state.

STIMULATING ENVIRONMENT
Dogs' hyperactive tendencies can be exacerbated by an excessively stimulating environment. For example, highly active and playful children can increase a dog's level of hyperactivity.

BREED AND GENETICS
Some dogs are more genetically predisposed to hyperactivity, due to being selected by humans for high-arousal activities such as hunting and herding. Understanding the make-up (original purpose) of your dog's breed will help you understand why they are hyperactive, and how we can modify these issues.

CHARLIE
Charlie, for example, is a Springer Spaniel-Border Collie cross, both working breeds that were selectively bred for high levels of work and energy. The Border Collie is traditionally a heading or gathering dog that might run 100 kilometres per day on a farm, while the Springer

Spaniel is a bird dog and similarly runs and hunts all day in a traditional context. This makes Charlie predisposed to over-activity, and when he doesn't have an outlet for his high energy, it's not surprising we see undesirable hyperactive behaviours. Both breeds are sociable by nature, which accounts for the soliciting behaviours, such as jumping up, that Charlie is prone to, and they're also both highly distracted and influenced by fast-moving stimuli, such as stock, vehicles, birds or kids. All these behaviours could have been modified or redirected in the formative period.

Treating hyperactivity

Hyperactivity is normally quite treatable and is, if anything, an indication that your dog is *too* friendly. However, some hyperactive dogs can also be aggressive. Careful training and understanding can resolve most issues associated with hyperactivity, and as this is primarily a juvenile issue in the wild, maturity often helps, too.

EXERCISE AND STIMULATION
Make sure your dog is getting an appropriate level of exercise, play and mental stimulation. Understanding which breeds are combining to contribute to your dog's genetics will help you make generalisations about how much exercise and stimulation he'll need, but as a general rule most dogs require at least 30–60 minutes of exercise and play per day (dogs like Charlie will need at least two sessions). Your dog should have slowed down and be content to relax once you've returned home after some exercise.

Try to give your dog a combination of aerobic exercise and exercise that is mentally and physically stimulating: chasing a ball, exploring a walking trail with new scents, engaging in a game, etc.

CHARLIE
Charlie loves water, and instinctively has a high hunting drive, so we took him for lots of swims and taught him how to play 'fetch' to satisfy his prey drive. Agility and other competitive activities can be great for

high-energy dogs, too. Charlie went on to be a film dog as well, so he has a repertoire of behaviours he can rehearse and undertake.

There is a fine line between excitable play and hyperactivity: watch that you don't cross that line. You need to be in control of any play activity and be able to turn it off when desired. If you can't, it has crossed over to hyperactivity and you will be rewarding the wrong behaviours.

It helps to have a ready supply of toys you can leave with your dog for entertainment when you're not home: a rubber toy stuffed with dog roll works well, as the delicious-smelling food inside holds the dog's attention and keeps him entertained for hours! Take care if you have left multiple dogs with toys when you are not home.

Training techniques

1. SWITCH YOUR DOG INTO A LEARNING STATE

Many hyperactive dogs are prone to distraction and constantly revert to an overly aroused non-learning state, with no capacity for effective training. Therefore, to calm a dog with hyperactivity, it's critical to get him into a learning state so he's focused on you and training.

To do this, set your dog up on a clip station and arm yourself with a clicker and a pouch filled with high-value food treats. Set up three or four clip stations around your place so that you have a variety of calm places for your dog. A clip station can be used as a place for time-out for your dog where he can settle and relax.

Once you are ready, begin by rewarding quiet and calm behaviour, as well as your dog having four feet on the ground. Never reward pawing, jumping up or vocalising. Remember that a reward includes any touching of your dog or speaking to him, and eye contact as well as traditional pats and food treats.

I normally start by delivering food rewards to the ground and try to work up to 'down', 'wait' and 'on your mat' commands that encourage quiet responses. You don't want your dog to go get the food reward and break his calm behaviour, so ensure food is delivered within easy reach. Deliver food rewards to the ground initially, as you want your dog to stay down and your food reward reinforces that. As your dog gets more consistent with four feet on the ground, you can start delivering the food reward from your hand, so your dog can learn to bring his attention to you while at the same time having four feet on the ground (learning he doesn't need to jump up to get your attention). If you find rewarding from your hand has started your dog jumping up again, then go back to delivering on the ground until the behaviour is better established.

Click and reward for calm behaviours. Once your dog is settled, the final reward is being released calmly onto a lead and doing some Joining Up. When your dog is settled, you can release him.

Examples

- If your dog is jumping up, when all four paws come back down to the ground, immediately click and reward as they hit the ground. Deliver the reward to the ground in front of the dog. Do this every time your dog's paws return to the ground. This teaches your dog it's good to have her feet down, which discourages jumping up. You can reward other calm behaviours on the ground, too.
- Click and reward your dog whenever she's not barking, jumping on or pawing you.
- Repeat this clicking and rewarding as often as desirable behaviour is present. You can't do it too often! Spread it through the day, with time-out on the clip station, too.

If you cannot get your dog to settle at the clip station, you may find it easier to start with a moving on-lead Joining Up. The same training techniques and principles apply: you will still click and reward for four feet on the ground and no vocalising — it's just that you'll be moving rather than stationary. Some people find their dogs respond to this more easily at first.

Once your dog is focusing on the food lures and responding to the clicker, she will quickly go into a learning state. (Watch for the signs: pupils shrinking down, calm demeanour, more calmly taking treats.)

2. TEACH THE CALMING COMMANDS

Next teach commands that will help establish ongoing calm behaviour: 'sit', 'down' and 'Zen down'. The Zen down is particularly great for pacifying a hyperactive dog, as it relaxes the dorsal muscles, switches on the vagus nerve and induces a state of calm. This training should be done while your dog remains on the clip station; you can find a breakdown of the steps involved in the Basic Commands chapter.

Once you've mastered all three commands, go through them during your training session. When your dog has held Zen down for a while, throw a food reward elsewhere so that he stands back up to reach it, then go back through 'sit', 'down' and 'Zen down' again. With each rotation, see if you can keep your dog in 'Zen down' for a little longer by continuing to click and throw treats between your dog's legs.

Each training session shouldn't last longer than 10–15 minutes, so that you're able to hold your dog's focus for the entire duration. To get the best results, have two or three training sessions like this every day, in the initial stages.

3. ON-LEAD JOINING UP

This training technique helps attune your dog's focus to you, establishing you as a mentor and encouraging your dog to look to you for direction and guidance. It's a great tool for a hyperactive dog, as it means you'll have control in situations that might usually lead to your dog getting over-excited and behaving inappropriately.

Refer to the Joining Up chapter to practise this technique with your dog. If your dog tries to jump up or paw at you during the session, give an 'off' command, and click and reward four feet on the ground. Keep moving; you do not want to stop and let your dog jump all over you. If he persists, give him a 'no' command. Click and reward four feet on the ground. If he persists, use your 'no' and an effective check, click and rewarding him for staying on the ground once he complies.

During these training sessions, continue to practise 'sit', 'down' and 'Zen down' at regular intervals. Be clear that no jumping up and pawing is allowed in the session. Try to finish with success. Do not finish a session with jumping up for reward and praise; finish with a calm sit.

Hyperactive dogs are prone to distraction, so once your dog has settled a bit, place a food lure in your hand and put it up to your eye-level to get your dog looking in your direction at intervals as well. You are trying to get contact with your dog without getting him too hyperactive. Intermittent periods of play with a ball or toy are great, but finish them with calm behaviour.

Teach good disciplines. Don't let your dog push ahead first.

Ask for a 'sit' and click and reward.

4. THE UMBILICAL PHASE

The umbilical technique is very powerful for a hyperactive dog, as your dog needs to learn to be in your personal space calmly and follow you as you go about your daily life. Refer to the Joining Up section for information on how to execute this technique.

Whenever you stop moving with your dog on the umbilical, ask for a sit and reward your dog for stopping when you stop. If you stay in one place for a time, go through your 'sit', 'down' and 'Zen down' commands, concentrating on a 'Zen down'. We want this to become an automatic response whenever you stop. Be conscious if you have any physical limitations that your dog doesn't knock you over or pull you over: a risk with a hyperactive dog.

5. TEACH DISCRIMINATION — THE 'LEAVE IT' COMMAND

Teaching the 'leave it' command is a good way to teach your dog to discriminate between appropriate behaviour and inappropriate behaviour, which is whatever we deem it to be. We want our dogs to know when we allow something, and when we don't allow something, as this gives us the ability to direct our dogs to understand conventions in the human world. This is especially important for hyperactive dogs, which are more likely to go off on their own tangents with little regard for what their human is saying! For example, if your hyperactive dog is about to rush off and jump all over another dog, you can use the 'leave it' command to tell your dog that it's not okay to do that, then recall her and put her on the lead for the meet and greet (dog handshake). Learn how to teach 'leave it' in the Basic Commands chapter.

6. DEVELOP GOOD DISCIPLINES

These are the basics you should remember and carry with you as you interact with your dog throughout the day — it's these that will ensure your training sessions are effective, and remain effective!

Teach 'settle'

Once you feel confident that your dog has a better idea of what appropriate behaviour is, work in a 'settle' command so you can cue your dog to calm down when he's starting to get hyped-up. I tell dogs to 'settle' in a neutral tone when they're starting to get hyperactive, then click and reward them for becoming more still. If they persist, use a 'no' command, and click and reward appropriate responses. If needed, on the second 'no', check effectively. I do this regularly, and it's something I keep up after I no longer have the need for so many formal training sessions.

Set good boundaries

Hyperactive dogs tend to have no boundaries whatsoever, so ensure you set some. For example, you may decide your dog is not allowed into your bedroom or on the couch. At a minimum you should certainly decide that your dog is not allowed to jump on people. It's important to get everyone in your household to agree on what the boundaries are, so that you're consistent and not causing confusion for your dog.

Learning boundaries and that 'no' means 'no' are critical, so continue to practise this with your dog after you've done the discrimination training and your dog has learnt that 'no' carries a consequence (taught with the safety slip and the contrast of pressure on/pressure off). You can, however, do most of the training using the clicker and reinforcing appropriate learning state first, and then appropriate behaviour.

Encourage good meet and greets

If your dog is hyperactive, it's likely she rushes up and jumps all over people and other dogs. To prevent this, encourage good meet and greets. This is covered earlier in the book (see video too), so I won't go into detail here; however, the main things to remember are:

o when meeting another dog, encourage your dog to calmly sniff the inguinal area of the other dog (the dog handshake), and click and reward the 'nicely' greeting. Pinch between her toes if she jumps up.

o ask your dog to sit before she receives any pats or attention from people; click and reward your dog for having four feet on the ground when around people.

o never pat, give eye contact or give attention to your dog when she is jumping up on you, and ask other people who interact with your dog to do the same.

Nothing in life is free

As part of setting boundaries, your dog needs to know that, as his mentor, you are in charge of resources. You need to control everything your dog perceives as a reward during the training phase: freedom, food, social contact, treats, pats, going through a door, being let out or let off the lead, etc. Rewards should be given for good behaviour, but never for undesirable behaviour.

Remember that having free access to you and the home is also a reward. When I am treating hyperactivity, I restrict the dog's access to me so that he is only allowed to be with me when calm (even outside of a formal training session). One way to do this is to have a crate or clip station set up in the house. When your dog is acting calmly, he can be with you (a reward for calm behaviour); when the hyperactive behaviours kicks in, he goes into the crate or clip station. Once settled, after a period he can then be allowed freedom again (a reward) for calm behaviours. Release with the clicker in a controlled fashion.

Practise good recall

Classically, hyperactive dogs don't have good recall, as they tend to be outwardly focused and easily distracted. Make sure you emphasise a good recall in your training, to help alleviate issues that come when your dog won't return to you on command. You'll find details on this training in the Recall chapter.

Finish training sessions well

Learning is mentally consuming, and hyperactive dogs tend to have short concentration spans and so get distracted easily. I always end every sequence of behaviours with a 'Zen down', which allows hyperactive dogs to regain calmness. When I finish a session, I use a play retrieve (throwing a toy for the dog, then calling her back) to let the dog release any energy she has pent up after a controlled training session, then again finish on a 'Zen down'. Praise your dog at the end of a session, but keep it low-key so as not to over-arouse her.

Some particularly difficult dogs can benefit from homeopathic or allopathic medications that have a calming effect on the sympathetic nervous system. Rescue Remedy can relax a dog, but more-difficult cases can be supported by other medications, so check with your veterinarian. Charlie got through without anything and most can, but medication is an option.

There are a number of toys and training aids that give dogs mental and physical outlets, such as manners minder, ball-throwing toys etc. It's important to give your dog an outlet and a purpose.

Conclusion

I don't want you to feel overwhelmed if you've just finished reading through this and it seems like a lot of hard work: it's important to just take it one step at a time, and as you cross each hurdle you'll find the next step seems more achievable. Start by making sure you stop rewarding hyperactive behaviours, then you can move into proactive training from there. Start your dog on the clicker quickly. I want to assure you that if you apply these training principles consistently, you'll see amazing results.

CHARLIE: STIMULATED, CHILLED AND MOTIVATED

Remember Charlie from the beginning of the chapter? These are the very same techniques we used to train him after we took him home. We focused on building a bond with Charlie, as well as giving him stimulation to burn his energy. We let him swim and taught him to play retrieve to satisfy his natural hunting instincts, as well as going through the training techniques I've given you in this chapter. Now he's the most loving and endearing dog. His energy is redirected into appropriate behaviours, and he is under good control while at the same time having a great sense of fun. We are able to walk him comfortably off-lead, let him roam freely around our other dogs, and have him at ease and resting by our feet in the evenings.

We gave Charlie another purpose as a film dog, so he has learnt lots of behaviours. Going to a mark, speaking on command and much more. He loves it on set, and they love him.

In fact, the story has a particularly happy ending. Charlie has become such a charming dog that my daughter Jaz was unable to part with him. He's now a much-loved part of her family, and has learnt to be perfectly calm and gentle with her young daughter, Nalu, who is his buddy. He is the one putting up with *her* excitability now, if anything!

Conquering the
fear of a vacuum
cleaner!

13

Phobias

When my three kids were little and there was a big electrical storm, all three would come bounding down the hallway and jump into bed with us to shelter near the safety of Mum and Dad. They grew out of it eventually, but it's not always the case for our dogs, who can be equally as frightened of loud sounds and unable to escape them. In fact, I think for dogs it must be even more terrifying, because it's hard for us to explain to them what is causing the noise and that they have no reason to be afraid.

This chapter looks at anxieties, fears and phobias in dogs. I use noise as the example, but you can use the same principles I'll take you through to help your dog move past other phobias he may have.

JO: THINGS THAT GO 'BANG' IN THE NIGHT

Such was the case with Jo, a Corgi cross who came to see us at my clinic with a multi-symptomatic set of phobias, including a fear of vacuum cleaners, firecrackers and thunder. Her owners, Julie and Brian, were very stressed and upset about Jo's phobias. She'd chew through doors and jump through windows to try to escape the noise. She would show all the symptoms associated with a phobia: shaking excessively, hyperventilating and at worst even vomiting.

Her problem started when she was three years old on a Guy Fawkes night. The neighbours were having a bonfire and a big party, with lots of fireworks going off very close by. Jo went into a state of extreme distress and chewed a hole in the back door around the cat door to escape. Poor Julie and Brian couldn't find her for four days, and their kids were desperate with worry.

Julie and Brian were trying everything they could think of, but the problem was just getting worse, as is typical of phobias. They found that Jo was not just afraid of fireworks and thunder, but of anything that signalled that one or the other might be coming — heavy rain, lightning, the neighbours having a party or a bonfire, you name it. She was also multi-symptomatic, also over-reacting to other noises, including the vacuum cleaner. It is relatively common with noise phobias that they become multi-symptomatic, so catching them early is important.

What is noise phobia?

Noise phobias are an extreme and excessive reaction to noise stimulus; It's very common — my clinical experience would suggest that 20–30 per cent of dogs suffer from moderate to serious noise phobia.

With this condition, certain noises will put a dog into a phobic state, which may cause them to become distressed, have dilated pupils, start shaking and panting, and stop taking food. In extreme cases, the dog can even defecate, urinate or vomit from fear, and may shake violently and have chattering teeth. Dogs in this state lose all rational awareness, and will make poor decisions, often doing everything they can to escape. These signs — particularly when a usually food-oriented dog won't eat — indicate that your dog is in a strong state of sympathetic arousal: the fearful fight-or-flight state.

Typically, the type of stimuli that cause noise phobia are firecrackers, thunder and gunshots, but dogs can also go into this same state from the sound of motorbikes, vacuum cleaners, lawn mowers or chainsaws, etc. Often your dog will begin to associate the precursors to the noise (such as heavy rain or lightning before thunder hits, or the vacuum cleaner coming out before it is turned on) with the fear, so that they become multi-symptomatic and even these events that precede their actual phobia can trigger their fears.

Dogs that have noise phobia often also have other fear-based issues that inhibit learning, which leads to other problems. Research has shown that around 40 per cent of dogs with noise phobia also experience separation anxiety. I consider these dogs prone to learning state issues, so switching into learning state will help stabilise these dogs.

Why does noise phobia occur?

Wolves are hypersensitive to unexpected noises, and will react very suspiciously towards them. A wolf will react to a loud and unexpected sound with extreme avoidance, going into a state of sympathetic arousal and stress (a non-learning state). This tendency is designed to keep the wolf safe from potentially dangerous situations.

Dogs are normally more robust and confident than wolves, as they inherited smaller adrenals and associated lowered environmental sensitivity, but nevertheless they can still be reactive to very loud noises. Some breeds are more susceptible, such as Pointers, Collies, Golden Retrievers and German Shepherds. Because dogs are confined to our properties, they are unable to escape the noise like a wolf would, which is why it's so important for us to desensitise them and rid them of their fears. If they do escape, it has the opposite effect of keeping them safe, and they can find themselves in dangerous situations, out in public and on busy roads.

As with all things we want our dogs to be comfortable with, it's best if we can expose them to noisy stimuli at a young age, during the 1–4 months formative period, especially if they show an early disposition to such fears. Good gun-dog trainers usually expose their pups to at first mild then increasingly loud gunshot-like noises from 6-8 weeks old. This early graduated exposure is highly effective, and I do the same with all my dogs. Exposing your dog to loud noises carefully and in a gradual way with the clickers too, is very important in preparing your dog for noisy modern life, with fireworks, cars backfiring and gunshots.

However, if you've missed that time, this chapter will help you work through resilience training techniques which help dogs to stay in a calm learning state while they adjust and adapt to the sounds we want them to become comfortable with.

How to treat noise phobia

As well as taking you through the training necessary to treat a general noise phobia, such as that of fireworks or thunder, I'll go through the techniques I would use to help a dog with a more specific fear, using the example of a vacuum-cleaner phobia. You can take the techniques I use to treat this fear and apply it to any item or stimuli that's causing your dog to become phobic — the same treatment approach underpins all phobias and fear-based problems.

1. KEY STEPS BEFORE STARTING

To begin, here are some key steps you should take before we start specifically treating a noise phobia.

Identify noises that scare your dog

Identify the noises that scare your dog, and list them in hierarchical order from least scary to most scary, so that you can create a plan for making your dog less sensitive to all of these stimuli. This is a called a desensitisation hierarchy (see diagram opposite).

Using the techniques given below, start with the least scary noises before working your way up to the most scary. For example, if your dog is scared of a hand-held vacuum but more scared of a big household vacuum and terrified of fireworks, you'll start with the hand-held vacuum cleaner first and work your way up to the fireworks.

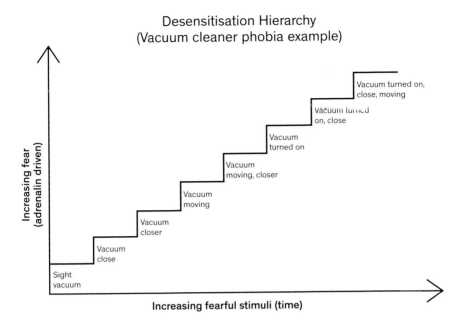

Desensitisation Hierarchy
(Vacuum cleaner phobia example)

Switch your dog into a learning state (counter-conditioning)

This is an essential step, as dogs who are phobic and suffer fear-induced problems are in sympathetic arousal, which inhibits learning. Getting them into a learning state helps them focus and learn. Use the clicker to access the rest and digest state that allows your dog to learn, and particularly focus on the extension of the calming 'Zen down' position. Don't reward soliciting behaviour such as pawing or vocalisations.

Be cautious about the use of the clicker, as the sound of it may make your dog fearful or uncomfortable. You can initially try muffling the sound of the clicker by covering it with some fabric (a thick sock works well). The clicker is a very important tool and must have positive associations, so take it very carefully and keep it muffled until you're sure your dog is comfortable with it. You may need to work with a soft whistle or word marker like 'Yes' if your dog is very sensitive.

Joining Up

Use Joining Up training to build a strong relationship with your dog, so she has confidence in you and looks to you for direction. Research shows that when a bona fide mentor is present, the secure base state is induced, so just your presence (if you follow the protocol outlined here) will help keep your dog in learning state. As you'll be exposing your dog to increasing levels of fear-inducing stimuli in this training, a strong level of trust between you and your dog is critical. This will ensure that your dog feels a sense of safety as you push her to confront her fear boundaries and desensitise her to things that currently frighten her.

Do not practise any corrections during Joining Up training when your dog is in an anxious, phobic state, as this will only make things worse.

2.   TREATING THE PHOBIA THROUGH DESENSITISATION — VACUUM CLEANER

I'll be using the example of a dog that's frightened by a vacuum cleaner for this segment of the chapter. You'll have earlier identified the things that scare your dog in order of increasing trigger points, so start with the item lowest on your list before moving up.

The sight of the vacuum cleaner can be a problem on its own, as it is a precursor to the noise the dog doesn't like. Therefore, the first step is to desensitise the dog to this lowest level of fear-inducing stimulus. Here is the desensitisation hierarchy for a vacuum cleaner: we desensitise the dog to the sight of it first, then to the movement of it, then to the noise of the vacuum from a distance, then closer.

Constantly click and reward your dog throughout for calm responses. This is what we call an exposure technique, and it's based on gradually increasing the dog's exposure to the fear-inducing item one small step at a time.

Joining Up

In another room (away from where the vacuum cleaner is set up), with your dog on a lead with you, start by practising some 'sits', 'downs' and 'Zen downs' to establish contact and focus.

Begin by introducing the stationary vacuum, turned off

Place the vacuum cleaner in the far corner of the other room. Bring your dog in, as far from the vacuum as is possible. Start by practising some 'sits', 'downs' and 'Zen downs'. Don't turn the vacuum cleaner on! If you start it straight away, your dog will go into sympathetic arousal immediately, and this will make training extremely difficult.

Begin dropping pieces of food on the floor systematically closer and closer to the vacuum cleaner. If your dog is taking the food, click and reward — that's a great indicator he's doing okay. If he's not doing okay (probably indicated by not eating), move further away from the vacuum cleaner and repeat click and reward for calm responses. If necessary, cover up the vacuum cleaner and start from there. Remember, food arousal tells you what state the dog is in.

Continue moving the treats you are dropping closer to the vacuum cleaner, then eventually start putting the food actually on top of it for the dog to take. We want to get the dog interacting with the vacuum cleaner. Pace how fast you go based on your dog's reaction: you need to push his boundaries, but not so fast that he can't cope. This might take more than one session, so go at the pace your dog needs.

Progress to moving the vacuum, while it is off

Once your dog is comfortable taking treats from the stationary vacuum cleaner, take your dog away from the vacuum and have someone pick up the nozzle and move it slowly and gently near the dog, again not turned on. Continue to click and reward your dog for calm behaviour. Slowly throw treats closer to the head of the vacuum as it moves, and encourage your dog to get the treats. Praise and talk to your dog in friendly 'up' tones throughout this process, and remember to be guided by your dog. If he seems okay, move him closer to the vacuum; if he seems too stressed, move away and give him more time.

Gradually increase noise intensity

Once your dog is doing great with the moving vacuum, take your dog away from the vacuum and have someone turn it on. As you've been doing work with the vacuum off and close to your dog already, having it on but further away is not so threatening. However, you might want to cover it with a blanket to muffle the noise if it seems too much for your dog. Start with it on briefly (about three seconds), then turn it off. Then extend the time on systematically. Click and reward for calm responses.

Start to move your dog toward the *on* vacuum cleaner in very small increments, closer and closer, clicking and rewarding throughout. (Move as quickly or as slowly as your dog accepts, based on his food drive.) If you can, encourage your dog to go into 'Zen down' as you're doing this. Your dog may be a bit more scared, but if he is taking food from you then he is doing well, and keeping him focused on the food lures will help to keep his mind off the noise.

Remember that it's fine to move very slowly through these steps: you want your dog to be really comfortable with each step before you move

Click and reward
calm behaviours.

to the next. Slowly and surely is good, as moving too quickly can cause you to go backwards in this training.

In each session, get as far as your dog can handle while still in a learning state. Finish any session on a good note, with your dog eating. You might not get through all the steps, but that is not a problem; just take it slow and allow your dog to desensitise. When you start the next day, go back a step or so from where you finished the day before so your dog succeeds early. Succeeding is the name of this game so that you build his confidence. This therapy will also require very high-value food (e.g. chicken).

Ideally, do the therapy once or twice a day. You can spend up to half an hour doing a session: just watch to see how your dog is coping. It will probably take between one and six weeks to see good change; it really depends on how severe the issues are with your dog.

3. TREATING THE PHOBIA THROUGH DESENSITISATION — FIREWORKS AND THUNDER

Set up your desensitisation hierarchy or list

Establish your hierarchy from least to most, allowing you to plan the desensitisation: with noise first, then add flashing lights (e.g. camera flash to simulate lightning), then sparklers from a distance (for smell).

Play fireworks and thunder sounds at low volume

Start this aspect of the training by sourcing a recording of thunder or fireworks sounds. You can do this by going to iTunes and searching for 'sounds scary'. There's a number of different ones you can choose from, or you can make your own. You can also search for 'fireworks noise' or 'thunder noise' on YouTube.

With your dog on a lead or at a clip station with you, play these sounds at a very low volume. As you play them, click and reward your dog for calm responses. You want to be working just at or below the threshold of your dog's fear: don't go overboard, keep it very soft and low in volume to begin with. If your dog stops eating, you need to reduce the volume.

Encourage your dog to go into 'sit', 'down' and 'Zen down' as you play the sounds.

Gradually increase the volume

As you continue the training, very slowly start increasing the volume of the sounds in increments, systematically clicking and rewarding your dog's calm responses. For each session, go as far as the dog can manage and stil! be in a learning state.

For thunder-phobic dogs, introduce flashing

First start with a torch, and turning it on and off — click and reward calm responses. Don't point the light into your dog's face, and buffer the light at the beginning. Slowly increase exposure. If your dog stops eating, slow down.

For firework-phobic dogs, introduce smell

This will include the smell of matches and gunpowder. Sparklers are good, as they have the smell but not the noise. Using the same principles as above, start slowly with the sparklers at a distance, then slowly bring them closer and closer. Take care with smell, as it is a dog's strongest sense. Again click and reward calm responses, and if your dog stops eating, retreat back a few steps.

4. SETTING UP THE ENVIRONMENT LEADING TO PHOBIC EVENTS

As well as doing this training, if you're anticipating an event in which there'll be noises your dog is afraid of (such as a big storm or Guy Fawkes night), it's a great idea to set up your dog's environment to help her feel safe and secure. Here are some ideas:

- Use toy-facilitated therapy to get your dog playing and distracted just as the noise gets started. Throw a ball, engage in a game of tug-o-war — whatever your dog likes.
- Close the curtains to lessen the visual impact, play music or have the TV on to help drown out the unpleasant noise, especially if you don't have your training tools ready or an opportunity to work on the problem with your dog.
- Provide your dog with a safe place to retreat to — her crate in a safe and quiet room works well.
- Some clients have built a sound-proof kennel inside for the dog to retreat to, which can work well.
- Revisit the training in the lead-up to events, e.g. if there's a forecast for a thunderstorm or before any fireworks nights.

Keep in mind

This is intense therapy, so you need to be committed. Go carefully and take it in stages. Remember to observe how your dog is coping — the more sensitive your dog, the more careful you should be and the smaller the steps you should take. Don't make the training context fearful; this is an exposure technique so you need lots of repetition, not big leaps. Go to our online programme to see me doing it.

Generally speaking, this training will take about 4–12 weeks, with between one and three training sessions per day. If you have a really difficult case on your hands which is creating major issues for your dog, please seek advice from a veterinarian.

Medication

Sometimes very chronic cases may require drug-facilitated therapies, which can be anything from basic homeopathic options (some dogs react well to Rescue Remedy) through to Prozac-style options. If your dog needs this level of support, then visit your veterinarian. Ask for an appropriate anti-anxiety drug that will suit your dog and not interfere with learning. These drugs can lower the fear-inducing sympathetic arousal state, similar to the click and reward technique, which allows you to move your dog into a learning state so that you can undertake the desensitisation therapy. You can then look to fade the drugs as they complete their purpose.

Also, your veterinarian may be able to supply you with a sedative drug, which you can use when there is going to be noise but you haven't had a chance to complete your therapy. Ensure you get good advice so that appropriate drugs are used. The important point is that your dog has a decrease in anxiety while not interfering too much with her learning state. You want to avoid having even one more episode of fear, so if you haven't completed the training and Guy Fawkes is coming up, use a sedative for your dog that night or two.

Conclusion

This is a challenging therapy for your dog, so pay attention to how he's coping, and respond appropriately. It will require both of you pushing your comfort zones a bit — you'll need to be diligent and patient. It can be a difficult issue to resolve, and it takes committed, dedicated therapy, but your dog's state of calm and happiness will be so much better for it!

JO: ON AN EVEN KEEL

Now Jo is no longer chewing holes in doors to escape when she hears loud noises. She's able to deal with big trucks barrelling past on the road, bangs around the house and the bigger scares like Guy Fawkes. As Julie and Brian continue to keep up her training, she is just getting better and better.

Excessive submission

Excessively submissive behaviour and submissive urination is a relatively common problem in two- to six-month-old puppies (rarely it is seen in adult dogs as well), and is often misunderstood by humans. When we don't understand why our pup is behaving this way, we can miscommunicate to our dog, and when we get it wrong, we actually exacerbate the problem. I see this issue so often, and I know how frustrating it can be for someone who just doesn't understand why their dog keeps doing overly submissive things even after being told off for them! In fact, that's the problem: misunderstandings between two cultures.

What is excessive submission?

Dogs and wolves have evolved a system of communication that relies on dominance and submission to facilitate harmony and decrease aggression within the pack. Dominance gestures communicate assertive control of resources, role (and elder status sometimes) and leadership; while submission gestures communicate non-threatening and compliant attitudes which are used to help resolve and prevent conflict within the pack. They are ritualised appeasement gestures.

The purpose of submission is to communicate that the dog gives up or acquiesces to the dominant dog, which tells the other dog to stop further aggression. When a dog goes into recumbent submission (when he fully lies down, exposing his belly), it's hard-wired into the dominant dog's brain to stop acting aggressively. This prevents unnecessary fights and loss of life within the pack over the control of resources such as food and mates. By using dominant or submissive gestures, the pack establishes a hierarchy and a smooth, synchronised social order.

In the wild, the dominant gesture is intended as a way of communicating to younger pack members what behaviour isn't appropriate. This teaches young dogs how they should and shouldn't behave, which contributes to the healthy functioning of the pack and keeps all members safe and happy. A submissive gesture indicates 'Sorry, I give up and will stop.' This indicates that the message has been received, and the dominant or aggressive gesture can be discontinued.

This behaviour has evolved over millions of years, and dogs are responsive to both dominant and submissive gestures within their human families as well. This is a natural and healthy part of learning. Dominant gestures are not harmful, cruel or over-the-top; they are simply a method of communication to establish how the pack (or human family) should act together. A dominant gesture from a human to a dog can simply be the use of a gruff tone of voice which says 'no, I don't want you to do that'. This is necessary, as it keeps us, our families, other people and our dogs safe.

However, because dogs have been bred for increased sociability, docility and submission over thousands of years, some dogs are now prone to being submissive to an excessive degree. A dog is particularly likely to display excessive submission when he experiences continued assertiveness or aggression.

Signs of submission include the dog:

O rolling onto his back

O attempting to lick the jowls of other dogs or people

O putting his tail down between his legs

O lowering his body posture

O urinating involuntarily, in extreme cases.

It is not healthy or normal for a dog to demonstrate these behaviours on a regular basis, as it leads to other anxiety-induced behaviours.

Why does it occur?

Excessive submission often occurs when an owner is not aware that their dog is signalling submission and the owner's behaviour continues to signal dominance (even after the dog has submitted). The owner may misread the dog's submissive communication and continue to do behaviours that the dog interprets as assertive or dominant, further exacerbating the excessive submission. This is a common misunderstanding, as many people believe that if a dog does something that they find undesirable (such as urinating), the best way to get him to stop is to tell the dog off. This is not the case.

Excessive submission is most likely to occur in young, female and more-timid dogs, as well as (but not exclusively) particularly sociable breeds such as Labradors, Golden Retrievers or toy dogs.

In Chapter 3 we saw a classic example. A man comes home and enthusiastically greets his dog, looking at her fondly and reaching over to pat her. The puppy interprets the direct gaze and the move as threat signals, and rolls over to submit. The man thinks the puppy wants her tummy rubbed, and reaches out over her, at which point she involuntarily urinates in an attempt to communicate submission. From there, matters deteriorate as the puppy is told off for 'bad' behaviour. This whole Catch-22 situation comes about from a simple misunderstanding between human and dog of what certain behaviours mean. That's why it's so important to understand what your dog is telling you, and to communicate with your dog in a language she understands.

Aside from the frustrating submissive urination, in some cases

See how the wolf pup lowers the front half of its body and keeps its tail down.

Adult dominance threat. The pup on the right shows submission, the pup in the centre (obscured) is in recumbent submission.

submissive dogs can show defensive threat to an approaching person. In these cases, often overly assertive methods have been used to solve the submission and submissive urination problems, and the dog has turned to punishment-induced aggression which is fear-based. The dog/pup can then end up doing a defensive snap or bite. The same methods apply to resolve this, but if it has persisted for some time there may be a need to rehabilitate your bond. If this is happening with your dog, then go back to Joining Up, eliminate punishers and work on your positive reinforcement techniques (clicker and food reward mainly).

You may be very familiar with this unintended, unhappy cycle. It's difficult to resolve if people don't realise their role in maintaining this unwanted behaviour. However, if you understand the root cause of the problem, it can be easy to treat.

Treating excessive submission

This issue is mainly a result of a lack of understanding about what the dog is trying to communicate, as well as our inability to adapt our body language so we are communicating appropriately to the dog. Therefore, this is the first step we take in correcting the issue. The chapter on Shared Language is a great place to start: we have to understand that our dogs can't change their responses, so we need to change ours.

Because this behavioural issue is fundamentally about a failed greeting, you begin this therapy by first creating a specific greeting routine to build your relationship as well as your dog's confidence. With most issues we do the Joining Up training before moving to treat the behavioural issue in question; however, with excessive submission we do just the opposite. We start by treating the behaviour in the manner prescribed, then, once we have made some progress, we go back and do the Joining Up and umbilical training (unless the dog has displayed signs of fear-induced aggression).

The key steps you need to take to address this issue are:

O Establish an appropriate greeting routine that encourages confident greets with your dog, which will both build your relationship with her and grow her confidence in you as her mentor without you having to exert excessive dominance.

O As your dog's mentor, you need to follow the instructions about

how to show non-threatening behaviours.
O Reward confident and upright behaviours (as opposed to lowered and submissive ones).
O Switch on the learning state.
O Build a relationship with your pup or dog, and teach her to be confident in your personal space, and to move confidently with you.

STAGE ONE: TREATMENT

Our aim is to create a good greeting routine and reward confident, upright behaviours — this includes standing tall or sitting up straight and looking up to you with confidence. The opposite of upright behaviours are lowered behaviours, in which your dog is lowering his body towards the ground, rolling over, putting his tail between his legs, or generally making his body smaller and more insignificant. You do not want to reward these behaviours when treating your dog for excessive submission.

Before you get started
O Get your dog or pup comfortable with the clicker, outside of the context of treating this problem.
O Teach a 'sit' and 'wait' only at this stage. Do not teach or practise a 'down' yet, as it is similar to the lowering behaviours of excessive submission, which are the ones you are trying to change.
O Take the 'wait' command carefully, too. Just use luring and no pressure; shape the behaviour with the clicker and reward only.

The greeting routine
O To start, appear as least dominant as possible. Each dog will need varying degrees of this. For example, you can lower yourself onto your knees or sit on the floor. Avoid looking your dog in the eye or staring, turn yourself slightly away from your dog so you are not facing him directly, and stay relaxed and gentle.
O Use positive, 'up' tones — 'good girl' / 'good boy'.
O Don't get too excitable or hype your dog up, as excitable urination could happen. Excitable urination is the other end of the spectrum to submissive urination, but you don't want to encourage either of these inappropriate behaviours with your training, so keeping calm is critical.
O Encourage and call your dog to you (friendly, high-pitched tone).

Recumbent submission and submissive licking.

Boy goes into recumbent submission in response to someone standing over him.

Do not approach your dog, as this is venturing into dominance behaviour for a timid dog. It's important that your dog comes to you, as this is less intimidating than you approaching him. As you progress, you will be able to approach him, but when you are starting out always call the dog to you.

O Click and reward your dog for approaching you. If your dog is very timid and hesitates to come to you, then drop food in front of him between the two of you to help lure him to you.

O Deliver food on the floor rather than directly from your hand at first. This will avoid you leaning over your dog to deliver the food and accidentally intimidating him.

O The less eager your dog is to come toward you, the more important it is that you do not approach him. Be patient if need be.

O Once your dog has come to you, ask your dog to 'sit' with an up tone and using a hand signal.

O As soon as your dog sits, click and reward, again by delivering the food on the floor. If your dog rolls over, again ask for a 'sit', luring him upright with a treat. Be careful not to lean over your dog and intimidate him: dogs feel dominated when someone is leaning above them.

O Gradually move to delivering the food from your hand to build your dog's confidence in his contact with you. It will help if you hold the food below your dog's head rather than above it, as having your hand above your dog's head can be intimidating. Then, systematically, gradually deliver the food higher and higher, a few centimetres at a time, to build confidence. Slowly you are getting your dog to anticipate the food coming from up high, which will also encourage eye contact and upright posture.

O As your dog's confidence grows, gradually handle him under the chin/chest area. This is the best area and the least intimidating.

O Click and reward your dog for staying upright. Only handle or pet him when he is upright.

O Don't reward your dog if he rolls over, either with food or by patting his belly, as this will only reinforce his submissive gestures. If he does lie down or roll over, then ask for a 'sit', and click and reward once he does that.

O Continue to handle the dog in upright/sitting positions, and click and reward when he is. You can use your hands to guide your dog's head upwards by gently lifting his head from the neck/chest area.

O If you are the dominant that your dog is submitting to and you're not progressing with these techniques, then a younger, female or less assertive member of the household might need to learn the routine first and work with your dog before the dominant members try. This builds your dog's confidence first and gives him some successes before he's asked to go to the next, more challenging level. You might want to let the kids lead on this one!

These techniques are designed to teach your dog to be confident and stay in upright behaviours when greeting members of the household. The clicker switches your dog into a learning state, and the food lure redirects his attention and behaviour to upright postures. This influences the neuro-chemicals in his brain that signal to him that he is safe and that you are a friend and mentor, not to be feared but loved. You want to encourage this as much as possible, so that our dog can feel happy and confident with you rather than fearful.

Continue with this training for around 15 minutes each day (you can split this up into a couple of sessions). After 2–3 weeks you should be seeing a great improvement in your dog's confidence, after which you can progress to the next stage of the treatment.

STAGE TWO: SWITCHING INTO LEARNING STATE AND JOINING UP — BUILDING THE RELATIONSHIP

Now that your dog (or pup) has more confidence with you, you can progress to building and strengthening your relationship. I have been very brief with the steps involved here, as you can refer back to the Joining Up chapter for more detailed instruction.

We reserve this training until after you have begun treating the problem of excessive submission, because a highly submissive dog may find it stressful or intimidating to be on the clip lead and be doing pressure on/pressure off work initially. Once you have established a calm and confident greeting routine, this work should become a lot more manageable.

1 Clip station

O Clip your dog to a clip station.

O Click and reward calm, upright behaviour by practising the 'sit' command only.

○ Once your dog seems confident and relaxed, practise your 'down' command, then graduate into 'Zen down'. Notice how the effects of this position are different to recumbent submission — how much more quickly your dog can calm down and learn, focusing on you. Her demeanour will improve and confidence grow, and overall learning speed increases dramatically now there is no longer excessive submission at play!

○ Fasten a half-slip collar (these are better for sensitive dogs than the full slip) to your dog while she is still on the clip station, to teach an effective check. Take care when putting the half-slip collar on that you do not elicit submission — click and reward for continued upright behaviours. If your dog rolls over, ask for a 'sit', then click and reward.

○ The half-slip collar will need to be used carefully and sparingly at the beginning so that you don't frighten your dog. Make sure you do not create any negative association with yourself or the clip station. Pressure on away from you on the long-line is the best place to start any 'pressure on' work.

○ This type of dog really challenges you to master the art of contrast training, and just how incremental and gradual you need to be. The use of graduated pressure on and pressure off builds resilience and confidence in your dog and you, particularly as your bond strengthens.

○ However, these dogs are so sensitive that if you go too fast and hard they will react submissively and associate it with you. Hence we start pressure on/pressure off on the clip station, with the wall creating the resistance.

○ For an even more sensitive dog, put her on a long-line and run it through the eyelet fastening on the wall. This offers the dog a little bit more freedom than on the shorter lead, but still creates some (limited) pressure, again not associated with you.

○ Starting very slowly, use pressure on/pressure off while your dog is on the clip lead, to teach her that it is uncomfortable to pull away from and resist the clip lead (pressure on from the wall), and comfortable and good to be sitting on the clip lead loose (pressure off). The second she takes the pressure off (the lead is loose), click and reward by dropping food on the floor inside the pressure-off area (that is, don't drop the food where your dog has to strain the lead to get it and create pressure on).

O Continue to do this for 5-10 minutes, clicking and rewarding all pressure off. Do this 2-3 times a day for as long as it takes to get your dog used to the pressure and staying on the click station by herself, settled. This will take up to 2-3 weeks.

O Be careful when you take your dog over to the clip station and clip her on that she doesn't get a fright and associate it with you. Go quietly and carefully, and be mindful.

O I can't reiterate enough that to begin with this should be done very slowly, very gently and with only slight pressure on the collar when your dog is resisting.

2 On lead

O Put your dog on the lead with a half-slip collar, and unclip from the clip station.

O Place particular emphasis on pressure on and pressure off. Don't use any firm checks for now: leave that for later when your dog has more confidence.

O The key behaviour to reward is your dog looking to you for direction. You want to build a relationship and confidence, so click and reward when your dog looks up at you.

O Your dog will likely be anxious looking at your eyes, so desensitise her to your eye contact by placing food in a line between your eyes and her eyes. Click and reward when you get confident eye contact and posture (not submissive). Ensure that you do not stare at your dog while you are doing this treatment. (you can glance).

O Continue with Joining Up along these lines.

3 Umbilical phase

O The umbilical phase is important for submissive dogs, as it reinforces them being safe in your personal space, without being submissive. It teaches them that it is okay for them to be near you and around you.

O Take care not to drag your dog around. It's important to do the on-lead Joining Up first and get your dog comfortable with it and following you well before trying the umbilical.

O Extend the 'Zen down' phase, because this increases the learning-state duration while active. When you stop for periods of time, click and reward when your dog goes into the 'Zen down' position.

o Take care that you are not standing on or tripping over your dog when you are rewarding her, as this might trigger submissive behaviours.

o As your dog's tolerance for standing over grows, click and reward her, as this will desensitise her to your more confident behaviours.

STAGE THREE: RETURNING HOME

When dogs are prone to excessive submission, I often find that a major trigger can be the owner's return home at the end of the day. For this reason, it's important to be ready to practise at this time. I recommend you keep your pouch full of treats and clicker up high and near your front door. When you arrive home, proceed through your greeting routine immediately upon entry. As it is the first greeting after you get home, it can be the most anxiety-inducing for your submissive pup or dog. You will probably need to do this each day for at least 2–3 weeks to get an established change.

STAGE FOUR: PROOFING FOR THE REAL WORLD

What we've just been through are the foundations of training that will help you turn your excessively submissive dog into a confident and happy one. Once you both become confident, you can start incorporating the next few suggestions to proof your dog for the real world, and desensitise him to a wider variety of less-controlled situations.

o You may want to teach your friends and family members the best way to approach a dog like yours (in fact, any dog) so that they can contribute to your dog's confidence and not his excessive submission. Remember, an appropriate way to approach a dog is to lower your body posture by crouching or getting down on your knees, asking the dog owner if you can pat their dog, calling the dog to approach you and/or patting the dog on the neck and chest area where it is not a threat. Giving this information to people who may be coming into contact with your dog may help you to eliminate these submission-based behaviours that you want to avoid more quickly. Submissive dogs need a gentle approach.

o Move from patting your dog's, neck, cheek and shoulder region or the chin/chest area to starting to pat him on the head. Click and reward him constantly as you do so, to teach him to accept it. Having a food lure in your hand and using the clicker will keep him more focused on the food and less focused on feeling threatened. It's almost inevitable that your dog will come into contact with someone who will try to pat him on the head, so desensitising your dog to this is an important part of preparing him to be confident with others.

O Start to approach your dog rather than always calling your dog to approach you. Only do this once your dog is consistently approaching you with confidence. Again, people are likely to approach your dog, so you want your dog to be prepared for this and not revert back to excessively submissive behaviours.

O Similarly, start to remain upright when approaching your dog (rather than lowering your body every time). Again, only do this after your dog has proven confidence with you in a lowered position. Continue to click and reward positive, upright behaviours as you do this.

Conclusion

By using these simple techniques, being careful not to impose a threat on your dog, and teaching him confidence behaviours builds resiliance. Imagine how much happier your beautiful dog will be, not having to live with so much tension and anxiety.

15

Dog-to-dog aggression

I cannot tell you the number of dogs with aggression toward other dogs that I have treated in my life. It's an alarmingly widespread issue, and naturally very upsetting for the dogs' owners (as well as the owners of dogs that are being targeted), particularly when you know that one of the defining features of dogs is their high degree of tolerance and sociability toward other dogs. This is, of course, if they get the right socialisation in the formative period: a dog doesn't know how to relate to dogs unless he gets socialised with them at the right age. Recent research showed that pups raised with kittens on a queen didn't know they were dogs (up until 12 weeks of age) — they behaved more like cats. It took weeks of mixing with dogs for them to realise they were dogs.

KANE: NOT SOCIALISED TO OTHER DOGS

Rachel came to see me at my behaviour clinic with a Siberian Husky she'd recently adopted from a family who were moving overseas. She'd fallen in love with this beautiful creature at first sight, and had spent a few hours with him in his home getting to know his nature and personality. Kane was affectionate to her and gentle with her young child, and he had a good understanding of all the basic commands, except recall. It seemed a match made in heaven!

However, the time she'd spent with Kane had been at the dog's home with only people around; he was very well-socialised with humans and had no issues there. But after she took him home and they went out for their first walk together, Rach discovered that Kane was aggressive toward other dogs, lunging and growling at them.

As you can imagine, she was mortified and extremely upset. She didn't have any experience with aggressive dogs and had no idea how to handle him or manage him. She felt like she was going to have to keep Kane locked away in her property, which was not how she wanted her dog to live, but she didn't know what other choice she had, as she couldn't risk him hurting another dog on her watch. Equally, the thought of having him put down was devastating, as she and her daughter had bonded with him closely and considered him a member of the family. This sadly has been a very common story in my clinical practice.

Why does dog-to-dog aggression occur?

Aggression is not an unnatural behaviour for a dog. In the ancestral wolf's world, aggression served several purposes, generally to assert dominance and order in the pack. Aggression is also largely a threat signal to threaten off intruders, though wolves (as opposed to ancestral dogs) can kill wolves from other packs that are intruding.

Dogs are normally not that extreme, though of course there are some exceptions, especially those bred for it, such as pit-fighting breeds. These breeds have had their natural inhibition, to stop attacking upon submission, bred out of them by us. The domestication of the dog enhanced this inhibition to attacking once an opponent had submitted, so reversing that through breeding is counter-productive and dangerous for dogs, as well as compromising their ability to live amicably with us and with other dogs. It is not something we should select for.

The postural communication that wolves primarily use actually evolved to minimise aggression, allowing these large predatory animals to live and hunt co-operatively and amicably together as a family pack. Dominance is communicated through upright postures and making themselves large, while subordinance is communicated through lowering postures and making themselves smaller. (See the Shared Language chapter).

The purpose of submission is to reduce and inhibit threat and aggression, by recognising the other's dominance. The dominant wolf recognises the meaning of the submissive gestures, and is able to back off without having or continuing a fight. Peace and harmony returns to the pack, with no blood spilled!

Dog-to-dog aggression usually occurs in dogs that have not learnt how to greet or socialise with other dogs appropriately. Generally, this happens when dogs miss being correctly socialised with other dogs in the formative period, and so never learn how to greet other dogs or read their postures in a correct manner. It's also seen in dogs that have been attacked by other dogs in the past and need to rebuild their confidence. Additionally, it can occur due to sexual drivers in males toward other males (especially entire males over 18 months old), as well as females toward females, who are worse when oestrogen is high, such as when they are in heat. Most commonly (except in mal-socialised dogs), males fight males and females fight females, so be conscious when you are choosing a second dog for yourself or when socialising with other dogs that a male and female are a safer choice.

A friendly greeting for dogs is an inguinal (groin) and/or anal (rear-end) sniff. The dogs approach from the side and sniff each other in turn (the 'dog handshake'). Once both dogs have done this, their relationship should unfold in a friendly manner. Aggression rarely happens from behind in a dog. If it does, you know you are dealing with a mal-socialised dog, or potentially a fighting breed, as such dogs lose their discrimination in this regard. When bred to do something so un-canine as to attack their own, they end up breaking cultural and intrinsic rules.

When a dog doesn't greet other dogs in this way, it can cause unnecessary conflict, because the dog's actions don't follow the normal social protocols, which may come across as threatening. This is especially true if the dog does do rush bluff behaviour (rushing up to other dogs with a threat bluff). If the other dogs feels threatened by this abnormal behaviour, they can act aggressively. Dogs that haven't learnt to greet other dogs properly can also feel threatened when other dogs try to greet them, because they don't recognise this normal greeting as social behaviour and mistake it for a threat. This can cause them to exhibit aggressive behaviours toward dogs that approach to greet them in normal ways. The Shared Language chapter explores how dogs understand these situations, and especially how to read their postures so that we can understand what they are communicating.

Treating dog-to-dog aggression

Because one of the primary causes of dog-to-dog aggression is the dog's lack of knowledge about a proper greeting routine, teaching your dog how to meet and greet other dogs is a crucial part of fixing this problem behaviour. You do this in a slightly different way than the meet and greet routine covered earlier, which is for generally well-socialised dogs. There are a few steps you take beforehand when you are dealing with a dog that has already exhibited aggressive behaviour.

The key steps to addressing this issue are:

O Consider whether your dog needs a muzzle (be conservative).
O Teach the key basics — a 'nicely' command, an effective check and the 'no' command.
O Build a relationship with your dog so that he looks to you first for direction and guidance.
O Make sure you can use the clicker and switch your dog into a learning state.
O Establish an appropriate greeting routine with your dog, which will also build your relationship with him and grow his confidence in you as his mentor — teach him the 'dog handshake' (see chapter 16).

STAGE ONE: TEACH THE BASICS
O Teach the 'nicely' and 'no' commands and an effective check

outside of this therapy context. These commands ensure that your dog is looking to you for guidance when she meets a new dog and will take your direction. 'Nicely' means 'Yes, that dog is okay, you can relax' and 'no' means 'Do not behave like that' or 'That dog may bite you, so listen to me, I'm your ally.'

O An effective check will ensure that if your dog behaves inappropriately, she will know that there is a negative consequence (coming apparently from the other dog) if she behaves like that. You are teaching your dog that listening to you can show her how to avoid the consequence. It is important that the check is effective, otherwise the situation might escalate: your dog needs a clear communication that 'no' means the behaviour is not appropriate.

O Initially, don't use a 'no' command when delivering a check, so it appears to your dog that the other dog is doing the correction. You want your dog to act nicely with other dogs even when you are not there, so it's important your dog thinks that there will be a negative consequence whether you are around or not.

O After a few sessions when your dog has consistently been behaving appropriately, you can start to introduce the 'no', which means 'Don't do that or the other dog will give you a correction — come back to me for safety and all will be good.' This gives the dog the opportunity to choose appropriate behaviour and avoid the correction.

O To do this, next time your dog behaves inappropriately, say 'no' in a growly tone, and click and reward your dog responding in a sociable manner. If not, do an effective check on your second 'no'. (Remember, your 'no' should already be trained and effective in other contexts before you use it here.)

STAGE TWO: JOINING UP

Before you get started on this therapy, establish a good bond with your dog by doing the Joining Up training. Practise all four stages — at the clip station, on a lead, on the umbilical and off-lead — before progressing to treatment. Joining Up is extremely important, as it will teach your aggressive dog to look to you for guidance on how to react when meeting new dogs, so you can teach him to be friendly and behave appropriately.

STAGE THREE: TREATMENT
Greeting routine

An appropriate greet is an inguinal and rear-end sniff: if your dog does this, it will prevent a multitude of aggression-based issues. An essential part of this therapy is teaching your dog an appropriate inguinal greet by encouraging him to first sniff another dog around the groin and bottom area, with you clicking and rewarding this action if safe to do so.

To start this training technique, you need an experienced and trusted friend who has a friendly dog that they have good control over. It's good to start with a dog that your dog knows, so you can trust their reactions but get a chance to practise your techniques. You will be using the rear-present technique, which involves turning first your friend's dog then your dog, and presenting each dog's rear end to the other dog to sniff.

Another dog is very unlikely to be aggressive to your dog's rear end unless severely mal-socialised. However, look for signs of aggression in unknown dogs, just in case they are mal-socialised. (This is why it's best to start with a dog you personally know, so you're sure he is friendly and well-socialised.) If you're concerned about either dog's behaviour at all during any stage of this training, remove your dog from the situation as calmly and quickly as possible. Remember, difficult cases will require a muzzle.

To undertake a greeting routine

- Always start with friendly dogs both you and your dog know, then next use friendly breeds like Golden Retrievers, King Charles Spaniels, etc.
- Make sure both dogs are on a lead. Your dog should be on a safety slip collar, and you should keep a firm hand on the lead so you can pull your dog away if you see him starting to react.
- Approach the other dog. Do not have the lead pulling the collar tight on the approach. It's important that your dog (the one with the issue) does the approaching while the other dog remains stationary. This is because it's less threatening for a dog to approach another dog than to be approached, and you want your dog to feel as non-threatened as possible.
- When you are first approaching and introducing the new dog, use your 'nicely' command to let your dog know that 'Yes, I have seen this dog and I have judged him as friendly.' The 'nicely' lets your

dog know that you are thinking about this situation so he don't have to — you are happy and in control.

○ Have your friend present their dog's rear end first, as that improves the chances of a social response. (Because your dog is more aggressive, he is likely to be more dominant, so having the more submissive dog be sniffed first will improve the likelihood of success.) Click and reward both dogs for friendly, appropriate responses.

○ If your dog shows signs of heightened arousal at any point, repeat the word 'nicely', and click and reward him if he shows signs of a good response. However, be ready for an effective check, as things can change quickly. (Effective is firmer in high arousal).

○ If there's no response and your dog is showing signs of early aggression, deliver an effective check as if the correction is coming from the other dog (an apparent natural consequence). Click and reward if your dog responds in a friendly fashion to the other dog, or actively moves away toward you (safety).

○ It is important that this correction is seen to come from the other dog, so don't say anything as you give the check initially.

○ Once your dog (as the more aggressive dog) has sniffed and greeted your friend's dog, turn your dog around to rear-present to the other dog. Place your dog's head and shoulders between your legs and present your dog's bottom area to the other dog for sniffing.

○ Click and reward your dog for accepting being sniffed and other sociable responses.

○ If your dog shows signs of heightened arousal at any point, repeat the word 'nicely', and click and reward him if he shows signs of a good response. However, be ready for an effective check, as things can change quickly.

○ If there's no response to your command and your dog is showing signs of early aggression, deliver an effective check as if the correction is coming from the other dog (an apparent natural consequence). Click and reward if your dog responds in a friendly fashion to the other dog.

○ It is important that this correction is seen to come from the other dog, so don't say anything as you give the check initially.

○ After both dogs have sniffed each other's rears, and when you think your dog is ready (he has shown reliable social responses), turn the dogs slowly head-on, continuing to click and reward non-reactive, quiet responses. Before you do this, check to see both dogs are in a learning state, with your dog very focused on the clicker and food reward. Don't rush to this stage; ensure you have had consistent, reliable social responses.

O Then walk off side-by-side, but some distance apart — click and reward good responses. Gradually bring the dogs closer together, continuing to click and reward good responses.

O When one or both dogs start play-soliciting or showing relaxed, social responses, and you are feeling confident, consider letting them off-lead on a long-line (so you can catch them easily by stepping on the dragging end of the line if you need to).

O Continuing practising your greeting routine with lots of different friendly dogs, then gradually with more and more difficult dogs. Introducing and exposing your dog to a variety of dogs will greatly benefit his confidence, ultimately allowing him to integrate into social groups.

O Timing is everything: don't rush your dog. Give him plenty of practice first with friendly dogs, and be guided by how your dog is progressing before moving to the next stage.

O If at any time you think the interaction is escalating beyond your control or skills, remove your dog quietly and calmly and go back to an earlier stage (muzzle if necessary).

O After a number of successful training sessions, you can gradually introduce the 'no' command at the same time as the check. Once your dog associates the 'no' command with the check, then the 'no' on its own will start to act as a signal to let the dog know that if he continues that inappropriate behaviour there will be consequences. Then you can start just using the 'nicely' and 'no' commands to get sociable responses, allowing your dog to choose to stop the inappropriate behaviour and avoid the correction. However, always be ready to use an effective check while training, in case things escalate. Know what is effective, remember that arousal is high.

Using this rear-present greeting technique is the best way to start interactions with new dogs to decrease arousal and increase sociable behaviour. It can go a long way to diffusing potential aggression, and will almost invariably stop moderate aggressive behaviour, thereby preventing fights.

Note how Bo (right) doesn't like the head to head. It's more threatening, hence a fear bark.

Inappropriate lunging and barking. Reggie (left) feels threatened.

If it doesn't diffuse a dog's aggression when done correctly, then you know you are dealing with a very mal-socialised dog, so remove yourself and your dog from the situation as quickly as possible. If your dog does not respond positively to this technique, then she may have quite a serious case of dog-to-dog aggression and you may wish to consult a qualified animal behaviourist.

De-sexing entire males, especially if done early, will lower inter-male aggression; that is, for those dominant males driven to be aggressive due to hormonal effects. Sometimes hormone-altering drugs can help also, so talk to your veterinarian. Similarly, for females that are more aggressive when on heat, de-sexing is recommended, as it's the oestrogen that makes it worse. (Don't de-sex during heat, though.)

If there is *any* risk that your dog could bite another dog, muzzle-condition your dog and then have her wear a muzzle for this training. You can read about these in the Dog Zen Toolkit chapter — this is essential to prevent any harm to another dog or a person getting in the middle.

Proofing

PRACTISING SOCIALISATION TECHNIQUES DAY-TO-DAY

As you go about your day-to-day activities with your dog, there are always opportunities to reinforce his social behaviours. When passing another dog in the street at any distance, say 'nicely' to your dog. Your dog is likely to look at the other dog and then look at you — click and reward as he looks to you and is not showing threatening responses (maybe say 'good boy/good girl' also). When sitting at a café or the like with your dog and a dog passes or is nearby, say 'nicely', bring your lure up between you and your dog, and click and reward if he is showing appropriate responses. If not, say 'no', then click and reward a good response (by now you would have introduced the 'no' command). If he doesn't respond appropriately, then check on your second 'no' and say 'nicely'. Repeat as necessary. (If your dog is reactive you can check on the first 'no').

This is one of the more serious therapies in terms of safety, so you must proof it very systematically and carefully. Ensure that you have identified the hierarchy of dogs that your dog reacts to, from slight to most, and work your way slowly through these, starting with the slightest. Always respond to how your dog is coping, and slow down the therapy if your dog is starting to show signs of issues.

It's very important that you establish a good greeting routine for your dog. Always ensure that your dog has greeted a dog he doesn't know correctly (on-lead), particularly if that dog is in the risk type for your dog. A quick 'no' to negative reactions is not enough. You need to make sure your dog gets a chance to greet the other dog properly and positively, otherwise the issue won't be solved long-term. You are the one who provides the guidance for your dog whenever he meets a new dog. After solid Joining Up work, your dog should look to you to determine if a strange dog is friendly, so always use the 'nicely' command to reinforce that your dog should take your lead on whether a dog is friendly.

Remember, have your dog wear a muzzle if there is *any* risk he could bite another dog — be cautious. A considerable amount of work is required to achieve results with issues of this kind, so do lots of practice whenever you can with as many different dogs as you can, and do not rush each step.

Also, don't put your dog in unsuitable circumstances when he isn't ready, like being off-lead at the beach or dog park, or going to doggie daycares. Proof and practise this therapy well before you decide to do this.

Dogs with very serious behaviour problems

If your dog has very serious aggression problems, then seek qualified animal behaviourist advice. Check the behaviourist's qualifications and experience, and talk to your veterinarian for a referral.

We have an in-residence animal behaviour clinic where we take dogs with more-serious behaviour problems. We have a whole range of additional sophisticated tools that need professional training to use well. These are beyond the scope of this book, although the techniques and rationale we use here extend into the use of these other tools.

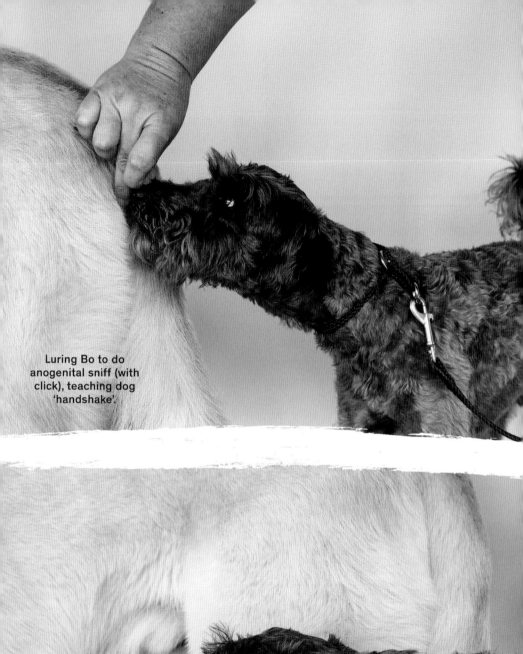

Luring Bo to do anogenital sniff (with click), teaching dog 'handshake'.

Conclusion

KANE: BACK ON TRACK

When Rachel came to see me about Kane, I walked her through these techniques, showing her how to do Joining Up, then how to use the rear-present introduction to meet new dogs. After watching her practise a few times with dogs at our place, I was confident this was going to be something she was able to do when she went out walking with Kane on her own back at home.

I called Rachel recently to see how she was getting on, and was thrilled to hear that things had been going well. She usually walks Kane with a safety slip collar and retractable lead now, just to be on the safe side in case they encounter a dog that Kane doesn't get along with and a check is needed. She uses 'nicely' whenever they are approaching another dog, so that Kane knows everything is okay, and she has used 'no' and her check occasionally as well, when she has noticed him stiffening and been a bit concerned that she was seeing the early signs of aggression.

This is something Rachel has done really well: she's become very attuned to Kane's body language, so she can see when he is relaxed and comfortable and when he is feeling a bit more aroused, so she therefore knows how to respond accordingly. This is an essential skill to learn to help you manage a dog like this with ease. Best of all, Kane is still with her and a part of her family, and no other dogs are getting hurt!

When you have a dog that has issues with aggression, it is going to be something you have to be conscious of for the rest of your dog's life, as it is hard to eliminate your dog's negative reactions completely. However, you can get to a stage where, like Rachel and Kane, you're able to go out walking and not be worried about your dog growling at or attacking another dog.

16

Human-oriented aggression

Treating human-oriented aggression can be challenging and holds risks, so we recommend you use a muzzle for any training that you undertake, to keep other people safe. If you have any concerns around the level of your dog's aggression, please seek the advice of a qualified animal behaviourist, having carefully checked on qualifications, experience and effectiveness.

I'm sure we can all unanimously agree that when a dog acts aggressively toward people, it is a problem. In some cases, it is a very big and very scary problem. There is a real danger of serious injury, or on very rare occasions even death, to a person if a dog is aggressive toward them — and, sadly, children are over-represented in dog-attack statistics. In fact, statistics show that male dogs in or near their own home attacking

boys under 10 are the most common. Eighty per cent of bites occur within or near the dog's home.

When people have a dog that shows aggression toward people, they understandably have a tendency to remove that dog from any potential interactions with new people. They don't go out walking with the dog, they keep her locked away separately when visitors come by, generally ensuring that the dog doesn't have any interactions with people she doesn't know, for fear that it will go wrong. Unfortunately, this exacerbates any issues relating to mal-socialisation, and so the problem worsens over time.

Why does this behaviour occur?

As we know, aggression is a natural behaviour in wolves and dogs, and served several purposes in the ancestral wolf's world. Generally used to assert dominance and maintain order in the pack (largely through threat signals), this enabled large predators to live and hunt cooperatively together. It also serves to guard against territorial incursions and as a response to fear.

The three major forms of human-oriented aggression that we will deal with here are:

O Protective aggression — protecting against people from outside of the extended family, normally in the dog's territory.
O Fear-induced aggression — often triggered by lack of socialisation and not learning the appropriate greeting routines.
O Dominance aggression — shown towards people within the family when the dog is trying to establish dominance using threat signals or aggression (e.g. growling and/or biting). It can also extend beyond the family.

Protective and fear-induced aggression

Generally, the root of this problem is that your dog hasn't been well-socialised with a broad range of people in her critical formative period of 1-4 months of age. It is the role of mentors to expose their dogs to a wide range of people during this time (including different ages, races

1 Stranger approaches Lucy – Lucy shows fear-induced aggression.

2 Muzzle on, trained in the 'nicely' command and greeting routine.

3 Mentor starts 2 metres away. In contact with sociable response. Then click and reward.

4 Start at 2 metres. Looking at visitor, use the 'nicely' command.

5 Mentor shields the visitor's hand for first interactions.

6 A later click and visitor rewards through the muzzle.

and sexes). If not, then dogs are likely to discriminate against people they haven't met. In essence, your dog doesn't have a wide definition of what kind of people make up her extended 'family'. By one year of age onward, mal-socialised dogs are likely to show fear-induced or protective aggression to anyone 'new' or considered a 'stranger'.

This type of aggression can also occur if your dog has suffered a negative experience with a person or group of people. People who adopt a dog from animal rescue shelters (my favourite kinds of people!) can find that their dog has been abused by previous owners or is mal-socialised, and has developed fear-induced aggression. The dog can end up being aggressive to all people he is unfamiliar with, or to a specific type of person who resembles someone who has hurt him in the past. In these instances, you have to re-establish those relationships with your dog. This can be done, but it takes effort.

Dominance aggression

Dominance aggression shown toward family members is less common, and occurs when the dog considers himself dominant over certain family members; often the younger, smaller members. More-dominant dogs, especially those who are reared without 'correct family rules', can start to use threat signals and even aggression to dominate resources or sites. If reared through the formative period in the recommended Dog Zen manner, with all the family sharing control over the resources properly, this type of aggression shouldn't develop. If it does, urgent action is necessary, and help may be potentially required from a trained animal behaviourist. Genetic factors can come into play, too. De-sexing entire males exhibiting dominance aggression is a must, as the male hormones make this dominance predisposition worse, particularly toward other entire male dogs and those perceived as subordinate humans.

Treating human-oriented aggression

Before I get started on how we treat this behaviour, I'd like you to evaluate how serious your dog's level of aggression is. If your dog is just starting to show aggressive tendencies, such as lunging and growling, and has his hackles up at people, this chapter should go a long way to helping solve the problem. If your dog has bitten or attacked somebody already, then although this chapter will help you understand the principles needed to treat this behaviour and put down foundations, I do recommend you seek assistance from a qualified animal behaviourist. The risks are just too high when a dog has already exhibited highly aggressive behaviour. You will need an expert overseeing any therapy and advising on any adjunctive therapeutic techniques that may be needed.

Dominance aggression toward family members is more serious and more challenging to treat, so again, for this issue it's worth consulting a qualified behaviourist first. However, you should find that establishing the clicker and working through your Dog Zen techniques may help solve the problem for simpler cases. For the more serious cases, it will provide a critical foundation for supported therapy and treatment. Modifying the hormones, particularly the androgens of a male, and some drug therapies may help, so talk to your veterinarian.

Given all that, here are the key steps in addressing this issue:

O Before any training session, teach the key basics: a 'nicely' command, an effective check, the 'no' command and a hand-touch target (see chapter 7, Basic Commands).

O Build a relationship with your dog, so that he looks to you first for direction and guidance.

O Establish an appropriate greeting routine with your dog that will also build your relationship with him, and grow his confidence in you as his mentor, as he should look to you for direction.

O Learn how to show new people how to best greet your dog.

Before you get started, it's important that you:

O Consider whether your dog needs to wear a muzzle for this therapy: be conservative with your judgement here — err on the side of caution. Be particularly careful with putting the muzzle on dominant dogs. They can be aggressive when you assert yourself over them or manipulate their mouth and head.

O Ensure that your dog is in a learning state.

O Know how to read your dog's body language so you can recognise when he is signalling problems, so that you can intervene early.

O Have the right tools with you: clicker, food rewards, pouch, muzzle, safety slip collar and retractable or long-line lead.

O   Remember the essential rules of training to make sure you have
    an effective session: keep it simple, start in a simple environment,
    be clear what you are training, and ensure that you are in the right
    frame of mind.

I cannot stress enough that if there is *any* possibility your dog might
bite and hurt someone, you must muzzle your dog for this training.
Dogs need to be taught to be comfortable with the muzzle, so refer
to the Dog Zen Toolkit chapter to learn how to help your dog build a
positive association with wearing it first. (See video if possible).

STAGE ONE: TEACH THE BASICS

Before you start any training for human-oriented aggression, teach
your dog:

O   The 'nicely' and 'no' commands. These commands ensure your
    dog is looking to you for guidance when she meets a new person,
    and will take your direction. 'nicely' means 'Yes, that person is
    okay, you can relax' and 'no' means 'Do not behave like that.'

O   An effective check: this will ensure that if your dog behaves inap-
    propriately she will respond to the correction.

O   A hand-touch target. The purpose of this in this therapy is to
    teach your dog to touch her nose to a person's hand to get a
    reward. This makes hands less threatening, and forms a positive
    association with the person's hand. Start with yourself. Smudge
    a little bit of food on your hand, then hold it out and ask your
    dog to 'touch'. Click as she touches your hand and deliver a food
    reward out of your other hand. Only have the food smudge for
    the first few times until your dog has learnt to touch your hand.
    This is very easy to teach.

O   Once established, teach your dog to do this with people she knows
    and is friendly with. To begin with you click and reward when
    she touches your friend's hand, then move to you clicking and the
    friend offering the food reward to your dog. If you are going to use
    a muzzle, then practise this whole routine with the muzzle on also.
    Practise with a range of friendly people.

STAGE TWO: JOINING UP

Aggression can result or be exacerbated by you not having a strong enough mentoring bond with your dog, in which your dog looks to you for direction and guidance in all situations. Once you do have a strong bond with your dog in this way, he should look to you for an indication as to whether a new person is okay: if you indicate that they are, your dog doesn't have to make the decision and potentially behave inappropriately. This is the role of the 'nicely' command.

Before you get started, establish this good bond with your dog by doing the Joining Up training covered earlier in the book. Practise all four stages — at the clip station, on-lead, umbilical and off-lead — before progressing to treatment. Joining Up is extremely important, as it will teach your aggressive dog to look to you for guidance on how to react when meeting new people, so you can tell him to behave in an appropriate manner.

STAGE THREE: TREATMENT

Before we start treatment, please note that for human-oriented aggression we use the 'no' command in conjunction with the check so that the correction is *not* associated with the other person. This is different to what we do when we treat dog-to-dog aggression, when it is okay for the dog to associate the correction with another dog. It is not safe to encourage your dog to think she is getting a correction from the person she is meeting, as this can create further negative associations and reactions.

As we progress, if the therapy is successful we will be using fewer and fewer 'no' commands and more 'nicely' — growing the dog's understanding that people are friendly. Because you are associated with the 'no' and 'nicely' it does mean that you will of course need to be around to support your dog in learning good meet and greets.

Greeting routine (see previous photo sequence)

When your dog encounters a new person, he should be looking to you for direction and guidance that this person is okay and not a threat. If you don't provide this assurance, he'll make his own decisions about the situation — and if your dog has protective or fear-induced aggression problems, that decision is likely to be an inappropriate one.

To alleviate this issue, you need to create a greeting routine for your dog when he encounters new people, in which you indicate that the person is okay, and the dog is rewarded for appropriate behaviours.

For this therapy, we will start with people your dog knows and likes, and practise the routine extensively before graduating to less familiar and less-liked people. For example, let's say your dog engages in fear-based aggression especially with tall men wearing hoodies and sunglasses. You would start by practising the greeting routine with family members and friends that your dog is familiar with, then you would move on to unfamiliar women, then short men, then tall men, then finally tall men in hoodies and sunglasses. In this way, your dog becomes accustomed to the greeting routine in incremental steps, with the situation getting gradually more challenging. Remember, this is called 'desensitisation' and allows the dog to learn in steps (see the Phobias chapter to understand the principles of desensitisation).

You will need a trusted friend (or a series of trusted friends!) to successfully carry out this therapy. You will need to instruct your friends as to what you want them to do to help you fix your dog's issue.

Here's what to do:

O Put your dog on a safety-slip collar and lead (as well as a muzzle, if necessary).

O Do your basic routine of Joining Up to get good contact with your dog.

O Have the other person stand still, sitting on a chair or crouching down, minimising eye contact with the dog, and positioning their body three-quarters on, so that they are not facing the dog straight. Ensure that the person does not reach out to your dog. The behaviour of the people your dog is learning to greet initially is fundamental and can change everything: they need to be demonstrating non-threatening behaviour.

O Have a good handle on your dog's lead, ready to deliver an effective check if needed.

O Approach the person with your dog on the lead, stopping at 2 metres away. Say 'nicely', then ask for 'sit' and 'wait'. Click and reward your dog for good, non-threatening, responses.

O Repeat the 'nicely' command, and click and reward your dog two to three times if he is relaxed and non-threatening.

O Your dog should be looking at you generally for direction, but also should be able to look at the other person and not be over-sensitive to the other person's intermittent glance at her. (Ensure that the other person isn't staring, as this is a threat.)

O If your dog is showing threatening behaviours, give him a 'no' command first, and click and reward an appropriate response. (A 'no' command without a check gives your dog a chance to choose to avoid the consequence, or otherwise receive a check.) Be prepared to move fast with an effective check if your dog's behaviour escalates.

O If your dog shows threatening behaviour, check firmly on a strong 'no' command. Circle around and away from the person, and reflect on whether or not you need to put your dog in a muzzle. If your dog is lunging and threatening to bite, a muzzle is definitely required to progress.

O Repeat the 'nicely' command as you approach the person, up until 2 metres away again. Do this until you get a good, consistent response, and you feel relaxed moving closer. Continue to click and reward good responses.

O Move now to within 1 metre of the person, then click and reward good responses. Be ready with your 'no', then a second 'no' and an effective check if needed. Ideally by now he is relaxed.

O Move now to within half a metre of the person, and click and reward good responses, or use the 'no' sequences, as above.

O In general, as you slowly approach in stages, progress in increments that allow your dog to succeed. Not too fast; don't rush this phase. Take guidance from how your dog is coping: is he eating, showing signs of aggression?

O If your dog is behaving in a non-threatening manner, move to the hand-touch target technique as above. Ask the other person to hold a hand out, palm facing slightly forward (do not reach the hand out very far). In happy, 'up' tones, say 'nicely', then 'touch'. When your dog touches the person's hand, you click and reward. Repeat several times. If this progresses well, then repeat with the other person giving the food reward. (If they find this difficult to do with the dog wearing a muzzle, then you reward.)

O For any negative responses, say 'no' and deliver click and reward if your dog responds. (However, be ready to check immediately if things escalate quickly.) If he doesn't respond, deliver an effective check at the same time as a 'no' command, then circle back out and away, placing yourself between your dog and the other person. You don't have time for just a warning 'no', so go straight to the effective check.

O Repeat the exercise if you feel you can progress safely.

O Timing is everything, so don't rush your dog. Give him plenty of easy practice first, and be guided by how your dog is progressing before moving to the next stage.

O If at any time you think the interaction is escalating beyond your control or skills, then remove your dog quietly and calmly, go back to an earlier stage and/or person, and consider whether you need to put a muzzle on your dog.

O Start with easy, familiar, friendly people, then move on to slightly more challenging, then very challenging people for your dog. (This hierarchy of people is dependent on your dog's triggers.)

Proofing the behaviour

This is one of the most serious therapies in terms of safety, so you must proof it very systematically and carefully. Ensure you have identified the hierarchy of people your dog reacts to, from slight to most, and work your way slowly through these. Also respond to how your dog is coping.

Once you are getting a consistently good response, you can proof your dog by changing the situation slightly. Have the person she is meeting standing up instead of sitting or crouching down, practise in other trigger areas, such as in your house and car, and generally vary and proof the training to practise in different situations. Continue to stay alert around any change of environment or context, and observe your dog closely so that you can respond. Make the changes incremental.

Remember, have your dog wear a muzzle if there is *any* risk she could bite someone — always better to be safe than sorry. A considerable amount of work is required to achieve results with issues of this kind, so do lots of practice whenever you can with as many different people as you can, and do not rush each step. If you have decided to use a muzzle, then it is best that you seek further professional help.

It's very important that you establish a consistent greeting routine for your dog. Always ensure that your dog has greeted a person she doesn't know correctly (on-lead), particularly if that person is in the risk type for your dog. You need to make sure your dog gets a chance to greet that person properly and positively, otherwise the issue won't be solved long-term. You are the one who provides the guidance for your dog whenever she meets someone new. After solid Joining Up work, your dog should look to you to determine whether a stranger is friendly, so always use the 'nicely' command to reinforce that your dog should take your lead on whether a person is friendly.

Conclusion

This is a challenging therapy to do: aggression is not easy to treat. However, putting the work in is worth it. Remember, you are taking your dog 'back to the den' to re-create similar diverse social experiences for your dog to adapt to. You need the dog in a learning state, and you need to reinforce this state and appropriate behaviour.

Take your time and get advice if needed. It is possible to help this type of dog, but you need to really understand this process and implement it consistently. For more serious cases we have advanced clinical techniques we have developed that are beyond this book to teach. Hopefully a behaviourist near you has similar skills and can help you. Seek advice.

I refer to the 'Family Rules of Conduct' for your dog and ask that you write down your family rules. It's important you sit down as a family and write these together – then stick to them!

Things to cover off are:

O Be friendly to all, including children, all kinds of people, other dogs and other species.
O Come when called.
O Understand our shared language.
O Don't soil in the house or car — and don't eat the house or car.
O Understand 'yes' and 'no'.
O Stay relaxed and calm, especially when alone.
O Practise a good 'Zen down'.

Good luck. Develop good situational awareness, be conservative and safe.

Barking

Yap, yap, yap, yap, yap, yap, yap. Delightful, isn't it? Don't you just revel in the joy of hearing the incessant sound of your dog's voice at all times of the day and night? Oh, not so much?

Most dogs do bark occasionally. This is to be expected, as it forms part of the way they communicate. But some dogs love the sound of their own voice, and get in the habit of barking with regularity (and perhaps not stopping for long periods of time), which can be incredibly unpleasant — particularly if you're constantly worried about whether or not you're annoying the neighbours. Worse still, if your dog barks excessively and complaints are made, it can result in a hefty fine or your dog being removed from you — not a situation any of us wish to encounter, I'm sure.

When a dog's barking is excessive, it can greatly affect the quality of life of that dog's family. I know of people who have been at their wits-end, losing sleep on a nightly basis because their dog barks too much. Then the effects start to roll out across other aspects of their lives: they're tired at work, irritable with the kids, too lethargic to go out and feeling drained.

Even if your dog isn't causing you this much grief, barking can still be very annoying, so if you can train your dog not to do it (or at least to stop when asked), then it can't be a bad thing, right?

Why do dogs bark?

Wolves rarely bark in the wild. Overly vocal behaviour didn't evolve in wolves, as it would have been a disadvantage when hunting as a pack, alerting prey to their presence. When wolves vocalise, it's usually either a bark or growl to scare off threats to the pack (such as other wolves or predators), a dominance gesture to other pack members, a vocalistion to solicit something from other pack members, or a howl when a wolf has become separated and wishes to find its way back to the pack.

Dogs, however, have developed much more vocal behaviour as they've been domesticated with humans who respond to these vocalisations, and they no longer need to hunt quietly as a pack.

Barking is easy for dogs to do, and very easy for us to unwittingly reward, which reinforces the behaviour, making it more difficult to correct. For example, some people give their dogs a toy or something to chew on when they bark to keep them quiet; or if the dog is barking outside and wants to be let in, they let her in. But these actions all continually reward the dog for barking, and encourage her to use barking again in future when she wants something. Why wouldn't she, when previous experience says it works?

How to treat this behaviour

The key steps to treat this behaviour are:

O Understand and treat the underlying cause of the barking.

O Recognise the ways you are rewarding your dog's barking, and stop these immediately.

O Put your dog in a learning state.

O Build your relationship with your dog.

O Teach the 'quiet' and 'speak' commands (and more advanced techniques outlined below).

O Work on the basic commands, especially 'come', 'leave it' and 'no'.

O Address any underlying behaviour issue.

UNDERSTAND THE UNDERLYING CAUSE

Though barking might look like one behaviour, dogs bark for different reasons, including protection, fear, separation distress, attention-seeking, in response to stimulus or play/excitement. If your dog's barking is caused by a particular behaviour problem like aggression, separation anxiety or fear, then it is critical that you address those issues as well.

Barking is hard-wired or intrinsic; that is, it usually can't be taught — it is a direct emotional response. The dog's communication is honest, so he is saying what he feels. Therefore, if you understand these rules/guidelines around these barks, you can trust your dog's communication.

In general, dogs' intonation will be a high-pitched bark or whine if they are soliciting and happy, and maybe if fearful. A low-pitched and growling intonation indicates a full aggressive, threatening or dominance state. Sometimes they might be barking deeply. Barking in dogs is a mix of tones influenced by varied environmental and emotional factors. For example, if they are restricted they will have a different bark than if they are free. If they are threatening you they will have a different bark than if they are fearful of you. If you are a family member they will have a high-pitched, soliciting bark, or if you are a stranger it will likely be low and growly.

When barking, some dogs will be conflicted in their emotional state, and so they mix up their bark signals, reflecting that conflict. For example, dogs barking in yards, on chains and in houses are often conflicted, because if they were free they would stay silent and avoid the threat, but because they can't leave they bark in fear and aggression. You might notice the varying tones of their bark, ranging from higher-pitched fear barks to a full deep-tone offensive, threatening bark (they can't leave, so they threaten). A territorial imperative is also often at play.

Below are a number of causes of barking to help you determine your treatment approach.

Protection

Barking is likely protection-based if your dog barks when someone or something approaches your property or front door, you, your car or a member of your family. This is a defensive through to offensive bark that's designed to scare off anything the dog perceives may be a threat. In this zone your dog will look alert and possibly aggressive, and the bark will be in a low tone. A threat growl or low-pitched bark occurs when the sender is aggressive and wants the hearer to withdraw: 'Back off, get out of my territory.'

Fear

This is likely to be the reason your dog barks if she is scared of people, dogs or some 'thing' (e.g. a strange object or animal). Your dog will be reluctant to go near the thing or person she is afraid of. This fear-induced bark is paired with fear postural signals and is conflicted. If your dog were free she would retreat, but since she is not, she indicates non-threat, then defensive threat the closer you get to her. The fear-induced bark is higher pitched or alternating pitch.

Separation distress

Dogs with separation distress when left alone often bark excessively in a high-pitched tonal cry, or even a howl, due to the anxiety and stress associated with this condition. This is attempting to call the owner back home, much like wolves use howling to regather the pack after the hunt, as the physical nature of the sound is easy to locate. It says 'I'm lonely' or 'I'm lost — come back to me.' When you hear it, you feel it!

These dogs usually exhibit other symptoms such as pacing, destructiveness, attempts to escape, self-harm, excessive panting and sometimes urinating or defecating in the house while you're out. (See the Separation Distress chapter.)

Attention-seeking

Many dogs bark or whine in a high-pitched tonal signal like a puppy whimper (it can be a whine, lost call or play bark) when he wants something or wants to get your attention; for example, a dog that wants a pat, to be let in from outside, to come into your bedroom or be taken for a walk. It tends to be motivated by care-soliciting, appeasement play or soliciting. He is not threatening but encouraging, and telling the receiver it's okay to come closer or please come to me.

The play bark particularly solicits play interaction! This bark is usually accompanied by high-energy behaviour, the play bow and tail wagging; for example, if your dog is playing and running around with other dogs.

Stimulus-oriented

This is when an animal or object stimulates your dog's barking — for example, a bird or cat outside. What she is barking at will determine the type of bark she uses. A cat on the fence will elicit a cross between a hunt bark and a threat bark. Hard-to-identify objects will cause a conflicted threat (a mix of high-pitched elements with a deep threat bark, as the dog can't see what it is) or arousal bark.

Treating the underlying cause

Once you have identified the cause of your dog's barking and whether you need to treat an additional behaviour problem as well, you can then go on to treat the barking itself. The Shared Language chapter will help you accurately identify through postures what is causing your dog's barking. Remember it is driven by internal state and environment.

If you have identified that your dog is barking for reasons such as separation distress, fear or aggression, then addressing these underlying causes will be an important part of controlling barking. The techniques in this chapter will certainly be helpful for addressing the symptoms, but fixing the main cause of the problem will be the best long-term solution; see the relevant chapters in Part D relating to your dog's issue to progress with this.

AVOID REWARDING YOUR DOG'S BARKING

Firstly, you need to ensure that you aren't rewarding the barking, otherwise none of your training will have any effect in the long run.

- Don't give your dog a toy, bone or anything to chew on to stop him barking; use it before for prevention, but not to reward him.
- Avoid patting your dog to stop the barking.
- Don't give your dog treats or his dinner when it's barking. Wait until he is quiet.

O If your dog is barking outside because he wants to come in, ignore the barking and wait until he is calm and quiet before he's allowed to come inside.

O Don't use high-pitched, friendly tones to speak to your dog when he's barking. I've seen people try to rationalise with their dog in a human way, using a nice voice: 'Buster, please stop barking, my darling. You're going to wake the neighbours.' Needless to say, this doesn't send your dog the message you intend it to — you are rewarding him with your attention! Conversely, often your shouting will make things worse because you haven't taught him what to do.

I know it's tempting to do whatever you have to do to stop your dog barking, but some short-term consistency will help to alleviate the problem in the long term, which will be better for everyone.

SWITCH YOUR DOG INTO A LEARNING STATE

Before you start implementing the following strategies, ensure that your dog is in a learning state. Use clip stations too.

BUILD THE RELATIONSHIP

Establishing a solid relationship with your dog will help immensely as, instead of automatically resorting to barking to get what she wants or alert you to something, your dog will look to you for direction and take her cue on how to act from you. Build this bond by using techniques from the Joining Up chapter, and practise your 'sit', 'down' and 'Zen down' commands.

TEACH THE 'QUIET' AND 'SPEAK' COMMANDS

Funnily enough, to teach your dog to stop barking you actually need to have your dog bark — the need for contrast. So for this training, you'll use something that generates barking from your dog to teach it the 'speak' and contrasting 'quiet' commands.

There are two training options. The first, in which you teach the 'quiet' command only, is preferable, but is more effective for dogs that have a minor to medium barking issue. The second, in which you teach both 'speak' and 'quiet', is a little trickier, but is usually better for dogs that have a really persistent bark. It provides a clearer contrast for your dog if he has a particularly tricky problem.

First, find something that causes your dog to bark: often dogs bark when they are clipped up, so that's the example I'll be using. However, if your dog doesn't bark when clipped up, use another stimulus — either a ball, a lead, holding a treat, waving something, shutting him outside the door, ringing the door bell, etc.

'Quiet'-only method

O Put your dog on a clip station in a quiet, distraction-free room.

O Practise your 'sit', 'down' and 'Zen down' commands, and click and reward calm behaviour.

O If your dog barks at all during this interaction, give her a 'quiet' command, and if you get three or more seconds of quiet, click and reward. Systematically extend the expected quiet period further — e.g. 5 seconds, then click and reward, 10 seconds, 20 seconds, etc. Once you are getting good, consistent quiet, then slowly work your dog into an intermittent schedule of reward (rewarding every three or so periods that she is quiet).

O Practise this lots, until your dog understands the association between quiet times and receiving a reward. She will then begin to associate these quiet times with your use of the word 'quiet' as a command.

O Be very careful that your dog doesn't learn that by barking she gets a reward. It can be easy for her to learn that by barking you will enter into this training session of barking, quiet, then reward.

O If you think that this is starting to happen, you will need to introduce your safety slip collar and long-line as well. If your dog barks, say 'quiet'. If she is quiet, click and reward; if she continues barking, say 'no' with gruff intonation, and if she continues, give her an effective check on the second 'no'. Then repeat the 'quiet' command, and click and reward if quiet. This is offering your dog a contrast to help her learn be quiet.

'Speak' and 'quiet' method

O If your dog is barking too much for you to get an opportunity to reward 'quiet', teach a 'speak' command first, then contrast with a 'quiet' command.

O This technique is trickier, and if done incorrectly you can end up rewarding your dog for barking and reinforce the behaviour. It's important to reward both 'speak' and 'quiet' so he learns the contrast. Only use this method if you need to for highly vocal dogs, and don't over-encourage the 'speak', as this is already natural.

O First teach a 'speak' command. Importantly, clip your dog up somewhere other than the clip station, so that he doesn't learn to bark on the clip station. (The clip station is the den associated with calm, safety and therefore quiet, so you don't want to ruin that association.)

O When you anticipate that your dog will bark, encourage him with a 'speak' hand signal. (Hold your forefinger and thumb together, then open and close them like a duck's bill.) Click and reward as soon as he starts barking.

O Continue this for 3–5 minutes, then introduce the 'quiet' command. When he stops barking momentarily, say 'quiet' and use the 'quiet' hand signal (with two fingers extended, move your hand from left to right in front of your dog's face), then click and reward.

O When you feel both are being done on command, slowly increase the repetition of 'quiet' and reduce the repetition of 'speak'.

O Be careful that your dog doesn't start soliciting your reward by barking — it must be under your stimulus control (command).

O Never reward your dog for barking unless you have given the 'speak' command and hand signal.

O Practise lots in a quiet room, then move to increasingly distracting environments.

O If persistent barking continues, introduce the conditioned aversive signal 'no' command. If your dog is not quiet when asked, say 'no' first, and if he responds click and reward; if not, check on the second 'no', then click and reward if quiet.

Extending the training

Above, you have taught the 'quiet' and/or 'speak' command by isolating the dog in a training context (a quiet room). Next you have to generalise this training into the actual contexts where your dog barks.

Clip your dog onto a long lead. Allow this lead to drag as she moves around the house or outside. If she barks, give the 'quiet' command. If quiet, click and reward. If not, say 'no', then click and reward quiet. If not, give an effective check on the second 'no'. Repeat as needed.

Speak.

Start to speak.

Speak.

Give hand signal. Click and reward after 5 seconds of quiet then slowly extend time for click and reward.

Click and reward appropriate quiet. See the techniques in the Proofing and Fading the Clicker chapter to show how to extend into a more challenging environment.

BASIC COMMANDS

I recommend working on a few of your basic commands extensively to help you manage your dog's barking going forward, especially 'leave it' and 'come'.

○ Leave it: This tells your dog to leave an external stimulus alone. For example, if your dog barks at birds or cats, a 'leave it' command will help to ensure your dog will come away from the stimulus that's generating the barking. This is particularly important for stimulus-oriented barking. Again use the 'no' command as well, as needed.

○ Come: This is an essential command for many reasons, and will enable you to call your dog back to you when he's barking. Similarly, in a high-arousal state like barking you might need to use your 'no' command to reinforce your command.

PERSISTENT BARKING

For persistent barking when the neighbours and council are involved, you might need to use one of the citronella collar or modern barking limiters with a warning tone (another form of conditioned aversive signal) to enable correction while you are not there. The warning tone will enable your dog to avoid the correction, so is more humane.

Go forth and conquer that bark and look forward to the peace and serenity ahead!

Separation distress

Separation distress isn't only distressing for a dog, it's distressing for the dog's owner, as I'm sure you're well aware if you're reading this chapter.

When your dog goes into a state of fear and panic whenever you try to leave the house, it's upsetting and can incite feelings of worry and guilt. I've seen it many times.

If you're in this situation, it may seem that no matter what you do to try to treat the separation anxiety, it doesn't work and even gets worse. It can be a daunting behaviour to treat, as it does take a significant amount of consistent effort; however, there are ways to cure it.

RUBY: WHEN CLOSE CAN BE TOO CLOSE

One particular dog was a Rhodesian Ridgeback called Ruby, whose owner Emily adopted her at eight weeks old. Emily worked from home, so Ruby was by her side all the time, following her from room to room and curiously keeping an eye on what she was up to. Whenever Emily sat at her desk Ruby was on her lap or lying under the desk; whenever she was out working in the garden, Ruby was there, too, helping her dig at the soil. Wherever Emily went, Ruby went — and Emily loved her loyal pup to bits.

Because Emily was a very conscientious owner, she made sure that she had cleared her schedule when she first adopted Ruby so she didn't have anything on that she couldn't take her to. She thought you couldn't leave puppies alone, so made sure she never did, and the two built an incredibly strong bond, with Ruby also becoming accustomed to sleeping in Emily's room at night.

However, the issue came when Ruby started to get a bit older and Emily began to want to leave the house and go to places where she wasn't able to take Ruby. Because she was used to having Emily around all day, every day, Ruby would become distressed and anxious whenever Emily left the house. As a result, Emily tried to avoid going out much, and always gave Ruby heaps of attention before she left and after she got back. Unfortunately, the situation kept getting worse, and Ruby kept becoming more distressed. This situation hit a low point when Emily had to leave the house and Ruby desperately tried to chew her way through the door to get out.

What is separation distress?

Separation distress (or 'separation anxiety' as it's also often called) in its extreme form is a phobia of separation. As with any phobia, when dogs are suffering from this they are highly anxious and go into sympathetic arousal (the fight-flight state): their pupils dilate, they start panting, salivating, pacing around, vocalising and become increasingly stressed. This is an extreme non-learning state.

Dogs with separation distress who are left alone will likely be barking, howling or whining, they may defecate or urinate inside, and they'll probably try desperately to escape — going so far as to chew through doors, ropes and fences or injure themselves trying to get out of wherever they have been confined. Highly destructive behaviours are commonplace in dogs that suffer from this issue. Many people work out that their dog has separation distress because they come home from being out and their house is in tatters, there is poo on the floor and neighbours report hearing the dog barking or whining. It's no fun at all, and horrible to see our dogs in such severe distress.

Why does it occur?

We see this issue in dogs that have never learnt how to be separated from the person or people they are close to (their secure base). It can actually be a symptom of a dog that has been too well loved, if anything!

Wolves are almost never separated from the pack in the wild, so if they are, they show severe distress and will make extreme attempts to get back to the pack. They will vocalise, howl, whine and dig. This is because when a wolf is separated from its pack, it's in dangerous territory. Wolves rely on 'safety in numbers' — being with the pack protects them from other predators, and enables them to hunt effectively so they can eat and stay alive. It's no wonder they become distressed when they are separated!

Dogs are by nature better suited to learning to be separated than wolves are. Usually at around seven weeks old, puppies are separated from their mother and go out to meet the rest of their pack (that's us, for domesticated dogs!). At this stage, puppies form a bond with their mentor (this is sometimes called their secondary socialisation period).

However, when the development of this mentor bond is not managed carefully and the puppy doesn't develop the ability to be alone, anxiety and fear of separation develops. The resultant fear state leads to the distressed (and even phobic) behaviours that are synonymous with this issue.

A common mistake that loving, caring owners make is going out of their way to ensure their beloved new puppy is with them all the time — tending to his every whimper or cry, always keeping him happy and entertained. However, our pups must learn to be alone for increasingly longer periods of time.

Though this stems from a place of love, in reality the dog is learning to become over-dependent and attention-seeking. These attention-seeking behaviours are often inadvertently rewarded by the owner, causing them to intensify; for example, a young dog whines when he wants to be patted, then the owner pats him and rewards the whining. Even just attending to the dog or even just looking at him when he shows anxiety can effectively reward this anxious behaviour and increase the frequency of it.

Separation distress is also a self-perpetuating behaviour in that because the dog is distressed about being left alone, he isn't left alone often. This creates further dependence, resulting in further distress over being left alone, and therefore the owner leaves the dog alone even less frequently or not at all. It's a vicious cycle that can develop into an extreme state of separation phobia, resulting in owners feeling trapped into keeping their dog with them at all times. I have had many owners who have scheduled their whole life around such dogs.

Prevention of separation distress

Prevention is better than cure! Separation distress can be easily prevented by teaching your pup how to separate appropriately in the formative period. For guidance on how to do that, go to Part C.

How to treat separation distress

This is a phobia of separation, therefore we use the same techniques and principles described in the Phobias chapter, using the principles of desensitisation and counter-conditioning (using the clicker). We are in effect desensitising our dog against separation fears.

The key to addressing this issue is to build your dog's confidence and independence. Most of the problems we treat are grounded in building a stronger bond, but in this case the current bond is too strong and unhealthy, so we reverse the process. Therefore, instead of first building a bond using Joining Up then doing the treatment therapy, we reverse this process. We do the treatment therapy first, then build an appropriate bond using Joining Up.

Healthily bonded dogs have as a part of their bond a secure base with the mentor, and so generalise this sense of safety (and stay non-anxious) in their home location, either a physical site or a den. Unhealthily over-dependent dogs don't transfer this to a physical site, so we have to re-cultivate that by building site-specific confidence. To do this we do a lot of clip station work, figuratively taking the dog back to the den.

The primary methods and tools for this therapy are:

O Understanding your role as owners and trainers in the issue.

O Counter-conditioning: switching the dog out of a non-learning state into a learning state through the use of a clicker.

O Desensitisation: the systematic exposure to gradually increased periods of separation (graduated departure) from key people your dog is close to. It involves increasing the amount of time you are apart from your dog while keeping her in a learning state and not showing distress behaviours. It slowly teaches your dog how to be separated from you, building her confidence and trust that you will return.

O Transfering social confidence to site-specific confidence, with graduated periods on the clip station and in other home sites. You might look to use social facilitation with a companion dog as well.

O Sometimes it helps to introduce a range of other approaches, such as anti-anxiety drugs, homeopathic and training aids to help to keep the dog in a learning state.

When you pair a desensitisation plan (graduated separation on the clip station) with counter-conditioning, you are systematically exposing your dog to greater fear-inducing stimuli (in this case, the increasingly greater loss of your presence) while keeping her in a learning state by using the clicker paired with food rewards. You then rely on habituation once rewarding is no longer feasible; that is, once you leave for a while.

Here are the key steps in this training:

O Understand your role.

O Create a secure base in terms of the clip station.

O Switch your dog into a learning state.

O Do generalised desensitisation through graduated departure.

O Undertake Joining Up to create an appropriate relationship.

O Set up the environment to minimise distress and prevent issues.

O Use training aids and medication to support your dog, if necessary.

STAGE ONE: YOUR ROLE

As discussed above, this is an issue of an over-dependent relationship, so by its very nature it relates to you. Your dog is overly attached to you, so your very presence can inhibit learning straight away, and as soon as you try to separate he will get anxious. So it is a challenging behaviour to treat yourself.

It is essential that you give your dog appropriate and consistent physical and verbal signals. Even if you are feeling anxious, remain calm, quiet and relaxed. Limit your verbalisations (friendly, 'up' tones if you have to), minimise your eye contact and limit your physical movements (don't move around too much or wave your arms). You are trying to present a calm, settling energy for your dog. Stay in this low-key state as you depart and when you return. Only reward calm.

STAGE TWO: ESTABLISHING A SECURE BASE AND SWITCHING INTO LEARNING STATE — COUNTER-CONDITIONING

We use the clip station to create a secure base (den site) — a physical place associated with you and safety. Because the clip station is related to you, it is a place that your dog can relax and accept separation in. It is a safe place that your dog can be whenever you are not around — a place he can trust.

You can help by making this spot the most attractive and comfy in the room: a place your dog wants to be, particularly when his other safe thing — you — is not around. It is good to place it in a familiar, social place so they are reminded of you. Being placed outside, far away down the end of the property, plus separated from you is two layers of separation. Instead, create the safe place near to your 'central den areas' — this is how dogs think of our lounge, dining room or bedroom. They know these areas are central by our habits and smells.

You can have three or four clip stations set up around your house to help with this therapy, including one in the car. Make sure they are warm, soft and welcoming. Using something that smells of you can also be supportive for your dog. Use them often, for gradually longer periods of time (a strong crate is a good idea, too, if your dog isn't claustrophobic, though many of these dogs will be, so take care).

○ Begin by clipping up your dog on the clip station. Be aware that clipping your dog up and separating yourself even the smallest distance can trigger separation anxiety, so watch for signs of distress. You do not want your dog to become distressed during this process, as it will make it harder to switch your dog into the learning state that you wish to achieve. You also do not want your dog to establish any aversion to the clip station, so take care.

O Minimise separation at this stage — sit right beside your dog, and focus on switching and maintaining a learning state and creating good associations with the experience of being at the clip station. You can start this with formal clip stations sessions, then move to having your dog beside you while watching TV at night or by you in your office or social area. (lots of this neutral contact is great).

O Practise this around 5-10 times a day until it's part of the routine.

O Click and reward calm, focused, non-soliciting, non-vocal behaviour. Teach and practice 'sit', 'down' and 'Zen down'.

O Click and reward independent behaviours, such as when your dog looks away from you and is relaxed. This is important, as normally your dog will be so obsessed by you that he can't look away. If he looks away, he's developing independence, so you need to reward this.

O Get your dog into a 'Zen down'. Click and throw food rewards between your dog's legs to encourage him to stay in this calm and relaxed state. (See section 7.3)

O Continue this for a period of time until you see your dog is consistently relaxed and calm. You are going to move to an 'on your mat' command off the clip station once you have mastered this calmness at the clip station, clicking and rewarding your dog when he stays on his mat for gradually longer periods of time while unclipped.

O Once your dog has learnt to be on the clip station, you can leave your dog for up to an hour on the clip station while you're at home.

O Do the same in the car or outside while in the garden, and leave your dog with other friends for intervals using the clip station. Most dogs have a preferred person that they are most phobic of being separated from. If that's you, it can help to let others take over more control of resources — walks, feeding, etc — to broaden bonding to more individuals in a relaxed fashion.

STAGE THREE: GENERALISED DESENSITISATION THROUGH GRADUATED DEPARTURE

The initial graduated departure therapy is started on the clip station, where your dog begins learning relaxed separation. You will need a family member or friend to help you with this technique, as they will click and reward your dog for being in a relaxed 'Zen down' position as you gradually leave the room for increasingly extended periods. At first, it's a good idea to have the helper be someone your dog knows and is comfortable with, so that it's not as distressing for her as you move away. Have your helper begin by giving your dog lots of treats with clicking and rewarding calm behaviour so their relationship is strong.

Before you start departing, your dog should be in a good learning state, calm and relaxed, in a 'Zen down' position. Below is a graduated departure plan for desensitising your dog to separation.

The food treats for this behaviour are of a lower value, so that the very high-value food can be used for when your dog is separated from you. If you think this therapy will be challenging for your dog, try Rescue Remedy beforehand (or other anxiety-reducing medication if your dog is on any) to help support your dog.

O To start, move yourself just 0.5 metres away from your dog. Click and reward your dog, throwing treats between your dog's legs as she is in a 'down' or 'Zen down'. If she stands up, ask for a 'sit', 'down' and 'Zen down' again. Click and reward each position.

O Stay 0.5 metres away for about 10 seconds, then return to your dog before she gets in an anxious state. Click and reward to relax her.

O Move back to 0.5 metres away and stay away for about 30 seconds. Click and reward calm behaviour, again tossing treats between your dog's legs so she stays in a 'down' position. Then return to your dog and click and reward calm behaviour.

O Repeat the above at 0.5 metres away for 1-minute, 2-minute and then 5-minute intervals.

O Then move to 1 metre away and repeat the above, starting again at 10 seconds, then 30 seconds, then 1 minute, 2 minutes, 5 minutes.

O You will be looking at a training schedule something like the following diagram. You can do this in an informal way while just being and moving around home doing things as normal, but use this kind of graduated approach.

O As you move more than 1 metre away, ideally you would have

	10sec	30sec	1min	2mins	5mins +
0.5m					
1m					
2m					
3m					
5m					
10m					
Out of room					

a friend who remains near your dog to continue clicking and rewarding her for calm, non-stressed responses as you are further away from her. If you don't have anyone who can help you with this, you will need to toss the food rewards between your dog's legs from a distance — however, this is much more challenging, and prevents you from moving right out of the room, which is a very important last step in the therapy.

O You may speed up or slow down the recommended staging, depending on how your dog is responding and the severity of her issues.

O Break the stages over a number of sessions. Make sure you start at the beginning for a short time whenever you start a new session (at 0.5 metres away), so you ease your dog into the longer intervals.

O Customise the times and distances dependent on your dog's level of anxiety. Only move on to the next distance or time interval spent away if your dog is managing to stay in a relaxed and calm learning state. If your dog is getting distressed, go back a step. If your dog becomes reluctant to take the food rewards being offered, you are pushing too far, too fast. It is best to go back to the stage in which your dog was comfortably able to remain in a learning state.

O You don't want your dog to get into an anxious or distressed state, so watch for signs that she is starting to get distressed, and ease back just before this moment.

O You will also have to go through a process of fading your friend using the same technique as above. However, the friend will have to toss the food rewards at your dog's feet.

Throughout this process, you should:

O remain calm and relaxed through the sessions, including when you depart and arrive,

O reward calm, focused behaviours.

O reward independent behaviours, such as looking away and non-soliciting, non-vocalising behaviours.

O keep your dog in a learning state by clicking and rewarding the 'Zen down' position.

O avoid long periods of separation during the weeks of therapy if possible, so that your dog can learn separation systematically rather than having long periods of separation in between sessions. This can be challenging if you go out to work all day, so think about how your dog can be supported during this period — every long separation can set your dog back. Possible ideas might be to arrange for your dog to spend time with friends and family or at a doggy daycare.

This is a challenging therapy for your dog, so pay attention to how she is coping, and respond appropriately. Your dog needs to be switched into a calm state for it to work.

STAGE FOUR: JOINING UP

After each session of graduated departure, make sure you finish with some Joining Up work to reinforce an appropriate level of relationship. As you do the on-lead and umbilical work, practice some 'wait' and 'stay' commands as you move around the room. Finish back on the clip station. Continue to keep the session relaxed and calm.

STAGE FIVE: PROOFING

To ensure this treatment carries over into real life and not just while doing a specific training session, here are some ways in which you can proof this behaviour for the real world.

O As your dog becomes more confident, you can start using the 'on your mat' command to have him return to the clip station/mat without clipping him up. Take your dog off the clip station and ask him to sit on his mat. Click and reward staying on the mat without being clipped, using the 'on your mat' and 'stay' commands.

O While your dog is on his mat, move around the house, going into other rooms. Go off and make a cup of tea or do your laundry — go about your everyday life. Once you return to your dog on his mat, click and reward him for remaining on his mat and his calm responses.

O Gradually go out the front door for short periods, extending those periods over time. Click and reward calm behaviours.

O Do a graduated departure session from your car or from the front gate of your house (especially if your dog is going to be left outside).

Environment set-up

Below are some suggestion to support your dog being separated from you. However, I wouldn't recommend leaving your dog inside for long periods of time, particularly through the initial part of the therapy period.

O Ensure the environment is secure, so your dog can't escape.

O When you leave the house, it's good to leave your dog in an area she associates with you, one you use and share with your dog (e.g. a sunroom or deck, rather than a garage or isolated area).

O Scatter high-value food items around the pen, kennel or run.

O Pack a Kong-brand toy with a high-value food item that is hard for your dog to get out and takes a long time, or give her a bone with some meat on it to help keep her entertained for hours.

O Take your dog for a big walk before you leave. This will help her to sleep when she has finished finding the treats and chewing the bone, etc.

O Leaving the TV, radio or music on can give your dog some comfort from familiar sounds — anything that is associated with you being around.

O Use doggy daycare services and friends to reduce the length of time spent alone.

O Give your dog social stimulation (facilitation) with a neighbour's dog: if you have a fence that divides your place from a neighbour's place, see whether there's a way you can leave your dog in a space along that fence line so she can have some interaction with the dog next door. Or even better, see if you and your neighbour can organise a schedule where both dogs are kept together sometimes to keep each other company (if they get along well, of course!)

Use of training aids and medication to support your dog

O You can look at a range of medications and or homeopathic remedies to support your dog. Please discuss with your veterinarian what suitable options might be. If your dog's separation distress is severe, also seek advice as to whether there might be underlying medical causes.

O Consider canine appeasement pheromone: this is an artificial version of a naturally-occurring pheromone that has a calming effect.

O Consider investing in a remote-reward training device that allows you to reward your dog for calm behaviours from a distance through the use of a remote control, (e.g. a Manners Minder).

O Look at the specially designed dog coats that use gentle, constant pressure to calm your dog, to relieve anxiety (e.g. Thunder coats).

Conclusion

RUBY: ON HER WAY

We've been doing some intensive graduated departure therapy lately with Emily and Ruby, to help Ruby understand that everything will be okay when Emily has to go away for a while — and give her the confidence that Emily will indeed come back to her!

As Ruby was an extreme case, it took several sessions moving Emily slowly just out of the room before we were able to get her leaving the room and house altogether for periods of time. But now, much to Emily's relief, she is at a stage where she is able to go out for dinner with friends and not come home to a highly distressed dog and utter destruction in the house. Hooray!

Good luck to you with this therapy. It is a challenging one, but stay committed — and remember, even though it's hard, it is for the best in the end for everyone.

19

House training

TOMMY: A LITTLE DOG WHO HAD NEVER KNOWN HOME LIFE

You have heard about my dog Tommy already and what a cutie he is. But it wasn't so cute when we first adopted him and he was soiling in the house. I'm sure we all have things we'd rather do than scrub the carpet to get rid of the smell of dog poo, right? But once I understood the background to Tommy's behaviour, I couldn't hold his excretal issues against him.

You'll remember Tommy was a breeding dog. I first met him when I was working on a set for a big TV commercial with a beautiful Jack Russell called Betty (sadly passed on now), who belonged to my great friends Kim and Tina. Betty was getting on in age, so to ease her rigorous filming schedule we employed a body double for her as back-up. (Yip, dogs get body doubles, too!) Tommy was scouted for the role,

and, being very similar to our darling Betty, was given the job.

It transpired that three-year-old Tommy had only lived in a kennel so he had not been house-trained. He was such a lovely dog and I couldn't bear the thought of him going back to that life (house-training problems or not), so I convinced the owner to let us have him, and the rest is history. I joke now that I needed to get Kim (my new partner at the time) a cute little dog to ease her into what I knew would be a crazy life with me, surrounded by troubled dogs (at the time I only had beautiful Blue, so I felt it was a bit of false advertising!). Luckily, she seems to have adjusted to the madness with flying colours — I reckon Tommy paved the way, so I owe him for that!

Understanding toileting behaviour

You may think the wild wolf isn't constrained to a house with a backyard, and can therefore toilet wherever it wants at any time it wants. This isn't the case. When the birthing season of spring is arriving, wolf packs create a den for the mother wolf to birth her puppies in, generally by digging a safe space into the soft spring soil. The mother will reside in this den with the new puppies for weeks after they are born. Initially, the infant puppies will toilet in the den and the mother will lick up the urine and faeces around her to keep the den clean.

As the puppies approach 6-7 weeks old, their instinctual desire to not want to spoil the den kicks in, and they'll naturally want to go outside the den to toilet. This is called 'nest site inhibition', and refers to a wolf or dog's natural instinct to not want to toilet in their nesting space. Puppies learn the difference between their den and the outside world through texture discrimination: the floor of their den feels different under their feet compared with the ground outside.

Using this natural learning process, you can also teach your dog to discriminate between indoor surfaces that are inappropriate for toileting on (such as carpet, tiles, lino or floorboards) and surfaces that are appropriate (newspaper or grass). By using textures and substrates to teach our dogs the difference between indoors and outdoors, we essentially teach our dogs that inside the house is the 'den'. This is an idea they can easily adjust to, as it's the area where we (as their

Meeko in his ideal house-training set up. Pen at back, the crate he's in leads to outside.

Take your pup outside after eating, playing and sleeping, to toilet on grass.

pack) spend most of our time. Once the whole house is generalised or established as the den, the dog will not want to toilet inside. In fact most dogs, if they get the chance early, will try to move away from the house as far as possible. Many of us have had a dog that defecates only off the property! Make sure you create a space as far away and out of the way as possible, and take your pup there whenever possible to toilet, and click and reward after he has done so. Say 'be quick'.

Starting house training when your puppy is 7-8 weeks old means that you are teaching him right behaviour at the same stage as he would have learned this behaviour in the wild, which will give you the best results, easily.

If you have an adult dog that still toilets inside, this is because he hasn't learnt to consider your house as his den, and doesn't discriminate between your house and outside. Although more challenging, the training principles for adult dogs are the same, so I'll take you through how to house-train a puppy first, then afterwards we'll discuss what to do if your adult dog toilets inside: we will take him 'back to the den'.

How to house-train your puppy

There are three main methods, each of which I'll take you through before showing you how to use them in conjunction with each other to the best effect. Choose which one best suits your home arrangements.

METHOD ONE: CRATE-TRAINING

This method takes advantage of your puppy's instinct to not want to toilet in her nest or den, and her ability to distinguish between substrates under her paws. Using a crate, we create a contained nest for her — just big enough to include a bed and food and water bowls.

Within the crate, half of the space should be a nice soft bed, and the remainder should be covered with a substrate that's unlike anything you'd usually have on the floor of your house — newspaper or commercial pads are my preferred materials. Tiles, carpet, floorboards and lino aren't suitable, as these are textures the puppy will experience in the home, so you do not want them associated with toileting.

Ideally the crate would be positioned alongside a dog door to outside, so the puppy can learn to let herself out; or at least positioned right by an external door, preferably to a fenced garden. Many people find a laundry works well, as it's a restricted space which often has an external door, but if you're unable to achieve this, just set the crate up anywhere convenient. The closer to your social areas the better.

Keep the puppy in the crate for periods of between one and three hours when she is not in supervision (except at night, when she can be longer), taking her outside to give her an opportunity to toilet on the grass as often as possible. However, if she needs to toilet while in the crate, she will do so on the newspaper as she will not want to toilet on her bed. Take the puppy out for short intervals of play time, but always return to the crate for sleeping and eating.

This method suits people who are at home more of the time with their pup so that the pup doesn't need to be in the crate for more than 2–3 hours. Otherwise, you need to use Method Two or Three below.

In general, it's great to crate-train any dog, as it has many advantages later in terms of travelling.

Once set up, here's how you use the crate:

O Pop your puppy in the crate during nap time and night-time, and she'll naturally want to hold on until you let her out.

O In the first few days to weeks after you've taken your puppy home, she will be able to hold for about 4–5 or maybe 6 hours, so you'll need to let her out right before you go to bed, once during the night, and then again first thing in the morning.

O Take her outside at regular intervals during the day to limit the chance of any accidents.

O Take her outside onto grass after food, sleep, exercise and play.

O Don't reward (with freedom or attention, for example) vocalising such as whining or barking — rewarding this now will turn it into a life-long habit.

O If you do catch your pup in the act of toileting inside, immediately and calmly pick her up and pop her on the grass or paper until she's finished her business. Don't make a big deal.

How does this generalise to the rest of the house?

As you extend this learning outside of the crate, gradually give your puppy access to different areas of the house. First let him free in the room his puppy pen was set up in until he proves he can be there successfully without toileting, then extend access to adjoining rooms, one at a time. That way you're gradually increasing your puppy's concept of the den across your entire house, so the whole home becomes the nest or den and he will choose not to toilet inside. A play pen helps, as does a dog door.

METHOD TWO: PUPPY PEN AND PAPER TRAINING

For this method, put together a small fenced area (a puppy pen) inside the house, with a bed in one corner and the remainder of the ground covered with newspaper. Ideally, situate the pen by an external door.

O The entire floor of the pen must be covered by newspaper or asubstitute for the first two weeks. After that, start to shrink the paper area down across the course of another week until it's only in one corner of the pen.

O Because your puppy doesn't want to toilet on her bed and newspaper is the only other option, the puppy will learn that newspaper is the surface she toilets on and will continue to toilet only on the newspaper as the papered area shrinks.

O After this, start to move the paper outside of the house, starting with it by the door, then gradually moving it further into the garden and on the grass. Give your puppy free access to outside to toilet as much as possible.

O Over the next week, remove the paper entirely, leaving your puppy toileting on the grass.

How does this generalise to the rest of the house?

As you extend this learning outside of the puppy pen, gradually give your puppy access to different areas of the house. First let him free in the room his puppy pen was set up in, for short periods initially, until he proves he can be there successfully without toileting, then extend access to adjoining rooms, one at a time. That way you're gradually increasing your puppy's concept of the den across your entire house, so the whole home becomes the nest or den and he will choose not to toilet inside. As you stretch the time out, try to keep him in under supervision where possible.

METHOD THREE: POP OUTSIDE

This method is very simple, but it requires someone who's around with your new puppy a lot!

O Put your pup outside (as far away from the house as is reasonable) whenever she would naturally need to go to the toilet — after feeding, drinking, playing, exercising or sleeping.

O If you're unable to supervise your puppy, put her outside in a safe, fenced area.

O If you ever catch your puppy toileting inside, take her out onto the grass immediately in a calm manner.

This way the puppy learns that the only time she toilets is outside, and therefore the house is the nest site and shouldn't be toileted in. With this technique in particular it can be helpful to learn the signs that your puppy is about to go to the toilet so you can pre-emptively take her outside. If your pup starts sniffing the ground, whining or indicates that she's about to crouch — put her on the grass straightaway. Having a dog door is great, too.

BRINGING ALL THREE METHODS TOGETHER

I think the best way to house-train your puppy is to use a combination of all three methods. This is done by using a puppy pen with a crate in the corner with a bed inside, having newspaper on the ground, providing ready access outside to a fenced area for the pup, and taking the pup outside as often as possible after feeding, drinking, playing, exercising or sleeping.

With this full set-up of crate and puppy pen:

O Pop your puppy in the crate overnight and for blocks of time during the day to help him learn not to toilet in his nest, and to learn to hold on as long as he can.

O During the day when you're not watching, leave your puppy in the pen area (ideally with free access to a safe, fenced area outside through a dog door). He will avoid toileting in the crate, so will choose to go on the newspaper or outside.

O Then shrink the area of newspaper inside the pen over a couple of weeks, moving the newspaper square closer to the external door, then eventually right outside.

O If you're around, pop your pup outside after all the appropriate times, like feeding, sleeping and playing.

O Once your puppy is going outside on his own, systematically open the house to your puppy one room at a time, making sure he doesn't start toileting inside the newly opened rooms. You may wish to start with rooms that aren't carpeted and are therefore easier to clean up if you do have a small accident! After a few days, give him access to the next room. This generalises the idea of the house being the den and ensures that he maintains his pattern of toileting outside.

You may find the crate becomes your puppy's preferred bed area: it's his den and he loves it and feels safe there! You want your puppy to like his crate, so consider feeding him in there on an ongoing basis. Then you can take the crate in the car, on holiday or to friends' houses, and it gives you an easy place to leave your dog without fear of any accidents.

REMEMBER:

O Always give your puppy the chance to toilet outside. If she has to go inside she will do so, so don't blame her for that.

O Never growl at your puppy or rub her face in her urine or faeces. This will only confuse and scare her. If you catch her midway through a toilet, just pick her up and pop her outside calmly, and encourage her to continue on the grass.

Ideal house-training set up.

O Soiling is largely involuntary, so punishment has little or no effect. In fact, because dogs urinate to indicate submission, if you as the dominant pack member tell them off for urinating they want to signal 'I give up!' and may urinate more — setting off a vicious circle that just gets worse and is the opposite effect of what you want.

O I use a 'be quick' command, and click and reward my dog after she goes to the toilet in the right place. She will quickly learn the command, and it's useful to let her know to toilet when you use the 'be quick' command. Wait until your dog has finished her business before clicking and rewarding. Don't do it during — you wouldn't like to be interrupted either, I'm sure!

How to house-train your adult dog

When adult dogs continue to toilet inside, it shows that they haven't learnt to consider the house their den, and therefore their instincts not to toilet in their den don't come into play.

MARKING

This was the case with Tommy. As well as standard defecation, he also leg-raised and marked (micturition) around the house, a common behaviour for entire males, and especially breeding males like Tommy. Once established it becomes a habit, and places like the edges of couches and curtains can become favourite targets. In the wild, wolves engage in marking behaviour to show other wolves what their territory is: it is done on prominent trees, rocks and the like that other wolves might pass. Entire males, of course, mark more consistently.

When an adult dog is toileting inside, you need to go back to basics and start from the beginning: taking your dog 'back to the den'. You have to go right back to the basic puppy house-training that I've just taken you through and complete it as if your dog were still eight weeks old, when this learning should take place.

Start working on the problem immediately: the longer the habit goes on for, the more challenging it will be to change. Be careful as you generalise the learning to the rest of the house — take it slowly and be consistent so your dog can succeed. Remember, an adult dog may well take longer to learn this than a puppy that is in his formative period.

Additionally, it helps to keep your dog on clip stations (or in a crate) to begin with while he is in the house (and definitely while he's unsupervised). With Tommy, I had a series of clip stations set up in all the main social areas where we spend our time: the kitchen/dining area, lounge and bedroom. Focus especially on getting clip stations set up in the areas where your dog is inclined to toilet inside (dog's usually have a few favourite spots to go). A clip station replicates a crate or den-type environment, so your dog won't want to toilet while on it. Then take your dog outside as soon as you let him off the clip station, to encourage him to toilet there.

With marking, once you've cleaned the sites — with a solution of one part white vinegar to three parts water — clip your dog to that area. This will help to establish the marking site as a sleeping site, which discourages your dog from marking there in future. Putting water and food bowls close to or on marking sites also helps to deter this behaviour, as dogs don't like to toilet where they eat.

If you have an entire male, de-sexing him will help greatly, and the sooner the better, so that the marking habit doesn't become firmly established. Puberty happens around 8-12 months for dogs, which is when they will start marking, especially if there are other males around or bitches in heat, so try to neuter before puberty to significantly decrease the chance that your dog will mark.

TOMMY: FINDING HIS ULTIMATE DEN SPACE

Kim wanted to keep Tommy close (he was our first dog together, after all!) and have him sleeping in the bedroom, so we set up a crate in the room at first to prevent him toileting inside, then moved to a clip station. Once he was consistently successful, he then just had his bed — this area for him is his ultimate den space — in the bedroom with 'Ma' and 'Pa'. Don't tell the shepherds!

For an adult dog defecating and urinating but not marking, it's a matter of setting up the clip stations and/or crates: a crate beside a dog door into a fenced yard is perfect. Leaving your dog for periods in the room where the dog door goes outside is fine. Gradually you will be able to move him one room at a time into the rest of the house. Use your clip stations religiously while your dog is not under supervision, and put him out often.

Conclusion

House-training a pup at the right time should be pretty straightforward, and if you follow these guidelines you'll get a bomb-proof adult dog. If not taught as pups, then it is a more challenging behaviour to change; however, persistence and supporting strategies will get you there. My Tommy isn't completely bomb-proof like my other dogs, and if I'm away for longer periods I often choose to leave him in a crate or the bedroom (his strongest association to the den) to help him succeed.

If I can give you one piece of final advice, it would be to simply keep at it: you will get there. If all else fails and you have a wee slip-up (no pun intended!), I find a mixture of white vinegar and water is a great solution to clean up with and eliminate the smell. Good luck!

20

Destructive behaviour and bite inhibition

Lots of people warn you that it can be expensive to own a dog. But not many warn you just how expensive it can be if you end up with a dog that is majorly destructive, and swiftly demolishes anything and everything within reach, whether it's your prized silk cushions, clothing, good leather boots, sports equipment or anything else in your house. Naturally, it always seems to be the things you love the most that go first — Murphy's Law!

RIMU:

I remember Lucy driving up one day in a Merc sports car with the roof down and a beautiful Afghan, his coat blowing in the wind beside her. As she pulled up, the scene was less romantic: the whole inside of the car's leather was gone — yes, gone — thanks to good old Rimu, that beautiful Afghan hound. She dropped him off with me at my clinic and never came back! Thankfully, I fell in love with Rimu, so he came to live with me. It took a while, but he lived happily ever after with me for over 10 years. I still remember that beauty, and thankfully my house stayed intact. (Well, except for the time he got stuck to my newly varnished wooden floor because the floor-sander had left the door open. But that's another story . . . they were literally Rimu floors!)

Why does it occur?

Wolves and dogs use their mouths like hands, an extremely useful appendage that helps them to investigate and manipulate the world. Complex analytical organs around a dog's mouth play a role in the dog's sense of smell, which is phenomenally perceptive and a highly important way for dogs to understand the world around them.

Young puppies naturally show a lot of interest in chewing, biting and mouthing everything and everyone, particularly when they're teething. During the 1–4 months formative period, they're learning to use the nose, taste and the mouth as an important part of their development, so this behaviour is to be expected.

In the wild, wolves would learn what to chew and not to chew through natural consequences: for example, if they bite a poisonous plant and get a burning sensation around the mouth or get sick; if they investigate a bee and are stung by it; or if they try to bite another pack member and receive a social reprimand such as a nip or a growling. They also learn what food makes them sick, even if it's a delayed effect, so leave it alone.

Dogs, however, don't usually encounter natural consequences when chewing inappropriate items in the human world, such as that favourite pair of your shoes. If they don't experience any negative side-effects from chewing these items, they'll continue to do so as it gives them entertainment: it's a self-rewarding behaviour. This can manifest in a dog that takes great pleasure in destroying all sorts of things around your house on a regular basis. They can, however, learn early what to chew and what not to.

Although this lack of distinction between household items and toys is the most common reason dogs are destructive, there are different drivers that can motivate destructive behaviours. The main causes are:

O your dog never learnt to distinguish between toys and household items
O boredom
O separation distress
O escape-induced (when your dog destroys property to try to get out)
O claustrophobia (a phobia-related issue)
O predatory drive (treating inanimate objects as prey and destroying them), e.g. chewing the squeaky out of the toy or the tennis ball
O a number of eating disorders can result from inappropriate chewing and eating, such as pica (eating inappropriate objects), coprophagia (eating faeces — it was on the proto-dog's menu for a long time), hyperphagia (excessive eating) and anorexia (loss of appetite that can be psychologically based).

Teaching your dog what's okay to chew and what isn't is a great place to start when treating this behaviour — particularly if you believe one of the first two causes listed here is the reason your dog is destructive. However, if the behaviour is related to a more serious issue, such as separation distress, then treating the cause of that problem will be a key part of the therapy (so therefore also go to the relevant chapter).

How to treat destructive behaviour

The key steps for treating destructive behaviour are:

O understand what (for you) are appropriate and inappropriate items for your dog to chew, so you can teach your dog how to discriminate beetween items that are allowed and not allowed
O set up the right environment
O switch your dog into a learning state
O do Joining Up and umbilical exercises
O teach your dog to retrieve the right objects
O discriminate the correct materials to chew.

This series of steps is the same whether you are starting out fresh with

Meeko with his favourite rope toy...
I'm a good boy!

a puppy who is indicating destructive tendencies, or if you are trying to stop your adult dog from destroying your stuff. If you start young (and provide a good environment to prevent destructive tendencies), you can usually avoid this issue. If it's your adult dog causing you grief, the same principles still apply and will be effective — it just may take a bit longer as you are curing rather than preventing!

STAGE ONE: UNDERSTAND THE CORRECT ITEM TYPE

When puppies are teething, the first thing I do is make sure the puppy has access to toys she can play with and chew when she desires. Same goes for adult dogs if they don't have toys like this already! However, it's important that these toys don't resemble anything commonly found in the house. If you give your dog a toy like an old chewed shoe and you encourage her to chew on and play with it, can you really blame your dog if she then chews your real shoes? It may be easy for you to tell the difference, but for your dog that's not the case.

Instead, choose toys like a rubber Kong-brand toy and rope toys for dogs or tennis balls, etc. Don't choose soft teddy bears, blankets or pillows, as having these toys can encourage dogs to chew on cushions, couches and bedding. They can discriminate material types if you teach them to discriminate.

If you are training older dogs who are no longer teething, it's still important they have access to toys for chewing and entertainment. Something that comes with an appealing challenge is a good source of stimulation that will likely hold your dog's attention (like a rubber Kong-brand toy that can be stuffed with food for your dog to try to get out) or a ball, etc.

STAGE TWO: SET UP THE RIGHT ENVIRONMENT

Making it easy for your dog to do the right thing is always a good way to start, so for the first few months of your pup's life inside your home, don't leave your shoes, slippers or clothes on the ground: it's just too tempting for him to chew these things! Dogs are particularly attracted to items that smell of your pheromones, so funnily enough underwear and shoes are often targets.

The same goes for destructive older dogs: leave them in a simple environment where there isn't too much they can destroy (with lots of toys as alternatives), particularly when you are still trying to fix the behaviour. Once you have done the training, you may be able to relax a bit, but certainly at first set your dog up to succeed by leaving him in a space with only appropriate items he is allowed to chew.

Also remember that providing adequate exercise and mental stimulation for your dog is an essential aspect of any training! Many dogs are destructive out of boredom, so ensuring that regular walks, social engagement with other dogs and people and active games are included as part of their lives on a daily basis will help immensely. Different dogs will need different levels of activity: high-energy and young dogs need more, lower-energy breeds and older dogs generally need less. If you work long days away from your dog, look into options such as doggy daycares, dog walkers, dog sitters or dog sharing (when you find another friendly dog that your dog can spend some of the working day with). Ask around your friends and family — you may find you know someone who would actually love to have your dog as company during the day when you're out sometimes.

STAGE THREE: SWITCH INTO LEARNING STATE, AND DO JOINING UP AND UMBILICAL EXERCISES

You'll be familiar with these techniques by now. Refer back to the relevant chapters to remind yourself how to put your dog in a learning state, and how to do both the on-lead and umbilical Joining Up work. Then do lots of practice: I recommend 5-15 minutes every day.

STAGE FOUR: TEACH YOUR DOG TO RETRIEVE THE RIGHT OBJECTS

It's well and good discriminating against bad behaviour, but dogs still need to bite and chew, so it's great to encourage this in the form of fetching or retrieving. It's not all about what they can't do, it's also about what they can do.

To teach a fetch or retrieve, tie a favourite toy to the end of a piece of rope and throw it away from you, followed by a 'fetch' command. When your puppy grabs it, pull it towards yourself while enticing your puppy in with a 'come' or 'bring here' command. Follow up with a click and reward when your puppy gets back to you. In this situation, be careful not to start a tug-of-war — unless that's what you want to teach your dog, of course! This is a multi-purpose exercise with many benefits:

O You are teaching bite inhibition by redirecting your puppy's biting you and inappropriate items onto a toy.

O You are teaching discrimination by helping her understand what items are appropriate to chew.

O You are fulfilling her natural prey drive and instinctive behaviour to hunt or chase things, but redirecting onto appropriate toys.

O You are enriching her learning: this is a form of playtime that is very beneficial to her development as a well-rounded dog, and it keeps her happy and fit.

STAGE FIVE: DISCRIMINATE THE CORRECT MATERIALS TO CHEW

Now you need to teach your dog the difference between correct items and incorrect items. You do this using contrast training, with a safety slip collar and retractable lead, and delivering an effective check. You can remind yourself about this technique in the Dog Zen Toolkit chapter.

The key is to make it appear that the item you don't want your dog to chew is the item that is correcting your dog. An effective check causes mild discomfort: you want your dog to believe this discomfort has been caused by the item you are encouraging him not to chew (e.g. a shoe), so he stays away from chewing shoes even when you aren't home. It's an 'apparent natural consequence': the shoe bites back. It is a technique that mimics natural consequences, allowing you to correct the behaviour while preserving your relationship with your dog.

Because you want it to appear that the correction has come from the item, not you, you will not say anything during this therapy.

O With your dog on a safety slip collar and retractable lead, lay out the correct and incorrect items for your dog to chew (a collection of shoes, clothes, underwear and other household items such as cushions, plus appropriate dog toys).

O Allow your dog to move towards the items.

O Click and reward your dog for mouthing the right items (dog toys).

O Click and reward your dog if he picks up and returns the right items to you (a retrieve).

O Deliver an effective check if your dog mouths an inappropriate item, but do not say anything (i.e. don't say 'No' at the same time as giving the check from a distance). Do the check remotely at this stage.

Good toys and
bad toys.

Learning to discriminate
between toys and
household objects.

By doing this consistently over a few training sessions, your dog will learn that it's no fun to chew on household items, shoes and clothes, but it's heaps of fun to chew on dog toys. This is the result you want. This is contrast!

Conclusion

I also find that having a safe den for my dogs helps to prevent destructive behaviour. This could be a clip station, crate and/or kennel for your dog to be in for short periods of time when you're out of the room. You should have three or four around your house. If your dog does chew, take care where and how you set these up, ensuring that only appropriate chew items are within reach.

RIMU

The basis of Rimu's destructive behaviour was caused by separation distress, so we had to resolve this as well as teaching him how to discriminate between appropriate and inappropriate toys. Once resolved, he was a lovely dog who played a central part in our family — the kids adored him. As a long-haired, rimu-coloured Afghan hound he was one of the most beautiful dogs I had ever seen and was very sought after for TV commercials. Not bad for a dog who started off in life unable to be left alone. He may not have learnt to drive the car, but he did learn not to eat it!

21

Recall

You're out for a walk in the sunshine, and your day is going beautifully. You've just taken your dog off-leash, when suddenly she spots another canine to befriend across the road. She starts running straight across the street through busy traffic, only just avoiding being hit by a truck, even though you've been calling her desperately to come back to you.

Perhaps you have found yourself in a situation like this, or one similar. If so, you'll know the trials and tribulations that occur when you have a dog that doesn't recall to you as quickly and consistently as you'd like. This is my first test when someone says their dog is trained: does he come reliably when called?

Having an unfailing recall with your dog is something you should perfect: it enables you to get your dog out of unsafe situations, and avoid unpleasant interactions with aggressive dogs. Make sure your dog is under control while off-leash so you don't get into trouble with other people, and make your off-leash walks pleasant and relaxing. There are myriad benefits to having this command completely reliable!

Why do recall issues occur?

Wolves in the wild have no problem with recall. They have strong attachments to their pack and hate being separated, so will always avoid it where possible. When wolves are distanced from each other, they will howl and show separation distress vocalisations so they can be found.

When it comes to the domesticated dog, it's a bit different. Pups when they are in the formative period and building their mentor bond are ripe for building a strong attachment, and recall comes naturally, especially if you cultivate the follower response using Joining Up. However, pups over the age of four months develop a strong outward focus and independence, which makes recall a challenge. Freedom is one of your dog's ultimate rewards, so if not well bonded to his mentor, he will often choose not to come back when called, instead preferring to run free. Certain breeds are more inclined to be less responsive to recall than others: generally, the more independent breeds that haven't been selected for a high level of trainability, the ancient breeds (e.g. Basenjis), the Spitz breeds (e.g. Huskies and Malamutes), sight hounds (e.g. Afghans and Salukis) and scent hounds (e.g. Beagles and Foxhounds). These dogs have been bred for different qualities. The working breeds and the herding dogs tend to be best, as we have selected them for co-operativity and trainability.

Additional factors that can affect good recall are:

O Predatory or prey drive: dogs focused on the chase and hunt are difficult to recall.

O Sexual drives in entire males and females in heat, as the sexual drive is strong.

O Dogs that haven't bonded properly with their owners.

O Dogs that are very interested in other dogs or haven't learnt an appropriate greeting routine, especially dogs that show dog-to-dog aggression.

O Juvenile and pubescent dogs are highly distractible if not trained
  — start early!

However, despite the challenges, all dogs can be taught to recall
consistently.

How to treat recall issues

The key steps to addressing this issue are:
O establish a learning state
O build a relationship in which your dog is attuned to your guidance
  using Joining Up and the umbilical lead
O play hide-and-seek games, especially when your dog is young
O teach recall in four stages: short hand-held lead, long-line or
  retractable lead, drag lead, off-lead.
O utilise a remote conditioned aversive signal (i.e., 'no') to reinforce
  safety and avoidance training.

STAGE ONE: ESTABLISH A LEARNING STATE

Refer to the Learning State chapter to go through the process necessary
to get your dog focused and attuned to you.

STAGE TWO: JOINING UP AND UMBILICAL

This stage is absolutely critical if you want to create a super-strong,
consistent recall with your dog. The more bonded your dog is to you,
the more she looks to you for direction and is attuned to you, the
easier it will be for you to call her back in any situation. It's tempting
to skip straight to the Teach Recall stage, I know, but don't skimp on
this Joining Up training, as it will make the next stage much easier for
you. It teaches your dog to enjoy being in your personal space, bonded
to you and following you. You can find details on this training in the
Joining Up section in Part B.

STAGE THREE: TEACH RECALL

Below, I outline the steps required to create a strong recall. Start indoors
at first, before moving to more distracting, challenging environments.
The instructions are similar across all types of leads and environments.

The key is slowly increasing the level of freedom and the challenge of the environment systematically.

It's really important that you absolutely master each step before moving to the next. Wait until you are getting a consistent result 95-100 per cent of the time before moving on to the more challenging step or environment.

Step one: Short hand-held lead

○ Set yourself up in a quiet, distraction-free room with your dog on a safety slip collar attached to a short lead.

○ Make sure you have your clicker in hand and a pouch full of treats.

○ Toss a food lure away from yourself to encourage your dog to move away from you to get it.

○ After your dog has eaten the treat, call your dog back to you with a 'come' command, using a food lure to entice your dog to you.

○ Click when your dog *turns* to come back to you, and reward your dog with a food treat when he gets right back to you.

○ Click and reward your dog any time he comes to you, whether called or not. This is an exception, as normally you would only want commands done on cue, but with this you want being close to you as your dog's default behaviour.

Step two: Long-line or retractable lead

In this stage, I prefer to use the retractable lead as it enables you to give an effective check from a distance while giving your dog some freedom to roam and be independent, without having to worry about tripping up and dealing with excess lengths of the long-line. However, you can use either option, depending on what you have and what you're comfortable with. Some people never quite master the retractable lead and get burned by grabbing the line. Put in the time to learn to use it properly, because it is a great tool. However, if it doesn't suit you, a long-line is fine.

○ Use the same process as you did in step one.

○ If your dog doesn't return to you, if she's looking and/or going away, call 'no', wait two beats, and if your dog doesn't respond repeat the 'no' firmly (with a slight growl intonation on the second one), and check at the same time if still looking and moving away.

○ Repeat 'come', and click and reward when she comes. Repeat as necessary.

○ Click and reward your dog any time she comes to you, whether called or not.

Once you have completed steps one and two in a quiet room, go through each step again in an outside environment before moving on to step three. Remember, make sure you are getting a good, consistent response 95–100 per cent of the time before you move to the drag lead then off-lead.

Step Three: Drag lead

Go through the same process again. At first, it's good to leave a long-line attached to your dog's collar while you practise this command off-lead. You can let go of it and let it trail on the ground behind your dog so that your dog has freedom, but if he doesn't immediately respond to your 'come' command, you are able to step on the trailing end of the lead to catch your dog easily. You can then use it to give him a check on the second 'no' to get him back towards you and remind him that he is supposed to come to you. You then start to proof this in more difficult environments.

Step four: Off-lead

Go through the same process, this time off-lead.

Step five: Proofing

Once you have completed these four steps, proof this behaviour, first in a low-distraction environment, then in increasingly high-distraction environments. So, first inside in a quiet room, then in a low-stimulus outdoor area such as a quiet garden, then a quiet park, then a busier dog park, then a busy beach . . . you get the idea. When starting, always make sure the environment is safe; e.g. not too near to busy roads.

Always start by doing a few practice recalls with your dog on a retractable lead or long-line at the beginning of each session, so that if your dog doesn't respond you can deliver an effective check. Then, once you've had a few consistent recalls with no trouble, try off-lead in the new environment. Remember to use a jackpot (an extra-special reward — say five times more than normal) for good recalls in the face of difficult environments (especially environments your dog would normally be challenged by). You can reward a couple of good responses with ball play, too, if your dog likes this.

If this has been a challenge for you with your dog, it's a good idea to always take a small handful of treats and a clicker with you when you go out walking off-lead, and make sure your dog knows you have them at the beginning of the walk (do a recall on a lead) — that way, she'll have double the motivation to return to you quickly whenever she is called!

Another fun technique is to play hide-and-seek with your young dog: it reinforces that your dog should look for you and come to you, in a fun and playful way!

For very difficult dogs you can replace your remote check and 'no!' with a remote citronella collar correction to enhance your 'no' signal. The same technique applies to other training aids. Make sure they have a conditioned aversive signal or warning tone to pair with your 'no!'

Conclusion

This is such an essential behaviour for your dog to know: it keeps him safe, and it keeps him under your control so that you can avoid any unpleasant situations.

Practise, practise, practise!

Proofing and fading the clicker – maintaining the good work

I couldn't say how many times people have said to me: 'It works in the backyard, but the minute I get to the park it all falls apart!' The most common problem people face with training is that they don't do the proofing stage well, and if you don't do this you end up wasting all the excellent training time you have put in.

Learning psychology emphasises how important it is to round out our training with what we call proofing and fading the tools and techniques used to teach the behaviours. Once the formalised training sessions are done, we need to learn how to sustain behaviour changes and translate them into the real world. This, maybe surprisingly, is one of the most important parts of the book.

Proofing

Proofing is taking our training out to the real world, and practising it in a variety of increasingly distracting and challenging environments. This is done in a systematic way, allowing dogs to grow their skills and confidence gradually as the environments become more challenging. This ensures you'll get to a stage where you can go out with your dog without taking tools and treats along, relying instead on just voice commands, hand signals and praise as a reward. When you get to this stage, life with your dog becomes much easier and more relaxed!

Changing the environment from simple to complex is one of the most challenging aspects of training. As we know, dogs have highly sensitive senses (particularly smell, response to movement and sounds), so once you head into novel environments with lots of new experiences and social stimulation, environmental influences will hinder learning if this transferral is not done in a systematic way.

Effective off-lead command is a sophisticated level of training in a complex, novel environment, so you need to follow these steps carefully. It can be very tempting to skip the steps when everything seems to go so well in your backyard or contained space. But when it all goes wrong in the park, it can be very frustrated and demotivating. Not only that, but the inappropriate behaviours your dog is doing in that environment are being reinforced (if not addressed), so he will do them again next time. Systematic proofing of cues, commands and behaviour supports your dog to succeed.

You need to be diligent and persistent in the early stages of proofing — failing to do so means you are failing to hard-wire the behaviour. The more systematic you are, the more you record it, the better the results will be. Once you have proofed the behaviour maybe half a dozen times (and it's gone well), then you won't need the diary discussed below.

A couple of failures here and there aren't an issue: it is when you get sustained inappropriate behaviour (when you have given up and thrown your hands in the air) that you are in trouble. Trust that your dedicated work will pay off — it will be worth it! Take the long view; we also have those days when we wonder if we're making any progress, but the accumulation over time will take place, and one day you will look up and reap the rewards.

By necessity, training is always started in simple, non-distracting environments so that your dog is able to quickly understand what is being asked of him, because he is focused on and attentive to you. However, once behaviour is established and you have confidence that you're getting a consistent result, you test and grow the behaviour in systematically more challenging and complex environments. This extends the training into the real world, so that these learned behaviours will remain in the face of distraction and unpredictable circumstances.

Fading the clicker

'Fading' is when you slowly and systematically remove from your training the tools and food rewards you used to teach a new behaviour. This is so that your dog will follow your commands without the need for rewards. For example, you use a clicker and food rewards to teach 'sit' and have practised the command using these tools and rewards in lots of different situations, and are confident with your dog's response to it; you'll then slowly start to remove the use of the clicker *and* food reward. That way, you will be able to ask your dog to 'sit' using just a voice command, and using only praise or a pat as a reward.

When is your dog 'proofed' enough?

There is a whole complexity of theory and language associated with proofing that we could go into. I will touch on it briefly; however, for our purposes I think it is best to keep it simple and to establish proofing to a level that is sufficient and adequate for our day-to-day lives. If you are looking to undertake higher-level obedience, then this might be an area that you explore in more detail.

Depending on what aspects of proofing you are interested in, you are looking for your dog to systematically improve in the following areas:

O Distance: how far away can you give your response? Just in front of you, or 100 metres away or more? Train for distance in increasing intervals.

O Distractions: to what level of distraction can you maintain a response from your dog?

O Duration: this refers to how long your dog holds a behaviour, such as a 'sit' or 'Zen down'. If you want longer periods, you have to train for it. Systematically delay your reward to extend the time the behaviour are held.

○ Latency: this is the time between your cueing (asking for) a behaviour and your dog performing it. If you want quick responses, train for it! Remember some breeds are often slower (giants and hounds), and some breeds are quick, like Border Collies.

○ Speed: this is the time between your dog starting a behaviour and finishing it. Again, train for it if you want it.

○ Stimulus (cue) control: a cue is said to be under control when the behaviour is always offered when that cue is presented; the behaviour is not offered in the absence of that cue; the behaviour is not offered in response to some other cue; and no other behaviour occurs in response to that cue. Depending on how precise you want your training, you can aim for this level of control.

○ Precision: how accurately does your dog perform a behaviour? This is likely to be of more interest to advanced trainers, e.g. in obedience.

For everyday purposes I see proofing as sufficient when your dog:
○ has a well-established bond with you (the most important aspect)
○ wants to be in close proximity to you — stays in contact
○ has a good level of control on-lead and off-lead
○ enjoys working with and responding to you
○ responds consistently and reliably to your commands
○ has good recall
○ understands your 'no'.

If you are so inclined (and here I'm speaking to those competitively minded types), you could start challenging yourself to improve on these areas across your sessions.

How to proof behaviour

The key steps are:
○ understand your dog's distraction hierarchy and triggers, and observe your dog's body language
○ slowly work in increasingly complex environments (e.g. location,

number of dogs and people, mix of movement and scents, busy versus quiet places, etc)
o in each environment, start on a short lead, then a long-line or retractable lead, then off-lead.

The following is the process I recommend going through as a way of transferring your training into everyday life.

STAGE ONE: UNDERSTANDING YOUR DOG'S DISTRACTION HIERARCHY

The more prepared you are the better, so it is useful to list in order (from low to high arousal) what your dog's key distractors are. Of course for each dog these are very different, so know your own dog. However, here is one example: moving trees, you moving, open doorways, interesting scents on the ground, tennis balls, traffic, moving small animals, other dogs, people.

By understanding your dog's distractions, when you move into new environments you can assess the level of distraction and therefore challenge for your dog, and manage it. This might include going somewhere else if it is too advanced, doing more close-contact work rather than off-lead or just being more vigilant.

Alongside this is the importance of observing your dog's body language and understanding her personal signals of going from low to high arousal. You'll remember in the Shared Language chapter that you have a window of opportunity between your dog alerting her behaviour, targeting (fixing on her 'target') and initiating her behaviour. It is critical for you to recognise this window so you can intervene at an early stage (usually up to the targeting stage).

Before your dog's adrenalin rises and the primitive brain kicks in, you have a window to make contact with your dog and get her focused on you, her mentor, so you can guide your dog toward the right decision (that is, appropriate behaviour). Looking to you is the key: in most instances, as soon as your dog looks to you, you can intervene effectively. Always check in to see that your dog is in a learning state.

STAGE TWO: INCREASING COMPLEXITY OF THE ENVIRONMENT

Determine the hierarchy of environments that you will build up to (e.g. inside, backyard, contained paddock or tennis court, quiet park, dog

park). Gradually increase the complexity of the environment you are
working in over time:

O Begin work in a simple environment, such as an enclosed room or
   backyard. Ensure it's a place your dog knows well, and there are
   few distractions — no unfamiliar smells and no other animals,
   people or loud noises.

O Then move to a medium-contained environment, such as a fenced
   paddock or tennis court. There will be more space to move, but
   it should still essentially be enclosed. It may have a few more
   distractions (such as new smells), but not many.

O Then move to a complex environment, such as a quiet park with
   just a few people and dogs. Slowly step up to the final stage, below,
   within 1-2 months, depending on how your dog is going.

O Finally move to a complex environment, such as a park with lots
   of other people, dogs and other species, in a place your dog doesn't
   know so well.

Within *each* of these environments, run through *each* of these tools:

O Work your dog on a hand-held lead — this is so you have maximum
   control as the behaviour you are training establishes in the different
   environments.

O Once you are confident you have a reasonable amount of control,
   move to the long-line or retractable lead. You still have control, but
   your dog has more freedom and begins to experience the concept
   of being off-lead.

O Then move to the long-line dragging: you have let go of the end
   and you are following your dog so that you can stand on the end
   of the line and pick it up if you have any difficulties. You still
   have some control, but your dog has more freedom and begins to
   experience the concept of being off-lead.

O Finally, after a period of time when you feel you're ready, move to
   off-lead. This is the ultimate test of the degree of control you have,
   and how well established the behaviour is. Make sure when you do
   start this off-lead work in the park that it is a safe, controlled place,
   as this stage will test you.

The smaller and more incremental the changes you make, the easier
and ultimately quicker it will be. Pay attention to how your dog is doing:

if he is going well, move ahead; if not, then slow down (even go back a few steps if needed) and take your time. If you have any problems with your dog off-lead, go back to using the retractable lead or long-line until you are confident. Be aware of your role and that your dog might pick up on your stress, so you need to stay as calm, relaxed and confident as possible. Your dog will be looking to you for direction and guidance.

Always make sure you start each session in the park on the retractable lead or long-line to test your recall in that day's distractions. Only when your dog is consistently recalling on the lead do you let him off in a safe environment. I'd recommend that this is a good habit to get into: ensuring that your dog is well focused and attentive to you, making sure you have contact with your dog before he goes off-lead.

How to fade the clicker and food reward

Remember that throughout your training, while establishing the behaviours you click and give a food reward each time you get the correct behaviour successfully (continuous schedule of reward).

Then, once established consistently, you move to an intermittent schedule of reward (randomly rewarding successful behaviour with a click and food reward) — this keeps your dog motivated as she's not sure which time she will be rewarded. Slowly over time you reward less and less, fading it out slowly.

It's very important that you never fade the food reward from the clicker: you fade them together. The click is always a promise that a food reward is coming, so you can never make a click and then not deliver a reward. Instead, reduce the frequency with which you are using the clicker, but continue giving a food reward each time you click. Once the behaviour is well established, you can stop using the clicker and just use the food reward intermittently, which can be more convenient.

If your dog goes backwards in his training, bring the tools back if you need to, practise again for a few training sessions, then fade again. When I have first faded the clicker and food rewards after training a dog, I still make sure I take the tools and treats with me when I'm heading out, in case I need to reintroduce them if behaviour deteriorates. Sometimes you might encounter particularly challenging situations, in which case you can decide if you'd like to use a click and

Simple environment.

Medium environment (but still some containment).

Complex environment – other dog breeds and open space.

food reward to ensure your dog stays focused on you.

I also recommend that you occasionally do top-up sessions using the clicker and food rewards, to keep your dog learning and remembering what he's supposed to do. The clicker isn't so important by this stage, so you also can use just food, toys or praise as the reward. Definitely use the clicker and food if you are getting fall-back in your training, to help re-establish it.

Remember, also every now and then you can jackpot the reward (increase the award amount reward by 5-10 times) for an extraordinary performance (e.g. when your dog comes back when called when there are lots of dogs playing nearby).

Good luck and finish off the good job.

Training diary

Here, I have provided a weekly training diary that you can use to track your training sessions. This is a comprehensive training system, so I recommend you start at the beginning and work your way through the whole programme to get the best results.

As you can see, there's a space to record your training sessions each morning and afternoon. You can use the blank boxes to give each session a score out of five, so that you're tracking your progress and performance throughout the programme.

I recommend doing at least 2-3 training sessions per day for six weeks to three months, as it will give you the fastest and most consistent results. This will reinforce your bond, establish your shared language and hard-wire the behaviours you seek.

Each of the early training sessions should start with Joining Up before you progress to the new behaviour, so that you ensure your dog is attentive to you (unless instructed otherwise). Remember, it's fine (in fact, necessary) to do training in small bites — try to achieve too much at once and you'll only confuse your dog. So just focus on one behaviour per training session to keep things simple, particularly when you are first training.

The payoff is that you will build a wonderful, harmonious relationship with your dog for life, where you will have confidence in the various situations you face together.

This is just the beginning, creating the foundations for you and your dog. From there, who knows? Remember Hercules? He had over 145 commands! We don't expect your dog to drive a car, but at least let's get him not to drive you bonkers — so enjoy and don't underestimate what kind of bond you can create, and what joy that will bring. Have fun and good luck!

BEHAVIORS	MON		TUE		WED		THU		FRI		SAT		SUN		NOTES
	AM	PM	AM	PM	AM	PM	AM	PM	AM	PM	AM	PM	AM	PM	
JOINING UP (Clip lead, umbilical lead)															
BASICS															
Sit															
Down															
Zen Down															
Wait															
Stay															
No!															
Leave it															
Heel															
Come															
Nicely															
GREETINGS															
Dogs															
People															

BEHAVIORS	MON		TUE		WED		THU		FRI		SAT		SUN		NOTES
	AM	PM	AM	PM	AM	PM	AM	PM	AM	PM	AM	PM	AM	PM	
JOINING UP (Clip lead, umbilical lead)															
BEHAVIORAL ISSUE (Please fill in – e.g. Hyperactivity)															
BEHAVIORS TO TRAIN (See the issues support document summary to help you identify)															
e.g. Calm behavior															

We extend this comprehensive resource in videos, webinars and blogs on our Dog Zen community and Facebook web page.

Final
Word

This poem from the wonderful Irish poet John O'Donohue embodies the essence of the dog and the wolf. You may have felt this state with your dog as I did when I saw my first wolf. It has a sense of something nature has gifted us; to have the good fortune to be in partnership and relationship with one of Nature's most successful and beautiful species. Nature herself speaks through this poem and it speaks to my heart. I hope it speaks to yours, too.

TO LEARN FROM ANIMAL BEING

by John O'Donohue

Nearer to the earth's heart,
Deeper within its silence:
Animals know this world
In a way we never will.

We who are ever
Distanced and distracted
By the parade of bright
Windows thought opens:
Their seamless presence
Is not fractured thus.

Stranded between time
Gone and time emerging,
We manage seldom
To be where we are:
Whereas they are always
Looking out from
The here and now.

May we learn to return
And rest in the beauty
Of animal being,
Learn to lean low,

Leave our locked minds,
And with freed senses
Feel the earth
breathing with us.

May we enter
Into lightness of spirit,
And slip frequently into
The feel of the wild.

Let the clear silence
Of our animal being
Cleanse our hearts
Of corrosive words.

May we learn to walk
Upon this earth
With all their confidence
And clear-eyed stillness

So that our minds
Might be baptized
In the name of the wind
And the light and the rain.

Dogs can take us back to this place, just with the wag of a tail, a play bow, a mesmerising look deep into our eyes and hearts. They are in the very here and now and they invite us in, in each conscious moment. We need to hear and see them on their own terms while helping them to live safely and happily in our complex human world.

It is the Zen in Dog Zen that asks us to step into the dog's heart and mind and to really *understand* them — to hear them, to listen to them. They are talking all the time, but through their actions not their words. They speak through their bodies with heart and truth. Deep down this honesty underpins both our cultures and binds us together.

The Zen of Dog Zen challenges you to be present, to be mindful, to listen and look with your understanding and your heart. Dogs so often speak directly to our heart, our intuition, our ancient language of animal nature we may have experienced in the hunt 30,000 years ago when we were more in touch with the call of the wild — our animal nature.

Go outside and walk with your dogs. Let them show you again the feel of Nature, the wind and the light and rain on your face. Let them show you the way back to your true nature and feel and smell the earth breathing with you. Something closer to the times when we traversed the great plains together, living from and of the earth. This is where and when this beautiful bond was galvanised, under the stars.

And if you can see and walk with your dog like this then you really will transform — your dog, your relationship and, maybe surprisingly yourself — a true sense of belonging realised, a bond for life.

Acknowledgements

My thanks go first to my true Dog Zen Masters, the dogs in my life. Science has been a great teacher for me but the greatest is Nature herself, and for me the dog. Scott was my first teacher and inspired my desire to understand dogs better. Our family dogs Pehu, Candy and the many rescues who passed through all taught me something, but Carlos was my first deep and successful bond. A beautiful big red German Shepherd, he raised my kids with me and taught me what loyalty and love from a dog could be. I still miss him. Hercules was the most amazing intelligent, deeply bonded dog I have had in my life. He taught me what dogs really can do. He moved thousands of people and had his own character and fame. He resides now in Sting's song *Fields of Gold*, played at his funeral, watered by my tears of love and gratitude. Jess and Deb, my heading dogs, taught me how to work sheepdogs and understand what balance and true co-operativity are. The 45 sheepdog pups I had for three years of my thesis study taught me about genetics and development — analysing their videos taught me diligence! The mighty sheepdog trialists Billy Reynolds, Les Knight and Alan Nisbett taught me the language of sheepdogs. Also, Blue, Tom and my friend Monty (the world's first driving dog). And Reggie, such a special friend that flew a plane for me, but most of all my true mate.

Many, many film and clinic dogs have taught me so much over the years. My heart remembers those few clinic dogs that did not make it. I still cry each time I bury such a dog but each one makes me recommit to preventing the conditions that led us both to that place. This work is the culmination of the understanding I hope will prevent others going that way in the future. Education is undoubtedly the only real answer.

"Something is complete . . .
not when there is nothing left to add,
but when there is nothing left to take away"
— *Zen proverb*

Kim, my dear partner, has lived and practised the quote above for the last year during the writing of this book. She has been an unflinching advocate, muse and editor on this four-year Dog Zen journey. She has watched my many dogs transformed by these techniques and inspired me to share it in this book, as she did for the TV series and our online programme Dog Zen. Kim is the doer; she makes things happen. This book would not be in your hands if not for her. Thank you my darling and Zen co-practitioner. I love you dearly.

To Jazmin, my beloved daughter and Dog Zen co-practitioner and photographer. Jaz has had a rapport with animals from the day she was born. She probably had no option, as she was born in a 120-dog kennel and behaviour clinic. She rescued everything from deformed rats to litters of pit bull terriers when she was seven. She now runs our behaviour clinic and stars on our TV shows. She is the happiest and most likeable person in the world and she creates magic with her dogs: Porter, one of the first driving dogs; Charlie our hyperactive dog in Part D; and her husband Russo's Tuss — Tupac off *Hunt for the Wilderpeople*. I love her so much. And her co-trainer Nalu — look at those lovable photos. Happy, proud grandad.

Thanks, too, to Alisa, also whanau and our PR and social media manager, who helped edit this book with Kim. They have together trimmed and refined it into a beautiful read. And to Koan, my son and Alisa's partner, who used to run my clinic. He taught me how to get rid of the bullshit and keep down to earth; dog training at its simplest.

Much gratitude to Marie Manderson, who has trained with me for well over 20 years and helps Jaz run the clinic. She offered a very helpful trainer's peer review and her insights have proven invaluable. Ádám Miklósi, a world leader in canine cognitive science and co-expert on the *Dogs Might Fly* TV series, has shared his formidable knowledge and expertise; he is a man and scientist I respect deeply. Alex Walker, a specialist vet and my best friend, has offered his formidable mind to the review too, as did his wonderful partner Megan Alderson, my GP vet. Professor John Craig, the supervisor of my Master's thesis on sheepdog behaviour and genetics 40 years ago and respected ethologist, has contributed his fine mind to the review, too. Many others have reviewed and contributed — you know who you are, and thank you.

To Captain Karl Vette, my dear brother who won the zoology award I didn't (!) and his dear Ngaire, both of whom have been there for me in so many ways over the years. To the rest of my whanau and team who have supported me and whom I love: Nalu, Bodhi, Suzie, Isla, Catchy and Gordy, and Alison, the wonderful mother of my children, who was there for those first 30 years of Dog Zen's evolution. And a deep thanks to my hero team who have all contributed to Dog Zen: Rosie, Kristy, Patrice and Sue. The A team.

To my human teachers, the late Professor Erik Klinghammer, my first canine behaviour mentor and the most influential. Thank you Erik, you have contributed to so many in the field. John Paul Scott the father of the critical period theory in dogs, the crux of Dog Zen and my work, guided me 40 years ago; as did Marc Bekoff, Michael Fox, Durward Allen and many others. Thank you for your early guidance and inspiration.

My heartfelt thanks to my publisher Margaret Sinclair at Penguin Random House whose belief in this project allowed it to come alive. And to Garth Badger and the wonderfully creative team at Thievery Studios, who created many of the beautiful images in this book and whose commitment and belief in us helped us so much in the mammoth task of creating Dog Zen online.

And finally, deep gratitude to my Zen Master and life-way teacher Thich Nhat Hanh, nominated for the Nobel Peace Prize by Martin Luther King and one of today's living saints, or as we say Bodhisattvas. His teachings of compassion, kindness, love and mindfulness underpin all my work and especially Dog Zen. I had the good fortune to give a Dog Zen workshop in Plum Village, our retreat centre in France, where one of the monks kindly described it as a Dharma door, a door into a truth. If Dog Zen can live up to this, then Thich Nhat Hanh's gatha or saying that inspired this book, Love *is* understanding, will have been realised.

It is with love (*metta*) that I offer this book to dog owners and their dogs. May you achieve a true and deep bond for life and find all the joy, freedom and happiness that it can bring.

REFERENCES

This book is written for everyday dog owners so the scientific references are noted as 'research says' or similar to ensure readibility rather than being cross-referenced in detail. The research facts are important, however, and are there to help reveal the broader story of the origin, intelligence and relationship capacity of the dog, as well as showing how the training paradigm Dog Zen was created. It is deeply based in science but is also based on my 40 years of clinical experience. It is designed to build a shared language to create a healthy, loving bond for life with our dogs.

Ainsworth, M.D., 'Object relations, dependency, and attachment: a theoretical review of the infant-mother relationship', *Child Development* 40, 969–1025, 1969.
Ainsworth, M.D.S., Blehar, M.C., Waters, E., and Wall, S., 'Patterns of attachment: a psychological study of the strange situation', *Erlbaum*, 1978
Beck, Alan M., *The Ecology of Stray Dogs: A study of free-ranging urban animals*, Purdue University Press, 1973
Bekoff, Marc, *Rewilding our Hearts: Building pathways of compassion and coexistence*, New World Library, 2014
— *The Emotional Lives of Animals*, New World Library, 2007
Bekoff, Marc, and Pierce, Jessica, 'For a Model of Fair Play, Look to Dogs', *Scientific American*, September, 2015
Belyeav, D.K., 'Destabilizing selection as a factor in domestication', *Journal of Heredity*, no.5, 70, 1979
Bowlby, J., *Attachment*, Penguin, 1972
Bradshaw, John, *Dog Sense: How the new science of dog behavior can make you a better friend to your pet*, Basic Books, 2011
Coppinger, R., and Feinstein, M., *How Dogs Work*, University of Chicago Press, 2015
Coppinger, R., and Coppinger, L., *What is a Dog*, University of Chicago Press, 2016
Fox, M.W., *Behaviour of Wolves, Dogs and Related Canids*, Harper & Row, 1972
— *The Dog: Its domestication and behavior*, Garland Press, 1978
Hare, Brian and Woods, Vanessa, *The Genius of Dogs*, Dutton, 2013
Horowitz, Alexandra, *Inside of a Dog*, Scribner, 2009
— *Being a Dog*, Scribner, 2016
— 'Attention to attention in domestic dog (*Canis familiaris*) dyadic play', *Animal Cognition*, 12, 107–118, 2009
Klinghammer, Eric (ed.), *The Behavior and Ecology of Wolves*, Garland Press, 1979
Lorenz, Konrad, *Man Meets Dog*, Routledge Classics, 2002
Mech, L.D., and Boitani, L., *Wolves: Behavior, ecology and conservation*, University of Chicago Press, 2003
Mech, L.D. et al, *Wolves on the Hunt*, University of Chicago Press, 2015
Miklósi, Adám, *Dog Behaviour, Evolution, and Cognition*, 2nd ed., Oxford University Press, 2015
Pryor, Karen, *Don't Shoot the Dog*, Bantam USA, 1999
Scientific American Special Collector's Edition, *The Science of Dogs and Cats*, Fall 2015
Scientific American Special Collector's Edition, *The Story of Us*, Autumn 2016
Scott, J.P., and Fuller, J.L., *Genetics and the Social Behaviour of the Dog*, University of Chicago Press, 1965
Stewart, G., *Behavior Adjustment Training*, 2nd ed., Dog Wise Publishing, 2016
Vette, M.A.G., 'The Onotogeny and Genetics of Sheepdog Behaviour', The University of Auckland (unpublished thesis), 1980
Wilson, E.O., *Biophilia*, rev. ed., Harvard University Press, 2011

The contents of this book are intended to assist readers in the raising, training and management of their puppies and dogs. The author and the publisher will not be liable for any injury, illness or damage to any person, animal, property or thing as a result of, or in connection with, the use of any instruction, advice, suggestion, information or other content in this book. All animals — including humans and canines — are very variable, so always act with caution when treating behaviour problems in dogs and use a muzzle in any aggression cases.

RANDOM HOUSE

UK | USA | Canada | Ireland | Australia
India | New Zealand | South Africa | China

Random House is an imprint of the Penguin Random House group of companies, whose addresses can be found at global.penguinrandomhouse.com.

Penguin
Random House
New Zealand

First published by Penguin Random House New Zealand, 2017

10 9 8

Text © Mark Vette, 2017

The moral right of the author has been asserted.

Design: Carla Sy © Penguin Random House New Zealand
Front cover photograph by Garth Badger, Thievery Limited.
Back cover photographs by Garth Badger, Thievery Limited (Nalu and pups); FCB New Zealand and SPCA/Mini (Driving dogs); Mat Ward (Flying dogs).
Photos © Garth Badger, Thievery Limited except: page 6 (wolf) © Mlorenz/Shutterstock.com; page 35 (wolves) © Michael Roeder/Shutterstock.com; page 40 (pariah dog) © Kulanun Chutisemachai/Shutterstock.com; page 120 (fear) © Sarah2/Shutterstock.com; page 237 (dogs socialisation) © Ksenia Raykova/Shutterstock.com
Instructional photos by Jazmin Vette Dal Bello, Dog Zen Limited; Driving dog photos courtesy of FCB New Zealand and SPCA/Mini; Pound Pup team and Bandit photo courtesy of Screentime NZ Ltd; Historical photos from the Vette family collection.
Prepress by Image Centre Group
Printed and bound in China by Leo Paper Products Ltd

A catalogue record for this book is available from the National Library of New Zealand.

ISBN 978-0-14-377081-7
eISBN 978-0-14-377082-4

penguin.co.nz